Duckworth Overlook

Bernard Taylor is an award-winning author of several suspense and horror novels, among them *The Godsend* and *Mother's Boys*, both of which were adapted for the big screen. He is also the author of non-fiction true crime accounts, including *Perfect Murder*, for which he won the Crime Writers' Association Gold Dagger Award (with Stephen Knight). He has also written for stage, television and radio.

Also by Bernard Taylor

NOVELS
The Comeback
The Godsend
Sweetheart, Sweetheart
The Reaping
The Moorstone Sickness
The Kindness of Strangers
Madeleine
Evil Intent
Mother's Boys
Charmed Life
Since Ruby

NON-FICTION
Perfect Murder: A Century of Unsolved Homicides
(with Stephen Knight) – Winner of the CWA Gold Dagger Award
Cruelly Murdered: Constance Kent and the Killing at Road Hill House
Murder At the Priory: the Mysterious Poisoning of Charles Bravo
(with Kate Clarke)

There Must Be Evil

The Life and Murderous
Career of Elizabeth Berry

Bernard Taylor

DUCKWORTH OVERLOOK

First published in 2015 by
Duckworth Overlook
This edition published in 2016

LONDON
30 Calvin Street, London E1 6NW
T: 020 7490 7300
E: info@duckworth-publishers.co.uk
www.ducknet.co.uk
For bulk and special sales please contact sales@duckworth-publishers.co.uk

978-0-7156-5120-9
10 9 8 7 6 5 4 3 2 1

Typeset by Fakenham Prepress Solutions, Fakenham, Norfolk NR21 8NN
Printed and bound in Great Britain by Clays Ltd, St Ives plc

This is for Jackie and Trevor

Contents

	List of Illustrations	ix
	Acknowledgements	x
	Introduction	xiii
1	A Grave Suspicion	1
2	Early Days	5
3	Love and Marriage	11
4	Another Marriage, and a Death	17
5	Old Ambitions, New Beginnings	23
6	Another Death	31
7	And Yet Another Death	37
8	The Oldham Union Workhouse	43
9	Death in the Workhouse	59
10	The Doctor's Suspicions	65
11	The Inquest Opens	71
12	The Wheels Turn	79
13	The Magistrates' Hearing	87
14	Repercussions	105
15	New Developments	113
16	The Trial Opens	125
17	The Verdict	145
18	After the Trial	159
19	The Inquest at Castleton Concludes	167
20	'A Very Small Heart'	177

21	The Earlier Deaths	183
22	'How Great the Fall'	193
23	Final Days	209
24	Strange Reunion – After the Mazy Dance	223
25	Last Words	231
	Select Bibliography and Sources	237
	Index	239

List of Illustrations

Elizabeth Berry and Edith Annie   35
Mary Ann Finley   38
Back Albion Street   41
Elizabeth Berry   44
The Oldham Union Workhouse   48
Edith Annie Berry   57
Edith Annie's death certificate   68
The Blue Pits Inn, Castleton   117
Elizabeth Berry, artist's impression   128
Edith Annie, pictured after death   147
Walton Gaol   195
Elizabeth Berry's petition to the Home Secretary   204
James Berry, hangman   225

Acknowledgements

I would like to thank all those who have helped me in the writing of this book. They have been unstinting in giving me their assistance. I must name among them Frank French, Dave Thomas, Mary Danby, Carolyn Caughey, Donald Rumbelow and Colin Crowe. My thanks also go to Sean Prins of HMP Liverpool, Debbie Brown of the Blue Pits Inn, Castleton, and those dedicated officers who staff the Oldham Archives, the General Record Office and the National Archives at Kew. I am also grateful to Stewart P. Evans; if he had not given me a copy of his excellent book, *Executioner*, this book would never have been written. In respect of certain illustrations used I have been unable to trace the author Jack Doughty, so if anyone could kindly help in this direction I would be most grateful. To anyone I have neglected to acknowledge, I offer my most grateful thanks now.

Bernard Taylor
2015

'Where there is mystery, it is generally supposed there must be evil.'

Lord Byron

Introduction

Since the middle of the last century, *known* instances of poisoning in Britain have almost disappeared. Indeed, we would be surprised to find a case of murder by poison reported in our newspapers today. Only a century ago, however, such cases were not rare, while further back, in ancient times, poison was one of the most common means of disposing of another human being – for reasons domestic, political and even military.

The fact is, murder by poisoning was relatively easy to get away with. While it would be hard not to notice an arrow in the chest or a knife in the back, when death was due to a little antimony in a glass of sherry or arsenic in a cup of cocoa it was a different matter. With poison easy to come by, and the victim's death often put down to natural causes, it was a situation that more or less continued until advances in medicine and forensic science made it all but impossible for a poisoner to escape detection.

Poison, it is said, is primarily a woman's weapon. Certainly it is the most secretive. Not for the poisoner a lashing out with the poker or a shot to the heart. Murder by poison does not require energy or strength; in fact it might require nothing more than stealth and trust.

These qualities, along with a cool detachment, were owned in good measure by the attractive young widow Elizabeth Berry, a nurse who, over the bitter winter of 1886-1887, found notoriety, first in the northern town of Oldham and then throughout the nation. In her hitherto little-told story, much of the drama was played out within the bleak and banal walls of a Victorian workhouse. Here it was that the death of her daughter occurred, an act perceived by many to be the cruellest of murders, performed with an ice-cold callousness that was almost beyond belief.

The tale that began to emerge of Elizabeth Berry's progress was, of course, meat and drink to the newspapers, and to some papers in particular. Telling her story would have been much more difficult for me without reference to the local Oldham papers, especially the *Oldham Chronicle*, the *Oldham Evening Chronicle* and the *Oldham Standard*. I am indebted to them, and impressed by the high quality of their journalism and their sheer, unwavering focus on their project – all the resulting coverage, unlike in today's papers, appearing without the reporters being named.

In addition to the invaluable newspaper reports of the time, I have also been allowed to study the Home Office file relating to the case, the dreadful murder that brought Elizabeth Berry's name to the fore. And in doing so I have been able to discover the most fascinating information from previously unpublished documents, documents that shone new light on the crime, and into the heart and mind of the victim's mother.

There were of course those faithful individuals who vociferously protested Mrs Berry's innocence in the affair, but the constabulary were convinced that they had their woman. As it turned out, however, their work was by no means over. In the pursuit of their inquiries they heard murmured suspicions surrounding another death – and suddenly the investigators were faced with the possibility that the child's murder – if such it was – was not a one-off, isolated killing. Elizabeth Berry's dark story was beginning to appear darker still. Had there in fact been an earlier murder committed on her route into the dock?

The question would soon have an answer. And this answer in its turn raised further questions, gave rise to further suspicions. What, one feels compelled to ask, of those deaths that had occurred earlier, the deaths of those others in Mrs Berry's immediate family – her loving husband and her two other young children? These deaths, I discovered, had all been accepted as due to natural causes. But were they indeed? I do not believe so. My investigations have convinced me that although Elizabeth Berry was indicted for one single, diabolical murder, she was in fact a cold-blooded serial killer of the cruellest kind.

1

A Grave Suspicion

The thick, smoky fog that had wrapped the town throughout the night had lifted by the afternoon, but the wind was still bitingly keen as the two men emerged from the main block of the workhouse into the bitter air. Curious inmates, peering out through the frost-etched windows, might have watched the men's careful progress as they carried the pallet across the frozen yard. Perhaps they wondered at its burden; they could see that it was not a heavy one, for it took up little space under its cheap covering. It was in fact the body of a child, a girl.

Just a few yards on and the men were out of the wind and entering the block that housed the small mortuary – known in the workhouse as the 'dead room'. Once inside, they laid the small body down and then went away to resume their usual duties.

By their very nature the nation's workhouses were frequently the scene of death, of the young and old alike, and the Oldham Union Workhouse in 1887 was no different from the rest. That week it had been home to over a thousand inmates, of whom nine had died, the little girl being the last to go. And while the deaths of the other eight might have brought varying degrees of grief, they had not caused any great surprise or given rise to untoward comment.

Unlike this particular death. The death of the child that January day had quickly become the subject of much conversation. When word of it was first heard, the grim news ran through the place like wildfire. To employees and pauper inmates alike who had so recently observed the girl so happily at play, her end had come with a suddenness that was surprising. She had not been some frail, sickly inmate, but a guest; moreover on her arrival in the place just a few days before, she had appeared the picture of health.

Along with the general sadness felt at the child's demise there was, in some quarters – and as might be expected – great sympathy for the mother. There were several in the place who had observed how she, Mrs Berry, had tended her daughter through the harrowing days of the child's decline. And those who knew the bereaved woman better would have been even more sympathetic. Poor Lizzie, they must have sighed, shaking their heads – had she not already suffered more than her share of heartache and loss? It wasn't fair. In the space of ten years most of her nearest and dearest had been taken from her, and now, adding to her agony, she had lost the last of her children.

But there was more to come. The initial feelings of sympathy were swiftly followed by amazement as further news was broadcast – news that marked a dark and sinister turn in the story.

The first published word of the new development came through an article in one of the local newspapers, the *Oldham Evening Chronicle*, a daily which, along with its sister weekly, the *Oldham Chronicle*,* was to follow the progress of the ensuing saga from its first to its last days some three months later.

The first report came on Friday 7 January in a single paragraph headed: SUSPICIOUS DEATH OF A GIRL. It was a hurriedly written piece, containing several errors of fact, and clearly cobbled together at the last minute. The article said:

A girl named Ada Berry, about ten years of age, died at the Oldham Union Workhouse on Tuesday, under somewhat singular circumstances. She was on a visit to her mother, who is a nurse at the Workhouse, and on Saturday morning was taken ill. She died on Tuesday morning. On Wednesday Dr Patterson, the medical officer for the Workhouse, made a post-mortem examination of the body, the result of which will be made known at an inquest to be held at the Workhouse this afternoon. The mother, who is a widow, has not now

---

* For the sake of brevity, these newspapers will henceforth be simply referred to as the *Chronicle*.

her full liberty. These facts, coupled with the reticence of the police and of the Workhouse authorities on the matter, would seem to point to a grave suspicion being entertained as to the way in which the girl came by her death.

The next day the paper went on to correct the piece, giving the girl's true name as Edith Annie Berry, and her age as eleven, following which it gave a brief account of the inquest's opening. These reports would constitute the start of what would soon become a storm of reportage on the case and keep the newspaper-readers enthralled. For all its brevity, the *Chronicle*'s news that the mother had been apprehended could mean only one thing – that she was suspected of being implicated in the death of her child.

Could it be? There were many who denied such a possibility. This woman is a nurse, they argued, one who has devoted much of her working life to the care of the sick. How, then, could she set about engineering the death of her own daughter? It was beyond the bounds of nature. And, if in fact she had done so, then what could possibly have been her motive?

2

Early Days

It was once remarked by a writer on true crime that in order for a case of murder to truly enthral him, there must be a woman in the business. Well, the story of what became known as the 'Oldham Poisoning' certainly has such an ingredient. In the starring role, and filling the part so thoroughly, is Elizabeth Berry, the dead child's mother, a woman reported variously as proud, intelligent, mendacious and highly excitable. In addition, notwithstanding that she was perceived by many as a cold-hearted monster, she is seen also as a most clever and fascinating woman. Undoubtedly, in her mysterious way, she was different.

Elizabeth Berry's story began, as it was to end, in Lancashire, and rarely strayed outside Greater Manchester and its environs. And by anyone's reckoning her tale is a remarkable one; not only for the fact that she should be accused of having committed the most vile of crimes, but also for the story of her dark and sinister progress.

Her birth certificate tells that she began life as Elizabeth Welch on 18 November 1853 in the Manchester inner-city district of Ancoats. On the certificate her parents are named as Joseph Welch and his wife Mary Ann, née Beven. These surnames, however, are not to be relied upon. In the various records that tell a little of the parents' lives – the census records and records of births, marriages and deaths – the name of the father, Joseph, is not only given as Welch, but also sometimes as Welsh and Walsh. For the sake of consistency, however, I shall refer to him (except when quoting from documents) by the name given on his daughter's birth certificate – that of Welch. It might be noted that varied spellings of family names are commonly found when making researches in the earlier parts of Britain's history – due almost invariably to the fact that so many of the lower classes were illiterate. Unable to write their names themselves, the spelling of them as recorded in official documents would depend on how the name was pronounced at a particular time, and how it was heard and perceived by the clerk who happened to be writing it down.

At the time of the Welches' wedding on 24 February 1852, Joseph was living at 5 Rowlands Buildings, Butler Street, Manchester, and it was there that the pair – he twenty-seven and Mary Ann twenty-six – set up home and where, a year on, their daughter Elizabeth was born.

From then on, events in the Welch family are somewhat clouded in mystery.

It is reported that Elizabeth claimed to have been born one of twins, of whom her twin sister died soon after birth. If so, it might be said that her lie illustrates a phenomenon that was displayed throughout her life – a compulsion to glamorize her history and existence. There were indeed twins born to Joseph and Mary Ann, but they were boys, George and John, born 4 August 1856 while the family were living at Wheelhouse Court, Ancoats. Sadly, however, John died on 12 November that year, and his brother George on 6 June the following year. According to the infants' death certificates, they both succumbed to convulsions. It is interesting to note that on John's death certificate his surname is given as Welch, while George's is given as Welsh.

We know also from the twins' birth certificates that Joseph was there at their birth – he is the registered informant – but we do not know whether he was present at the time of their deaths. All we know for sure is that at some time during this period he left the household, never to return. Mary Ann said that he went away leaving her with a boy and a girl, which, if correct, suggests that he left in the period between the twins' deaths. Whatever the facts, he was never to play any part in his family's lives again. As for his reason for going, none has ever been given.

With her father having gone out of her life before she was three years old, Elizabeth had no first-hand knowledge of what had become of him, but it would appear that she was told that he had died – and died not only tragically, but heroically, killed fighting in the Crimean War. However, as she and her mother would later admit, there was not a word of truth in the story. No matter – in time, when it suited the abandoned Mary Ann, another romantic scenario would be invented to account for his absence.

Whatever the facts of Joseph's whereabouts, Mary Ann and her daughter were left to manage as best they could, a situation that was made a little easier when Elizabeth became old enough to go to school.

And fortunately for her, times were changing. Unlike her mother, Elizabeth would not grow up illiterate. In earlier Victorian days illiteracy was widespread. Education was neither compulsory nor always free, the only free schooling being that offered by what were known as the 'ragged' schools, introduced in the late eighteenth century to provide free education to the children of the poor. These institutions, however, were few and far between until later in the nineteenth century. Further, to make matters worse, with no reliable contraception and couples tending to have large numbers of children, it became the custom to educate only the sons. After all, it was reasoned, it was they who would eventually have to be the breadwinners, so what was the point in spending hard-earned money in teaching a girl to write and do arithmetic when she was unlikely ever to have need of such learning? In the general order of things, the working life of a girl from the lower classes would be spent in domestic service, or on a farm or in a factory – after which, with luck, she would marry and raise a family. In any such situation book-learning would have no place in her life. This phenomenon of female children being denied education is demon-strated in the marriage record of Elizabeth's parents. Mary Ann, born in 1826, was typical of the many illiterate working class girls of her time. On her marriage she 'signed' the register with a cross, while her groom, Joseph, penned his name. It is similarly the case with the witnesses to the marriage. They are named as John Hamilton and his wife Ann, and while John signs his name in the register, Ann can only make her mark with a cross.

It would be different for Elizabeth. With the proliferation of the free schools more and more children were being given some kind of education. With Mary Ann working long hours at the local cotton mill, Elizabeth could not be cared for at home during the day, so the answer was to send her to school – which would not only ensure that she would get an education of sorts, but also see her in safe hands while her mother was out earning a living. No records exist of Elizabeth's scholarly progress but there can be no doubt that her education, such as it was, suited her well. Clever and ambitious as she was, she made full use of her tuition, and in so doing sowed the seeds of the dissatisfaction that would colour the rest of her days – and eventually see her go on trial for her life.

Unlike today's more protracted terms of education, Elizabeth's schooling was unlikely to have taken her beyond the age of twelve, at which time she was sent out to earn her keep, working alongside her mother at the mill.

So many people at the time worked in the cotton industry. The Industrial Revolution had seen mills springing up all over the north of England, and the lure of steady employment became a magnet to men and women all over Great Britain and Ireland who were eager to make a better living. But while tall tales circulated of men in the northern towns walking around with £5 notes stuck in their hat bands, the reality was very different; the reality was a life of long hours of hard graft for low pay.

And Elizabeth was soon to discover the hardships at first hand, and to discover also that labouring day in, day out as a cotton-weaver was not the life for her. With no alternative, however, she had to take what was available, and even then, mill work was not always easy to come by. Over the latter part of the 1860s mother and daughter would move around Manchester finding employment where they could, frequently changing their living quarters, renting rooms at a succession of addresses in the city's various sub-districts.

The 1871 census finds them living in Werneth, an area of Oldham. Elizabeth was seventeen now, and developing into a handsome young woman. Known to all as 'Lizzie', she was petite in build – fully grown she would be only four feet nine-and-a-half inches tall – and had the added charm of the most attractive chestnut hair. Known to be reserved in her disposition, and with an inclination for dressing 'tastefully, but not gaudily', she was also said to be a hard-working young woman.

For all the positive comments about her deportment and work ethic, however, she also attracted many negative observations – which comments would later come thick and fast when her name was making headlines throughout the kingdom. And there would be no shortage of individuals ready to air their memories of her. Many of the negative comments came from her erstwhile colleagues at the mills. Declining to mix, she was never a popular girl, one former workmate typically remarking that in her relations with her co-workers she was most reserved, and as a rule kept aloof from them.

One positive thing that all agreed on, however, was her superior intelligence. There is no doubt that she had a fine brain, and perhaps in a later age she might have amounted to something dynamic in the most positive way. And the fact that she was well aware of her mental abilities inevitably contributed to her discontent. Never happy with her lot, she made no attempt to hide her dissatisfaction with the humdrum quality of her life. In her work in the mills her days were spent in the same wearisome routine, and in the full knowledge that, being female, she had no chance of advancement other than in the most modest terms. And while those around her expected nothing more than their lot, she at every turn showed a desire and determination to escape her situation. And when that ambition was not accomplished she used her imagination to invent for herself a persona that would raise her above her peers, and separate her from the common herd. In her striving for a better life she sometimes comes over as a kind of northern English, angry Madame Bovary – deeply dissatisfied with the unattractive reality of her existence, and, in seeking some kind of social elevation, resorting to lies, romance and illusions.

That she intended to escape her situation there is no doubt, and it would not be long before she was attempting to climb those first precarious steps on the steep social ladder, steps that would lead to scandal and, eventually, death.

3

Love and Marriage

While the young Elizabeth was making the best of things at the cotton mill, Mrs Welch too was hoping for an improvement in her situation. Since her husband's departure she had lived the life of a single mother. However, some fifteen years on it looked as if there might be a welcome change in store.

Mary Ann Welch, who was regarded as a hard-working and respectable woman, wanted, like most women of her time, to be settled in a secure, domestic relationship, and, hopefully, to leave the matter of the bread-winning to a husband. And there appeared to be a chance of this when, in 1869, while she and her daughter were working at the Springhill mill in Royton, she met Manchester-born William Finley, who had come to work beside them as a cotton-weaver.

Whatever Mary Ann's hopes, Finley doesn't appear to have been the best possible catch for a secure and happy married life. In his late thirties, he was referred to by some at the mill as 'the tramp weaver', which soubriquet gives some hint as to his character. He was a rather happy-go-lucky, if not shiftless, rover – notwithstanding one with charm – and one who was somewhat too fond of propping up the bar at the local tavern. Whatever his failings might have been, however, Mary Ann took to him. He was, though, she soon discovered, a man with something of a past. He had previously married, in 1853, and had fathered five children. But he had not proved a good provider, and in 1866, homeless and jobless, he had taken his whole family as paupers into the Manchester Union Workhouse. And it was there, in the following October, that his thirty-six-year-old wife Margaret died of tuberculosis.

With his children motherless and totally dependent, Finley should have remained with them, to work and support them, but he chose not to, and soon after his wife's death he gathered his things together and quit the place, leaving his children behind.

Five years later, with his children no longer playing any part in his life, he was starting a new life with Mary Ann, and on 22 July 1871 the two were married. On their marriage certificate the bride's 'condition' is given as 'widow'. They each give their age as forty – Mary Ann having knocked off five years. The two witnesses were Smith Duckworth and Mary Ann Duckworth. The certificate shows that all four – bride, groom and the two witnesses – were illiterate, all 'signing' the marriage register with their 'mark' – in each case a cross.

Was this a genuine marriage?

Although for years it had suited Mary Ann to present herself as a widow, she had no evidence or knowledge to support such a claim. And now she came out with a totally new account of how she had become widowed. According to reports, she said that the story of her husband dying in the Crimea had been invented out of shame over her abandonment – when the 'true story' was very different. This story, it appears, was the one she told to William Finley. Years later, Finley would be interviewed by journalists from two or three Oldham newspapers. Asked by the *Chronicle*'s man what he knew of Mrs Finley's first husband, Finley replied, 'I can't answer that. She always told me that he went to America, and left her with two children, twins, a boy and a girl. The boy died and the girl was Elizabeth. He never wrote afterwards, and whether he was dead or living I never knew.'

So Finley's words show that he himself didn't know whether or not his 'bride' was indeed a widow, and, therefore, that he might knowingly and happily have entered into a bigamous marriage.

Mary Ann's account, only slightly different from Finley's, was that following Joseph's departure she received a letter from him saying that he had gone to live in the USA. Later he wrote again, she said, sending money, and saying that he had enlisted to fight in the American Civil War. After this there was no further word from him.

This story of his having vanished somewhere in America would not do, of course, not when she was anxious to be seen to be free to tie the knot with Finley. After all, Joseph would be only in his mid-forties and could very well be alive and thriving somewhere. So, it was said, keen to make plans for her wedding, she made inquiries of the 'American War Authorities', and as a result was informed that following her husband's discharge from the army he had retired to Louisiana, where he had died.

There are many questions raised by such a scenario, and they can only lead to the conclusion that the whole story was just another invention. How, one might ask, did Joseph, in 1857, send his wife money from the USA? US monetary notes were certainly in use at the time, but is it believable for one moment that he would have sent Mary Ann a wad of dollar bills in an envelope? Furthermore, *why* would he do it – send her money? In walking out on her he had made it abundantly clear that he had finished with her. Also, with regard to Mary Ann's seeking information on his movements abroad – and his *very* convenient death – how would she have known which body to write to in her quest? Even with today's internet and its all-powerful search engines one would find it a most daunting – if not near-impossible – challenge. Further, any exchange of correspondence back in 1871, even without the time taken for the 'American War Authorities' researches, would have taken several months. And as for the 'official information' on Joseph's demise – nothing more specific than that he died between 1865 and 1871, somewhere in the vast state of Louisiana – it is worthless. If indeed the authorities had been able to discover details of his history, they would surely, at the very least, have given his widow the time and place of his death.

So what indeed did become of the errant Joseph Welch? Unfortunately it has not, at this time of writing, been possible to discover – in spite of extensive searches. It would appear that he remained with Mary Ann for only three years before packing his bags. And one has to wonder, too, at the reason for his going. Though perhaps the answer is not so difficult to fathom. Unhappy in his marriage, with a wife and children to support on a very small income, along with the constant necessity to be on the move in the pursuit of work, did he one day, following the death of baby John, decide that he had had enough?

And did he then leave the country? In those times of a growing British Empire, with the world opening up to enterprising young men, many were getting their one-way tickets to foreign lands. Was Joseph among them, and does he now lie buried in some foreign field? Possibly – but it is more than likely that he remained in England and merely moved to another part of the country or even of the town. Perhaps one day in his work at the mill he had met someone else, and determined to start a new life and marry again. Or perhaps he was already married when he met Mary Ann, and simply decided to return to his true wife.

It must be acknowledged that this is a strong possibility. Bigamous marriage was no rarity in earlier times. With divorce more or less out of the question for the lower classes, for someone with a wish to remarry it was just about the only answer. For a man to up sticks and leave his wife for a new life can't have been so difficult an operation. In an age before telephones and the internet, National Insurance numbers, Council Tax records and electoral rolls, and any number of other means that are available today, there was no procedure by which a wife could trace a straying husband if he was determined not to be found.

Whatever the facts surrounding Joseph's departure, Mary Ann, left in the lurch and eager to remarry, invented his emigration to the USA. And who on earth could have proved it false? Only perhaps Joseph, and he was keeping a low profile.

It is not difficult to understand Mary Ann's actions – and even to sympathize. A middle-aged woman abandoned by her husband had no option but to support herself, and if that proved impossible it meant going into the workhouse. It can hardly be wondered at, then, that if the chance of love and security came to her she should want to reach out and take it. After all, it could make no difference to anyone else. Joseph Welch was most unlikely to come back into her life, so perhaps the simple answer for her was to stick to her story of being a widow, and in the eyes of all be eligible to remarry.

Regardless of Joseph Welch's whereabouts, it would appear that the newly married Finleys were in no fear of his coming back to upset their applecart, and they must have started their married lives with great hope. So it was that, along with Elizabeth, they set up home in rooms in Drury Lane, Hollinwood. Unfortunately, what dreams of happiness they nursed were not to last. Within weeks William Finley was gone from the scene, dragged away by officers of the constabulary.

Had he and Mary Ann been on their own they might have made something of a go of it, but there was conflict. He was later to say of Mary Ann that he 'couldn't do with her relatives', citing one instance where one of her sisters came for a visit and did not address a single word to him in the course of five hours. But the real thorn in his side was – and not surprisingly – Elizabeth.

It was, of course, almost inevitable that Finley and his stepdaughter would not get on. There was she, a fastidious, socially ambitious young woman who kept herself aloof from the common crowd, and there was he, a beer-drinking, shiftless, illiterate, roving mill-worker – a man who would not even take responsibility for his own children. Disapproving of him from the start, Elizabeth soon came to dislike him with a passion, making no effort at any kind of rapprochement, but openly showing that she despised him. It suited her too to cause friction between him and her mother, and as he worked alongside the two of them at the mill he found no respite from the ever-present tension and disagreeable ambience. Consequently he sought comfort through beer and friends in the local public house of an evening, which resulting expenditure further blackened his relationship with his wife and stepdaughter, leading to furious rows between them.

In his interview with the man from the *Chronicle*, Finley would speak of some of the difficulties he encountered right from the first days of his marriage. Notwithstanding that Elizabeth was, in his words, 'a hard-working lass, and the cleanest girl' he had ever seen, she was also, he said, 'a regular beggar'. He told the reporter: 'She wouldn't speak to me when she came in, and you know it's very fretting for a man to sit there a whole day, and for a young woman that I never did harm to not to speak to him…And the very first day I was married she didn't do right. When we were having a bit of a jollification after the wedding a friend of mine says to Lizzie, "This is your father now." And she tossed her head in disdain, and says, "I'll never call you father, and I'll never try."' Continuing his melancholy account of the big day, he said, 'That night she went to Manchester to see a relative, and as it got late, and she didn't come back I thought she was going to stay all night, but at twelve o'clock she knocked us up, and that was on my wedding night too.'

There was worse to come. One Saturday morning, five weeks into their marriage, Finley was setting off to work when Mary Ann told him bluntly that when his work was finished he was to come straight home with his wages. 'Mary Ann,' he said, 'all you thinks about is money,' to which she replied, 'Yes, that's all I do think about.'

There would be more sharp words later. Disobeying instructions, after work that evening he went drinking and became the worse for it, and not surprisingly his wife and stepdaughter were waiting for him when he got in. There was an almighty scene between the three of them, during which Finley managed to do some damage to the house, or as he put it, '… there was some bother, and I broke some windows'.

If he thought that this would be the end of the matter, however, he was soon to be proved mistaken, and in the most shocking and dramatic manner.

As noted, Mary Ann and Elizabeth were well aware of certain parts of his history, not least how after the death of his wife he had abandoned his children to the care of the workhouse, and left the workhouse guardians no means of reaching him. This knowledge was all that Elizabeth needed. Determined to get him out of their lives, she did the most remarkable thing. On the Monday morning following the row she didn't go immediately to her work at the mill, but set off for the Manchester workhouse where Finley's children had been abandoned. There she informed the Board of Guardians of her stepfather's whereabouts. As a result, members of the constabulary promptly came to Drury Lane and arrested him for the desertion of his children. He was then hauled up before the magistrate in the police court and sentenced to three months in the squalid environs of Manchester's Belle Vue Gaol.

Speaking of the episode to the *Chronicle*'s man fifteen years later, Finley remarked, 'Lizzie informed on me, and it ended my married life for a bit.'

And there was more disappointment in store. On his release from prison, he sent a woman to the house to fetch his clothes, only to learn that they had been pawned – for twenty-eight shillings.

He made no attempt to mend the situation but went on his way, leaving Mary Ann and Elizabeth there alone.

The sordid circumstances surrounding the early break-up of the Finleys' marriage, marked by Elizabeth's betrayal of her stepfather to the authorities, demonstrate, if nothing else, a ruthlessness and singleness of purpose in Elizabeth's character. They were characteristics that would become apparent on several occasions in her life.

4

Another Marriage, and a Death

So, there it was – five weeks into Mary Ann's marriage and she and Elizabeth were alone again. It was not a situation that would last, though, for soon Elizabeth herself would be spreading her wings and building a life of her own. It was not long after William Finley's departure that she met the young man who was to become her husband.

Thomas Berry was born in Salford in 1847. It appears that his parents might have died while he was still young, for the 1861 census reveals him, at the age of fourteen, along with his three sisters – Ann, aged sixteen; Jane, nine, and Elizabeth, seven – to be lodging with their uncle and aunt and five cousins at 22 Sycamore Street, Manchester.

Ten years on, and he is lodging with his sister Ann, who has since married and is living with her husband John Sanderson, a machine printer, in Saville Street, Newton. The couple have a year-old son, Herbert. Also lodging with them is younger sister Jane. While she is working at the mill as a silk weaver, Thomas has left mill-work for employment with the Lancashire and Yorkshire Railway Company.

It was somewhere about this time that Thomas and Elizabeth met, and the two were subsequently married on 7 June 1873, their wedding taking place at the Parish Church of St Stephen Hulme, Lancaster. Their marriage certificate shows Thomas – described by an acquaintance as 'a very decent sort of fellow, a little pale-looking, and quiet' – as twenty-six years of age, his occupation that of 'iron turner', and living in City Road, Manchester. His bride, Elizabeth, is shown as nineteen, living at 30 Park Lane, Royton. Somewhat surprisingly, her father is not denoted as 'deceased' but is shown as having an occupation – that of 'maker up'. There is no mention of an occupation for Elizabeth; in all probability she quit her employment at the mill shortly before the day of her wedding. She would never return to such work.

At the time of their marriage Thomas's occupation with the railway company was based at Manchester's Victoria Station and for some months he commuted daily between Manchester and Royton, where he had moved in with Elizabeth and her mother, and where the following year, on 9 March, almost nine months to the day, the Berrys' first child was born, a son whom they named Harold.

It is reported that the doctor who attended Mrs Berry at her son's birth was one Dr John Kershaw, who was in practice at Royton. He was to feature in her story again years later and, as will be seen, would become her greatest support and champion. She was going to need all the help that she could get.

In the matter of the situation of the newly married Mr and Mrs Berry, it has, of course, ever been common practice for many young newly-weds to live for a time with the parents of one spouse or the other. But while it might work for a great many brides, it did not suit the young Elizabeth, and she was very soon showing her eagerness to move on and improve her situation. Added to this, her desire to be mistress in her own home, was the fact that she and her mother did not get on – a situation which Mrs Finley bitterly regretted.

The parting of the ways for Elizabeth and her mother came soon after baby Harold's birth, with the Berry family moving out of Park Lane and renting a house at 45 Saville Street. It was there, a year later, on 29 April 1875, that Elizabeth gave birth to a daughter. On the new baby's birth certificate she is given the name Annie, with the added information that she is 'Edith Annie on certificate of naming'. Throughout her short life she would be known formally as Edith, and by family and friends as Annie. Mrs Berry herself, so records show, would sometimes refer to her as Eda.

By the time of the new baby's birth Thomas had gained promotion at the railway company, and was now working as a railway carriage examiner. Said an acquaintance: 'He was one of those fellows who go about with a long-handled hammer testing the wheels of the carriages at Victoria

Station,' adding, 'Of course, he wouldn't have had a very large wage, but he kept respectable on what he had.'

Regardless of Thomas keeping 'respectable', however, Elizabeth was not content. Not only had her relationship with her mother further deteriorated, but she was also on less than good terms with her Saville Street neighbours. She was noted for her reticence, it was reported, and for the little acquaintanceship she had with them. As a journalist for the *Chronicle* later wrote, following her trial:

> This want of familiarity on her part was put down to pride – to the belief that she deemed herself better than they – and consequently the feeling between them was not the kindest. All the residents… say that she was a proud, haughty woman, who dressed beyond her station, held little or no intercourse with her neighbours, but strode along the street 'as if they were nobody, and she was everybody and for all the world as if the whole street was her own property'.

This, it would appear, was usually the way wherever Elizabeth was to live, and it is safe to say that she probably wouldn't have cared tuppence for any neighbours' opinions of her. In her high ambitions and aspirations they would have played no part.

Whether her over-arching aspirations also encompassed being mother to a growing number of children, however, is extremely doubtful, and it is most unlikely that she would have been pleased to find, towards the end of 1876, that she was once again pregnant.

On 13 June 1877, two years after the arrival of Edith Annie, Elizabeth gave birth to her third child.

Whatever the young Mrs Berry's feelings at this time, to many an outsider she would have appeared to be in an enviable position. She had three handsome children, an agreeable home, no need to work outside the home, and a hard-working young husband. As for Thomas himself, observations from individuals who had known him were invariably positive. He would be described by William Finley as 'a steady, honest-looking gentleman', by another who knew him as 'a kind and affectionate husband, one who, in order to gratify his wife's inordinate vanity, stinted himself of the ordinary requirements of life, so that they might keep up appearances beyond their means...' and by yet another as '...a superior man for his position, deeply wrapped up in his wife, whose every wish he ministered to, and who denied himself many comforts to minister to her pride'.

There is no doubt that with his devotion to his wife and children, Thomas strove to provide for them a good home, and due to his diligence they lived in relative comfort and appeared to have every reason to be content. As becomes ever more clear, however, contentment was never to be a notable factor in Elizabeth's life, and if such ever did show its face it was not for long. Certainly any outward appearance of happiness was shaken that autumn, for tragedy came. Sadly, the new baby did not survive infancy. After a short illness, on 26 October, at the age of four months, the babe was dead. The cause of death, Mrs Berry announced to her relatives, was 'teething'.

The sad and sudden death of the Berrys' youngest child will be examined further along in this book, but for the present it is sufficient to say that very soon after the funeral the bereaved mother was showing dissatisfaction with their home at Saville Street, and was set on moving again. This time they went to the nearby locality of Newton where they rented a house at 13 Jackson Street. Superior to their previous home, it caused a few raised eyebrows among neighbours as they wondered how it could be afforded on the modest income of a railway carriage wheel-tapper.

What Thomas himself felt about their domestic situation we cannot know. Was he happy in his marriage? As observers remarked on the controlling character of Elizabeth's nature, and Thomas's readiness to work long hours to provide her with her wants, it is hard to escape the conclusion that it was a marriage in which, as the old saying goes, it was the wife who wore the trousers.

Whatever the state of their marriage, it was to end in tragedy. In the summer of 1881 Thomas fell gravely ill, and on 16 July he died. He was thirty-four years old. Present at his death was Elizabeth, who, two days later, registered his sad demise. He was buried in Harpurhey Cemetery beside his late infant child.

Thomas's death was later to give rise to some comment in the vicinity, and even at the time of its happening his young widow caused outrage

when, the very day following his death, she set about making arrangements to sell the household furniture. When a relative commented on
what he termed her 'undue haste', she protested, 'You know I'm not now in
a position to keep on the house and pay the rent.'

Notwithstanding the negative light in which she was viewed at
the time by her neighbours and some members of her family, there was
nevertheless truth in her response. The simple fact was that at the age of
twenty-seven she was a widow with two small children to raise on her own,
and without an income. But she was not to be defeated. On the contrary;
she was determined to find a way and, at the same time, to make for herself
a better life.

5

Old Ambitions, New Beginnings

Thomas Berry's weekly wage from the railway company would not have been great, and with children, and a wife with expensive tastes, it is unlikely that he would have been able to put anything by for a rainy day. And now, for his widow, that rainy day had arrived. Thomas's death did not leave Elizabeth completely destitute, however. He had been insured, and on his death she collected £18 4s. from the Rational Sick and Burial Society, and a further £60 from the Prudential Society. £1 in that year, 1881, would be equal to about £110 today in 2015, so she had in her purse something in the region of £8,500. To this would be added whatever she was able to realize from the sale of the furniture and Thomas's effects, his clothes, his watch and chain, his razor and other personal belongings. While in all it made up a decent sum, however, it was not a fortune, and it was certainly not enough to keep a family of three for long. The young Mrs Berry had no choice, then, but to provide a living for them on her own. While her husband had been alive there had been no need for her to find employment outside the home, but her situation now was different.

In the present day our welfare benefits ensure that no single mother with children will have to sleep on the streets. Not so in earlier times. Before our government's largesse provided round-the-clock care and financial assistance from the cradle to the grave, individuals could rely on the state for very little. For some without paid employment there might have been a few shillings coming through the parish's poor relief, but otherwise the only real barrier against starvation was to join the many thousands of paupers who crowded into the workhouses that were scattered throughout the land.

Britain's citizens were expected to take responsibility for their lives, and for the young widow Elizabeth Berry things were no different. The options open to a woman such as she, and in the position in which she found herself, were few. She could expect no financial help from her impecunious mother, and her only experience in the workplace came from her time in the mills, and while such work was available to her still, it would have brought insufficient financial reward. Further, it would have seen her condemned to such unremitting graft for years to come, and while she could have survived in such a situation – thousands did, and she was strong – it was a move that she would never have considered. That earlier part of her life was over for good.

So, with mill work out of the picture, what, then, was she to do?

The best of all solutions to her problems was, of course, to remarry, and it very swiftly became apparent to those around her that this was her aim – and not simply to remarry, but to remarry soon, and, more importantly, to remarry well. Not for her some lowly clerk, or weaver in a mill – or even some railway carriage wheel-tapper. As she was to demonstrate, her aims were considerably higher.

A good marriage, then, was her aim, but in the meantime she had to find a means of providing for herself and her children. She must, therefore, find employment without delay – and ideally employment that offered a promise of some security until her ultimate goal was achieved.

Eschewing any kind of mill work, she cast around for something more promising. And it seemed that she had found it in a newspaper advertisement for a resident housekeeper/general servant to a local medical practitioner. He was Dr David Shaw, a bachelor, thirty-four years of age, living on the Oldham Road in nearby Newton. His housekeeper, it appeared, was departing his employ, so leaving him in need of a replacement, and to Elizabeth Berry's great pleasure her application was successful and she was offered the post. However, in order to take up the situation she would first have to deal with the inconvenient presence of her two small children. To put it plainly, seven-year-old Harold and five-year-old Edith Annie were an encumbrance. But it was one that could be dealt with.

Nearby in Miles Platting lived Elizabeth's sister-in-law, Ann Sanderson, with her husband John. As noted, Ann was the sister of Thomas, Elizabeth's late husband. The Sandersons were now living at 68 Albion Street with their sons Herbert and Arthur, while lodging with them still was Ann's sister Jane, still working as a silk-weaver in one of the mills.

It was to her sister-in-law Ann that Elizabeth turned for help. Without wasting any time she made her way to Albion Street where, after some discussion, it was arranged that for the foreseeable future Harold and Edith would go to live with their aunt and uncle and attend school with their two cousins. The agreement reached was that Elizabeth would pay her in-laws six shillings a week for the children's keep, along with any extra that might be required for clothing. In addition she would pay their school fees, which ran to 3d. a week for each child. She was also committed to paying a weekly premium of 2d. to an insurance company on policies she had taken out on the children's lives. At that time this arrangement was a common one, whereby a parent would pay a small weekly sum to insure the life of a child, the premiums collected by the insurance company's agent who would call from door to door. Paying into these 'burial clubs' would, if nothing else, realize in the event of the child's death at least enough to pay for an inexpensive funeral.

So, that summer, with all arrangements in place, the children were delivered to their aunt and uncle, leaving their mother free to begin her work as housekeeper to Dr Shaw. And it seems likely that she saw in her promised employment with the doctor the possibility of a relationship that was something quite different from that of master and servant. She did not, of course, see herself as being nothing more than a paid house-keeper for the rest of her life, and in her wish for a new husband the young, unmarried doctor might well have seemed perfectly cast in the role.

So much for her ambitions. Unfortunately for her, things did not work out as she had hoped. We shall never know what transpired, but whatever it was she so displeased the young doctor that she was quickly dismissed, departing his company on the very day of her arrival. A correspondent to the *Chronicle* later wrote that the doctor 'found something out and would not even allow her to bring her box'. What could it have been that so swiftly turned him against her? Did she make some inappropriate gesture or come out with some ill-chosen words? Bearing in mind her determination to acquire a new husband, it seems highly probable that she might have been rather over-familiar, and perhaps dropped some not-so-subtle hint that she was after more than steady employment, and was perhaps ready to be more than a mere servant to him.

How she accounted to others for her dismissal can only be guessed at, but that evening she was back in Albion Street knocking at the Sandersons' door, and there she would remain until she made the next move in her career.

Following her rebuff by Dr Shaw, Elizabeth turned her thoughts of employment away from domestic service and decided to do something that might hold more in the way of promise and security. She announced her intention to become a nurse, and to this end she went to the Manchester Royal Infirmary and enrolled for the necessary course of training, the £20 fee for her tuition coming from her late husband's insurance settlement. The course would take about six months, after which time, when she had passed her examinations, she could set about finding worthwhile employment in her new career – and at the same time continue to look for a new husband. It was surely not beyond the bounds of possibility that once she had qualified she could perhaps find a post caring for some wealthy widower, or land a position working alongside some eligible doctor or other professional gentleman of promise.

Elizabeth's efforts to remarry might strike some in today's society as rather strangely desperate, but in those times marriage was the goal of almost all young women. In Georgian and Victorian times the world was very much a man's world. Professions and careers in all walks of life were dominated by men. Such a situation still exists today in certain professions, such as engineering, architecture and the military, but in other professions the scene has changed. We read that more females than males are making careers in medicine today, and that female GPs outnumber male. In earlier times, however, a woman who wanted any kind of medical career could not realistically consider anything higher than nursing. It was not until 1876 that women were allowed to become doctors, and even then only a handful took up the opportunity and studied medicine at university – a situation that lasted until well after the Second World War. In general, the women of yesterday simply did not have careers. They were usually expected only to marry and be good wives and mothers. Men were the breadwinners, and as Jane Austen succinctly put it, marriage was 'the best preventer against want'. Without marriage or legal paid employment, a great many young women turned, in their desperation, to prostitution, leaving their home towns for the cities – notably London, which metropolis in mid-Victorian times is said to have boasted upwards of 60,000 prostitutes (one for every twenty men, went the reckoning).

It is not surprising, then, that Elizabeth Berry was out to get a husband, and with the exacting social situation being what it was, she moved with some alacrity, for her goal was not likely to be one that could be realized overnight.

It would not be long before she made her move.

Elizabeth had been raised as a Catholic like her parents, but with her marriage she changed her religion to that of the Protestant Church of England, and with Thomas worshipped regularly at their local church, St Luke's, where Thomas sang in the choir. Now, following her dismissal by Dr Shaw, the widowed Elizabeth resumed alone her attendance at St Luke's, and very soon began to have some sympathetic meetings with the church's curate and to offer to help him with his work, giving out tracts and such. And the association quickly became the subject of gossip. As one contributor to the *Chronicle* wrote, 'The grass over her husband's grave was scarcely green when she was often seen, flaunting about in a white dress, walking about with a curate...'

The young widow's meetings with the curate took place at weekends when she was free from her nursing studies at the Manchester Infirmary. And it wasn't long before the meetings developed into something rather more personal than might usually be the case for a grieving widow in need of a little tea and sympathy. In Mrs Berry's book the relationship became somewhat romantic in nature – though how far, in truth, it went in this direction we cannot know. She, however, was both experienced and determined. Though while *she* was in no way naïve, the same cannot be claimed for the reverend gentleman. Although he was regarded as a victim of her machinations, and unlikely to have made the running, it was said that 'she enamoured' him to such a degree that – so she contended – he proposed marriage. The truth of the matter is now beyond discovery, but whatever happened it was not long before the young man's relatives began strongly objecting to the union as a mésalliance, and the 'courtship' was broken off. In response, Mrs Berry, as determined and imaginative as ever, immediately threatened to sue for breach of promise, claiming in compensation the sum of £1,000 (£110,000 today).

The case did not go to court. While the young curate claimed to be well aware that her action was a 'plant' to obtain money, and stated that he was quite ready to defend the action in court, his mother had other ideas. She had no intention of seeing her son forced into such a scandalous situation, and went personally to confront the gay young widow. Speaking to her 'in no stinted terms', she told her plainly that she was on to her game, which was to obtain money regardless of the damage that such a court case would do to the character of her son, a young man just beginning to make for himself a position in life. 'What sort of a woman are you?' the curate's mother asked. 'I know that all you want is money. Tell me what it is and if it's reasonable it shall be paid.'

The upshot was that Mrs Berry did not get her £1,000 – but she did receive from the curate's mother the sum of £150.

So concluded that particular adventure – a 'discreditable incident' as the *Chronicle* described it, and one which further illustrates the darker side of Elizabeth Berry's character. And while the affair didn't bring her what she had hoped for – marriage – she ended up financially better off. She was, of course, well aware of the negative gossip that the affair provoked, but there can be no doubt that had she managed to land her fish she would have borne the contumely as she had borne such in the past. Although the clergyman's mother accused her of being after her son's money, there can be little doubt that it was indeed marriage that Mrs Berry was after, and with it the elevation of her social status. To rise from cotton-weaver and daughter of an illiterate mother to that of wife of a wealthy cleric would have been right in line with her ambitions.

Breach of promise is of course an antiquated concept now, and since the law was dropped in 1970 there can be no more prosecutions. And while no abandoned woman sues for damages today, neither does she, like some latter-day Miss Havisham, stay shut away in a darkened room in a greying wedding gown beside the remains of her rotting wedding breakfast, clutching her heart and murmuring that it is broken. As we well know, in the modern age with women no longer dependent on men and marriage, a scorned woman is less likely to seek financial redress than revenge. And while it has been known for some to go to the police with cries of rape, others have demonstrated other means of settling scores – perhaps pouring paint-stripper over the ex-loved one's Mercedes or cutting up his Armani suits.

Elizabeth Berry, though, was a different kettle of fish. And it might be argued that in her particular situation she made the best of a bad job. Faced with the humiliation of being discarded, she could have faded into the background. But this was not her style, and although she had failed to catch the husband she wanted, still there was comfort in being given a handsome pay-off by the curate's mother. And the fact that it was paid over so swiftly can only demonstrate how gravely the situation was regarded. But there again, perhaps the curate's mother got the measure of the young widow, and realized that she was dealing with a very dangerous woman.

6

Another Death

Undeterred by the scandalous outcome of her affair with the curate, Elizabeth Berry would resume her efforts to find a new husband before too much time had passed. In the meantime, having come to the end of her medical schooling, and now a qualified nurse and midwife, she was ready to take the first steps on the path of her new career.

While undergoing her training at the Manchester Royal Infirmary it is likely that she had hopes of her future work taking place in pleasant surroundings. If so, she was to be greatly disillusioned, for she soon discovered that the options open to her were very limited. Generally, the only realistic offers of steady employment came from the country's workhouses.

Her nursing career would last for six years, and all of it would be spent in a succession of workhouses in and around the towns of northern England. And to say that she detested the work would not be an exaggeration. Apart from being highly intelligent and regarding herself as superior to others of her station, she was fastidious to a degree. The milieu of the workhouse, then, would not have suited her for a moment, and it is hardly surprising that she was never content and kept moving on.

The last of the workhouses closed in the last century – but they were once ubiquitous, with hundreds scattered throughout the land. A brief look here at the institution will give some idea of the backdrop against which Elizabeth Berry's life was played out over the six years of her nursing career.

For hundreds of years before our present national welfare system came into being in the mid-twentieth century the care of the destitute had been the responsibility of the parishes, housing the homeless in poorhouses or workhouses. The Union Workhouses, as they were called, came into being in the nineteenth century when it was decided that it was time for such institutions to be centrally controlled, with the same governing rules in place across the country. So rules were laid down. Pauper inmates would have food, clothing (uniform), and a bed provided. Those who were fit were made to work. No coming and going at will was permitted – so gates were locked and guarded, liberty being allowed only to trusted inmates at certain times. The sexes were segregated, inevitably leading to families being split up. Not only were the healthy poor given shelter, but the sick also, with care given to the blind, the lame, imbeciles, lunatics and the terminally diseased. Each workhouse was run by a Master, or Governor, some of whom, as is the way of the world, abused their positions, so that over the years numerous instances came to light of the most dreadful cruelties meted out to inmates. Charles Dickens's workhouse setting for *Oliver Twist* was very much based on reality.

An illustration of the conditions found in some of the workhouses in the mid to late nineteenth century can be seen in a report made by an examiner from the Poor Law Board. It paints a remarkable picture – one which graphically reveals some of the horrors associated with the workhouses, and adds to their dark mythology.

The examination took place in October 1866 at the Oldham Union Workhouse, by coincidence the same workhouse which, twenty years later, was to be Elizabeth Berry's last place of employment, and the scene of Edith Annie's death.

The government inspector sent to look over the place was Poor Law Board officer Mr R.B. Cane. Judging by his subsequent report, his investigation appears to have been fairly thorough and, one might hope, led to some much needed changes. It is worth quoting part of his report. He wrote (his underlinings conveyed here in italics):

About one fifth of the inmates are Roman Catholics; about half the remainder are Dissenters, and the rest belong to the Church of England. All the inmates who are able to do so, go either to church or chapel out of the workhouse on Sundays. A clergyman of the

Church of England voluntarily performs a service in the workhouse on Sundays. "Town missionaries" visit the workhouse daily.

The ventilation of this workhouse is very imperfect, and the defect is immediately perceptible to the senses upon entering the wards. Many of the wards are close, dark, and gloomy. The water-closets are so imperfectly constructed that much of the foul air arising from them is drawn into the wards.

The children of both sexes are all quite young and small. They readily obtain employment as soon as they are old and strong enough; the boys go to the coal pits and factories; the girls become "nurse girls" and domestic servants. When in school, these children, boys as well as girls, are partly under pauper superintendence.

The men sleep together two in a bed, a most objectionable custom, and one that I hope to see entirely done away with very soon in this district. Smoking tobacco by the women as well as by men is prevalent in most of the wards here, as in many other workhouses in this district.

A woman who had been blind from her birth complained to me, though with much apparent hesitation and reluctance, that the pauper superintendent of the ward, of which she was an inmate, abused, swore at, and ill-treated the infirm women under her care; I inquired into the complaint, and came to the conclusion that it was well founded. The other inmates of the ward whom I questioned assured me that the superintendent ill-used them constantly; they seemed quite in fear of her. After consulting with the master and matron, it was arranged that this woman should be immediately superseded and removed from the ward, and her place filled by someone else.

There is a detached infirmary at this workhouse, and there are also detached wards called "fever wards"; there are no convalescent wards in either of these places. The number of sick and others requiring medical attendance at this time is eighty. Some of these cases, owing to the want of room, are placed in the ordinary sleeping wards, occupied by healthy persons in the main building.

The nursing, attendance, and general management of the sick in these wards is insufficient and unsatisfactory. Efficient nurses are urgently required, and they should be superintended and guided by a person of superior intelligence.

The sick are not always supplied with separate beds; in one ward *two old men were in the same bed together.* In another ward I found together a girl 13 years old afflicted by a "urinary complaint", a woman with "itch",* a child four years old with "whooping cough", a middle-aged woman with venereal disease, and an aged woman who, from infirmity, was unavoidably of extremely offensive habits. Into these wards was lately sent a case of cholera, which shortly afterwards terminated fatally. The convalescent patients from the fever wards are sent to the infirmary, and they mix with the other patients there.

There are no proper dining tables for those who are able to sit up and take their food. Consequently, they are obliged to place their plates upon the beds, their knees, their seats, and on the tops of the night stools [commodes]. Tables and table linen are much required.

Mr Cane's compelling report is interesting in many ways, not least in his recording of how a sub-standard nurse was removed and replaced on the spot for her unacceptable behaviour. That incident aside, the report presents a picture akin to hell, and shows well why individuals would consider anything rather than go into a workhouse – and in many cases end their miserable days there.

As noted, Mr Cane's examination of the Oldham workhouse was made in 1866, twenty years before Elizabeth Berry would step over the threshold, and by which time many improvements had been made. However, during her nursing career she would have been faced with conditions very similar to those observed by Mr Cane, and with her fastidiousness she must have recoiled from some of the demands made of her.

---

* A skin disease correctly named scabies, caused by *Sarcoptes scabiei*, a minute oval-shaped mite, just visible to the naked eye. The female burrows in the skin, forming small tunnels in which she lays her eggs. The eggs hatch and it is the movement of the larvae which causes intense itching, so giving the disease its common name. In earlier times in Great Britain scabies was rife among the population and virtually untreatable. Even today it requires the most careful treatment.

We are told that Mrs Berry's first post on completing her nurse's training was at the Prestwich Asylum in Manchester. But as with her brief employment as housekeeper by Dr Shaw, it didn't last, and after a very short time, for reasons not known, she was dismissed. Her next employment was somewhat further afield, at the Wellington Union Workhouse in Shropshire. She is said to have remained in this post for about nine months. Before leaving her situation, however, there took place a most surprising and tragic event.

Now and then, in between the periods of her employment at the various institutions, Elizabeth made calls at the home of her in-laws, the Sandersons, at Miles Platting, where Harold and Edith had been sent to live. And it was to their house in Albion Street that she repaired when she had been given some time off from her duties at the Wellington workhouse

Elizabeth and Edith Annie, c. 1882. From a photograph
likely to have been taken on a trip to Blackpool.

in the late summer of 1882. On her arrival she announced that she had come to take the children away on holiday.

The coastal town of Blackpool – 'where enjoyment is the watchword of the day', as the *Chronicle* would have it – was a popular and not overly expensive resort for those northerners who wanted a breath of sea air, and Elizabeth Berry had gone to stay in the town on more than one occasion. Early that September, a year after her husband's death, she packed up Harold and Edith's things and, with the excited children beside her, set off for the coast and the bright lights of the town.

After finding lodgings they spent their days enjoying the beach and the other diversions and amusements on offer, and taking refreshment in the seaside cafés. All seemed to go well, and it is likely that Harold and Edith enjoyed themselves. Tragically, however, on the return journey home on 18 September the children fell ill. By the time they arrived back at Miles Platting their condition was giving cause for concern. Fortunately, Edith recovered, but Harold's condition worsened. Two weeks later, on Thursday 27 September, he died.

His death will be examined later in this book.

Harold's body was laid to rest next to his father's in Manchester's Harpurhey Cemetery. His life having been insured with the Prudential Insurance Company, his bereaved mother promptly collected the due sum of £5.

7

And Yet Another Death

The year following Harold's death Mrs Berry left the Wellington Workhouse to seek new employment, and in April 1883 took up a position at the Union Workhouse at Burton-upon-Trent* in Staffordshire. A new building, it was a cut above many other such institutions, and possibly as a result of its relative comforts and mod-cons Mrs Berry's period of employment there was to be the longest in her nursing career. Even so, it was still a workhouse, and the future she had in mind did not embrace years on end of tending to the needs of the neighbourhood's down-and-outs, imbecilic vagrants, disease-ridden ex-prostitutes and incontinent septuagenarians.

She stayed until the end of October 1885, after which she went to Miles Platting to spend the rest of the year with the Sandersons and Edith Annie, her remaining child, and there to be joined for the Christmas period by her mother, who travelled from Castleton.

While staying in Miles Platting Mrs Berry had applied herself to the matter of finding new employment, and in January she applied for a post at the Chesterfield Union Workhouse in Derbyshire. The year now was

---

* By coincidence, some years later one of the ward attendants at the Burton-upon-Trent Workhouse would be one Dorothea Waddingham. A petty criminal with convictions for theft and fraud, she would later run a small nursing home in Nottingham, and, notwithstanding her lack of formal nurse's training, would nevertheless style herself 'Nurse' Waddingham. In 1936 she was hanged for poisoning one of the paying guests at the home. Waddingham was one of the last women in Britain to suffer the death penalty.

1886. It would prove to be a momentous year for her, and yet another year of drama and loss. She could not know that it was also to be her last year of freedom.

Her application to the workhouse meeting with success, it was arranged that she would assume her duties on Monday 1 February. As things turned out, however, she was to spend only one day in the job.

As agreed with the Board of Guardians, she arrived at the workhouse on the 1st and put in her first day's work, but on returning at eleven the next morning she informed an astonished Mr George Shaw, Clerk to the Guardians, that she would have to leave. That morning, she said, she had received a letter from her mother in Castleton, Rochdale, saying that she was seriously ill. Therefore she would have to go to her at once. By half-past eleven she was out of the building, and next day was on her way to Castleton to see her mother.

As we have seen, Mary Ann and William Finley had separated soon after their marriage. The break, however, didn't mark the end of their relationship. Following his spell in prison for deserting his children, Finley didn't see his wife and stepdaughter for some time, but eventually he and Mary Ann got in contact again and made up. Two years following their separation they were back together. The reunion didn't last. Only six weeks later, following quarrels and disagreements, he was gone again.

Mary Ann Finley.

Later, after Elizabeth had married and moved out with her husband, Mrs Finley left Manchester also, going alone to Rochdale. And there, some three years later, she got in touch with her wandering husband once more and they decided to make yet another new start together. This proved to be no more successful than the previous attempts, and in April 1880 they separated for the third and last time. Following William's final departure, Mrs Finley moved outside the town to Castleton where she rented a small house, at the same time supporting herself as a cotton weaver at a nearby mill. It was there, on Wednesday 3 February, that she received an unexpected visit from her daughter.

Arriving in Castleton, Mrs Berry made her way at once to Back Albion Street, the row of humble terrace houses where her mother had made her home. As it happened, Mrs Finley had that morning left to go to Manchester to visit relatives, so when her daughter came knocking on the door of number 6 she got no answer. Knowing that her mother must return before long, Mrs Berry knocked on the door of a neighbour at number 11. The door was opened by Mrs Sarah Wolfenden, to whom Mrs Berry introduced herself, saying that she was Mrs Finley's daughter Lizzie, and that she had come to call on her mother but had found her not at home. Mrs Wolfenden, impressed by her caller's appearance and manner – later describing her as 'quite a lady' – invited her to come in and have some tea.

Mrs Berry gladly accepted the invitation, and over their teacups she told her hostess that she was an infirmary nurse, and had just obtained a new situation in that capacity at the Birmingham Union Workhouse. She had been to Birmingham that morning, she said, to take up her new appointment, but on arriving there had found that the nurse whose place she was to take would not be vacating her position until a week later, the result being that she, Mrs Berry, would not be required to start in the position until the nurse alluded to had gone away. It was for this reason, she said, that she had decided to visit her mother. All lies, of course, and Mrs Wolfenden might have wondered why it was necessary for Mrs Berry to travel all the way to Birmingham to discover that she couldn't start work there for another week. Britain's postal service was second to none at that time, and Mrs Wolfenden might have questioned the fact that the guardians of the Birmingham workhouse did not think to save her a journey by writing and informing her of the changed situation.

Be that as it may, Mrs Berry continued to impress her kind hostess, speaking 'in good style' and giving the impression that she was a lady who 'knew Latin and foreign languages'. At one point in their discourse Mrs Berry spoke of wanting to find a pharmaceutical chemist, upon which Mrs Wolfenden told her that there was none in Castleton, but that she would find one in Rochdale, and gave her the name of the street on which he could be found.

As their conversation moved on, Mrs Berry said something that Mrs Wolfenden would not easily forget. The night before, she said, she had had a remarkable dream, and that whenever she had had such a dream in the past a member of her family had died. Mrs Wolfenden would later have good cause to remember Mrs Berry's words.

At some point in the evening Mrs Berry must have gone back to number 6 to see whether her mother had returned, for shortly after nine o'clock the two of them were reunited.

There is no doubt that Mrs Finley was pleased to see her daughter. Matters between them had not always been as Mrs Finley would have liked, and there had been a prolonged period when Elizabeth would have nothing to do with her mother. Mrs Berry would later claim that they had fallen out over 'a religious matter', but whatever the reason for the rift, it was well known among Mrs Finley's relatives and friends that there was an estrangement between the pair, and among her Castleton neighbours Mrs Finley had made no secret of the fact that Lizzie had not 'owned' her for some considerable time. It was known also that Elizabeth had declined to help her mother financially, even when she knew her to be in very poor circumstances.

Happily for Mrs Finley, however, the estrangement between them appeared to have been mended, for in December had come the invitation from the Sandersons to spend Christmas at Miles Platting along with Elizabeth and granddaughter Edith. She had gladly accepted the invitation and on returning to Castleton two or three days afterwards had happily told a neighbour that she had seen her daughter and 'made it all right with her at last'.

Back Albion Street. The modest street in Castleton, where Mary Ann Finley was renting a house when Elizabeth visited her in February 1886. *Photograph: Jack Ireland, c. 1986.*

It was shortly after her return from Miles Platting that Mrs Finley began to suffer bleeding from the nose. She recovered from it, however, and was in good health when her daughter made her surprise visit on 3 February. Certainly any observer would have noted that, contrary to what Elizabeth had told Mr Shaw at the Chesterfield workhouse, her mother was *not* in the grave state of health that she had reported to him. She had given him to understand that her mother was at death's door, but this was clearly far from the case.

This was not to be the last that Mr Shaw heard from his briefly-employed nurse. On 5 February, three days after her hurried departure, he received a letter from her telling him that she could not return to her post as her mother was 'sinking fast'. Included with her letter was a formal letter of resignation.

Although Mrs Berry's statement that her mother was 'sinking fast' could not have been further from the truth, her words turned out to be sadly ominous. All too soon Mrs Finley's health would be giving cause for grave concern.

None of Mrs Finley's neighbours had met Mrs Berry before that February, for she had never before visited Back Albion Street. However, they knew that she was a qualified nurse, so on learning of her arrival they would have been glad to know that their neighbour would be in the best possible hands. To their shock and sadness, however, they saw Mrs Finley's health begin to fail in the swiftest and most alarming way. Over the space of a few days those friends and neighbours watched as her condition deteriorated. Come the Saturday morning, she was dead.

The day after her mother's death, Elizabeth wasted no time in making arrangements for the funeral, and Mrs Finley was buried a week later at the Moston Catholic Cemetery, after which Elizabeth set about selling her mother's possessions. The dead woman's clothes were the first things to go, followed by her other effects. Elizabeth also set about collecting the payments on the various insurance policies that came due on her mother's death.

When the small rooms of 6 Back Albion Street had been stripped of anything of value and the keys returned to the landlord, Elizabeth Berry must have felt some sense of relief. Another chapter was closed; it was over, and she could look again to the future.

If these were her thoughts, however, then she was wrong. It was not over. Those neighbours who had come to call on the ailing Mrs Finley had remained disturbed by the dramatic happening, and whispered among themselves. And though they might also have thought that the unhappy business was over and done with, they too were to be mistaken. Mrs Finley was dead, her remains lying in a cheap coffin in the cemetery, but they were not to lie undisturbed for long. In a year there would be gravediggers hacking at the earth to bring her coffin back up into the light. Much then would be revealed, and some of the dark questions would be answered.

8

The Oldham Union Workhouse

After leaving her late mother's house in Back Albion Street, Elizabeth Berry went to lodge in nearby Whitworth Road. While staying there she saw advertised in the local papers the vacant post of nurse at the Rochdale Union Workhouse, and she wrote applying for the position, stating in her letter of application that she had considerable experience in a nursing capacity, adding, 'If given the situation it is my earnest desire, under the Divine blessing, to do my duty truly and well.' Her application, however, proved unsuccessful.

Some weeks passed, and then in May, still from her lodgings, she answered an advertisement for a situation in Oxfordshire at the workhouse at Henley-on-Thames, the small, pleasant town known for its annual rowing festival. The position, offering a complete change of scene, far away from the grim, grey mills of the north, promised much, and she was delighted to learn that her application had succeeded.

Sadly, however, her happiness was soon to be dashed, for she arrived at the workhouse and departed on the very same day. With echoes of earlier incidents, she somehow managed to outrage her would-be employer almost immediately upon her arrival. We cannot know exactly what passed, but the *Chronicle* later reported: 'Her conduct there was so insolent to the Master of the workhouse…that she was told to pack up and be off, not having been on the premises more than an hour.' It has to be surmised that this information came from the Master himself, as it is inconceivable that Mrs Berry would have chosen to let it be known.

So she remained out of work, but not for much longer. The next month, June, she saw advertised a nursing position at the Union Workhouse in Oldham. The post, that of senior resident nurse in the female wing of the infirmary, offered an annual salary of £25, plus free board and lodging. She wasted no time in making her application and, following submission of references from the Burton-upon-Trent workhouse, she was invited for an interview on 7 July. It was to be a seminal event in her life.

One of six candidates for the post, she was interviewed by the governing body of the workhouse and, most notably, by Dr Thomas Patterson, a thirty-six-year-old Irish bachelor who had been the workhouse's medical officer for eleven years. With the doctor having a prominent voice in the choice for the post, Mrs Berry was selected. She would later claim that when offered the post she initially declined it – we

Elizabeth Berry. A newspaper illustration
taken from a photograph, c. 1886.

are given no reason – and was only persuaded to accept it by Dr Patterson, who followed her out of the boardroom and asked her to reconsider. He very much wished her to take up the appointment, she said, and assured her that if she accepted it he would see that she had 'efficient help and every comfort'. So, she said, 'I consented to accept the office, and went again into the Board room and was re-elected.'

Had she been able to see into her future she would have learned that in meeting the good doctor that day she was meeting her nemesis. Later she would make the most dynamic and infamous charges against him. Guilty of them or not, the doctor was to have the most profound effect on her life and prove a vital instrument in her dark fate.

If the Board of Guardians imagined that after Dr Patterson's intervention all would be well with Mrs Berry's appointment, they were swiftly disabused of their expectations. The capricious element in her nature would soon again come to the fore.

It was agreed that she would begin her duties a week later on Wednesday 14 July, but when that day came she failed to turn up to begin her duties. Then, at 8.15 that evening, the workhouse master, Mr William Lawson, received a telegram. Addressed to 'Workhouse Master', it stated:

MRS BERRY CANNOT COME TONIGHT DAUGHTER MET WITH A SERIOUS ACCIDENT THIS AFTERNOON WILL BE THERE IN THE MORNING.

So Mr Lawson waited. But come next morning there was still no sign of her, and no further word came all day. And then, about 7.45 the next morning, Friday, Mr Lawson received a letter. Giving the sender's address as '99 Wilmott Street, Stretford Road, Manchester', with a message even briefer than that of the telegram, it said:

Mrs Berry can't undertake the duties of nurse to your hospital owing to her daughter's illness.
[signed] E. Berry

This very surprising news placed Mr Lawson in a most awkward position, and he decided that he must at once acquaint Mr Mellor, the Clerk to the Guardians, with the state of affairs, and with this in mind he set off for Mellor's office. On the way, however, as he reached the corner of King Street and Manchester Street, whom should he meet but Mrs Berry herself. Greatly surprised, he asked her what she was doing in Oldham, and she replied that she was of course on her way to the workhouse to begin her duties. Not a little puzzled, he told her that he had received a telegram and then a letter from her saying that she would not accept the situation, and he was now on his way to Mr Mellor's office to see what he must do to get someone to fill the place.

To his further surprise, she said, 'What do you mean? I never sent any letter. Let me look at it.'

He handed her both the letter and the telegram. Looking first at the letter, she said, 'I know nothing at all about it,' to which Mr Lawson remarked, 'It's strange – there's your name and all there.' She did, however, confirm that she had sent the telegram, and told him that her child had indeed fallen downstairs at a hotel in Scarborough where they were staying, and sustained concussion. She had called out a doctor to her, she said. She herself, she added, had been travelling all night, reaching York at two o'clock that morning. There, after sleeping the rest of the night in the waiting room, she had caught the first available train to Oldham, where she had then gone straight to Mr Mellor's office.

After this strange meeting, the two together, Nurse Berry and a very bewildered Mr Lawson, made their way to the Oldham workhouse, where, at 10.15, Mrs Berry commenced her duties.

Mr Lawson had no further discussions with her about the puzzling matter, but over the coming months he would come to know her distinctive handwriting very well, and he would be in no doubt whatever that the letter had been written by her – his conviction firmly endorsed by other persons in the workhouse. This being so, it indicates that Mrs Berry did indeed have second and third thoughts about accepting the position, and then, for some reason, had changed her mind again. As for her tale of Edith Annie having fallen downstairs while staying in Scarborough, there was no truth in it. Ann Sanderson would later state that the child had never fallen downstairs, had never been to Scarborough, and at the time cited was safe in Miles Platting.

Altogether it was a most astonishing incident, and one wonders how Mrs Berry could have thought for one moment that her extraordinary story would be accepted. After freely admitting sending the telegram, she had denied having written the letter. But it is surely not within the bounds of possibility that the letter could have come from some other party. Furthermore, although she said that her daughter had suffered an accident at a hotel in Scarborough, the telegram had not come from that north Yorkshire town, nor from anywhere near it. Like the letter that followed, it had been sent from Hulme, an inner city ward of Manchester, only about twelve miles from the Oldham workhouse. This is borne out by the telegram itself, on which was clearly written: 'Handed in at the Manchester York St office at 7.47 p.m.'

Another question arises concerning the very odd business, and the strange scenario that it suggests – a question that Mr Lawson might have been tempted to put to his new nurse – and that is with regard to her claim that her daughter had fallen downstairs. What then did she, Mrs Berry, do about the child afterwards? She claimed that Edith's accident was 'serious', that she had been concussed, and that a doctor had been called out to her. And yet here was the child's mother in Oldham – with no sign of the child. If Edith had been injured in Scarborough, then what had become of her? Where was she? Had Mrs Berry simply abandoned her, leaving her at the Scarborough hotel? As far as is known, there is no record of such a question being posed.

As was later established, there was no Scarborough hotel, there was no holiday with daughter Edith, there was no serious accident. In all likelihood, during the intervening week between her interview for the post, and the day of her proposed commencement in it, Mrs Berry was all the time staying close by in Hulme, near Manchester's city centre, there chopping and changing in her mind as to whether or not she should commit herself to her new engagement at the workhouse.

As for the bewildered Mr Lawson that morning, one thing that must have become disappointingly clear to him from the bizarre business was that his newly engaged nurse was the most unconscionable, unsubtle and outrageous liar. And such a realization could not have boded well for the future.

The Lancashire town of Oldham, where Elizabeth Berry was to spend her final period of employment, was one of the most important centres of the textiles industry until the decline of the cotton trade in the last century. The workhouse, where she came to live and work in that summer of 1886, was situated on the Rochdale Road (now known also as the A671), leading north to Rochdale and Burnley. As we have seen, the shocking report from the Poor Law Board officer of 1866 (see pp. 32–4) was made on this very institution, though in the twenty years since Mr Cane had made his investigation the place had seen many changes.

Photographs of the building show a wide-fronted, red-brick building with numerous additions, and it was much like this in its layout and appearance when Elizabeth Berry began work there. The main building's construction had been completed in 1851, after which time were added wards for the sick, for 'male and female imbeciles', accommodation 'for lunatics', a school to hold 350 children, plus a chapel, dormitories, wash-houses and dining hall and, later, workshops, kitchens and a boiler house. In the degree of its self-sufficiency it appears an extraordinary place – it not only had its own gardens, wherein inmate gardeners worked to provide vegetables for the kitchens, but boasted also what was rather generously called a farm – a plot housing pigs, chickens, etc.

The running of the place was overseen by a Board of Guardians who met every Wednesday, a report of which weekly meeting would be published the following day in the *Chronicle*.

The Oldham Union Workhouse, where Elizabeth Berry took up employment in 1886. Photograph, c. 1900.

The report of the meeting of 14 July, two days before Elizabeth Berry's arrival in the place, gives a typical picture of the institution. With twenty officers present it was reported that in the previous week there were 847 souls resident – these in addition to the paid staff, the manager, the guards, the porters, the nurses, and so on. The pauper inmates, as they were known, were made up of 315 adult males, 276 adult females, 129 boys, 97 girls, 30 infants. Of the adults there were 42 men and 52 women in the imbecile wards. There had been one birth, and three deaths. Nineteen souls had been admitted during the week, and 23 had been discharged. The Guardians' report also noted the number of vagrants who had come to the workhouse in search of succour, a total of 218 men, women and children. These would have been fed and watered and sent on their way. The institution was also the regular recipient of various charitable donations from certain members of the public; in this case it was reported by the Master that 'Mr Asa Binns Kershaw of Greenacres Road had forwarded a parcel of copies of the "Quiver" and "Cassell's Magazine". He also mentioned that Mr Hargreaves, of High Street, and the scholars of the Friends' Meeting House, in Greaves Street, 'came and practised the children for the Whitsuntide hymns'. The thanks of the board were ordered to be forwarded to the parties named.

This, then, was the Oldham Union Workhouse, the setting for Elizabeth Berry's last period of employment, and scene of the death of her only surviving child.

Regardless of her personal feelings about the place, there can be no doubt that in her new position Mrs Berry had improved her lot. She held the most responsible senior post and enjoyed very comfortable living quarters. Workhouse Master Mr Lawson, who described her as 'a most extraordinary woman, possessed of more than ordinary intelligence', later remarked that she occupied 'the nicest and cosiest sitting-room about the premises'. 'The room contained a marble mantelpiece, and the hearth was tiled,' he said, 'which couldn't be said of any other room occupied by an official. In addition she had a bevy of inmates to serve her both in her professional capacity and in a personal one. She was considered very clever at her business, and the workhouse officials had the highest opinion of her abilities.' As for her general conduct, he remarked, in something of an understatement, that 'at times she became somewhat excited'.

Lawson was certainly correct in describing her as an extraordinary woman. And she very quickly let it be known that she was no run-of-the-mill workhouse infirmary nurse. Immediately on assuming her post she surprised the Guardians with the announcement that she had taken up the study of physiology, and wished to pursue it further by taking a course of lectures that were being given in Manchester. Her reasons for this could bear some examination. She surely didn't believe that the lectures could enhance her work as a nurse, so it is more than likely that her reason for wanting to take the course was the opportunity that she thought it might offer – that of meeting, on a regular, weekly basis, eligible men – young doctors in training, as likely as not. Unfortunately for her dreams, however, she couldn't be spared; the lectures were given on Wednesdays, at the same time that her attendance was required at the weekly meetings at the workhouse. In an effort to assuage her disappointment and accommodate her, the Guardians arranged for their new nurse to be given the loan of some books on the subject. It soon became clear, though, that it was not expertise in physiology that she was after, for her supposed enthusiasm was seen to evaporate as quickly as it was born. As was reported to one of the men from the *Chronicle*, '...she was not a great student, for her inclinations in that direction were just as changeable as her temper'.

Whatever disappointment she felt at being denied attendance at the lectures, it is clear that she regarded her engagement at the workhouse as a mere step in the process of bettering herself, to which end she remained intent on procuring a good second marriage. By no means put off by her scandalous failure with the Royton cleric, she had continued over the years, whenever possible, to make the acquaintance of divers promising men. While employed at the Burton-on-Trent workhouse she was said to have 'captivated a medical gentleman', confiding to friends that she several times visited him in Torquay. Unfortunately for her, however, the affair ended with no satisfactory conclusion. Undaunted, she was soon to embark on another romantic liaison. The *Oldham News* was later to report that while employed at the Oldham workhouse she frequently travelled to Derby, where she had 'secured a lover, a gentleman of means, a widower with an only son'. Judging by contemporary accounts, this appeared to be a most promising liaison and Mrs Berry set great store by it, daring to see in it, eventually, the realization of her dreams. To her great disappointment, however, when it came to the crunch, the gentleman would not commit, telling her that he was reluctant to remarry until his son came of age. Whether this was the truth we shall never know. It is doubtful; it rather appears that the man was having second thoughts about the affair. In any case, and tragically for Mrs Berry's hopes and ambitions in the matter, word came to her that the gentlemen had died.

This must have been a considerable blow to her, but she did not give up. From her Oldham workhouse residence she resumed her quest, whenever an opportunity arose going in her finery to various social functions such as parties and balls. One such outing, which she would later have reason most vividly to recall, was to a policemen's ball in the town that summer where she met a certain gentleman who, at her invitation, joined her in a dance. They got on well, and in the course of their conversation she told him something of herself and her work. Whether he in turn mentioned that he was married, or spoke of his occupation, we do not know. As for the latter, perhaps due to its unusual nature – which we shall come to later on – he was reluctant to reveal too much, though she would most certainly learn of it before long. At the end of the evening they shared a cab and a train compartment on their ways home, and when their journeys diverged said their goodbyes, not expecting to meet again. Their meeting, though, was not to be their last. The man with whom the gay young widow flirted and chatted and invited to join her in the 'mazy' dance was soon to come into her life again, and in the most dramatic circumstances.

For all her personal comforts within the workhouse, Elizabeth Berry can have found little pleasure or contentment in the place. And going by reports of her behaviour with fellow staff members, she was not by any means an easy woman to befriend. The building itself offered no amusements or diversions, and she was likely to have spent much of her free time alone in her sitting room, reading.

By all accounts she was a voracious reader, with a love of romantic novels and poetry, added to which, through the plethora of newspapers available, she would have kept abreast of happenings in the world. That year of 1886 saw its share of upheavals on the international scene, while in Great Britain there was great political change, there being two governments within a year – Gladstone leading the Liberals to power in February, and then being replaced by the Conservatives under Salisbury in August.

Away from the political scene there were happenings of a more scandalous nature making the headlines, among them several sensational murder trials. In April, Mrs Adelaide Bartlett had stood trial in London accused of poisoning her husband with chloroform. Lucky for her, she was acquitted. Not so fortunate was forty-two-year-old Mary Ann Britland, of Ashton-under-Lyne. A factory worker by day and barmaid by night, that July she was in the dock charged with the murder of her neighbour's wife, through poisoning by strychnine, though it was accepted that she had also poisoned her husband and her nineteen-year-old daughter. At the conclusion of her trial she was found guilty and soon afterwards hanged. One of the witnesses at her trial was Dr Thomas Harris, a Manchester medical expert. He was a man whom Mrs Berry herself was soon to encounter. Fortunately she could not see into the future, and it is safe to say that she would have read the reports on the murder trials with nothing more than interest, and probably, like other readers, a certain amount of enjoyment.

As observed, Mr Lawson, the Workhouse Master, in remarking that Elizabeth Berry at times 'became somewhat excited' was not exaggerating. On the contrary, he was putting it mildly. And if the bizarre events that had surrounded her arrival at the start of her employment had rung no warning bells he would soon have real cause to wonder if the Guardians and the medical officer had done the right thing in electing her. On *her* part, bearing in mind her claim that she initially refused the post when it was offered, and then, after accepting it, wrote to the Master declining it yet again, it is clear that she cannot have entered into her new employment with any great enthusiasm. The fact is that, less than happy with her situation at the start, it was downhill for her from then on.

Her growing dissatisfaction and discontent with her lot was swiftly to become apparent to everyone around her, with the Guardians soon being informed that the behaviour of their newly engaged infirmary nurse was giving cause for concern. Making her mark in the most negative and extraordinary way, to the general surprise and growing alarm, Nurse Berry was soon found to be 'not the kind, motherly person that was expected and desired' – as the *Chronicle* put it – but to be regarded by employees and inmates alike as not only difficult and demanding but possessed of a most fearsome and violent temper. Later, when her time at the workhouse was over, several of those associated with the place came forward to report on their experiences with her. All her patients, it was said, had come to be in dread of her – and not only her patients, but also many of those with whom she worked. In particular, her treatment of the women who acted as her servants was frequently violent. Indeed, it was said that when the least crossed she would not hesitate to throw a bottle or a boot at anyone whom she considered had offended her. If such reports on her behaviour appear perhaps a little extreme, they were not in fact untypical. And as the weeks passed, the instances of her shocking behaviour increased in number and in their intensity.

Today, observing her most marked personality disorder, she would be regarded by many as a psychopath or sociopath. There can be no doubt that she was finding her continuing situation in life a massive disappointment, and in all probability was beginning to despair of finding any solution to her chronic problem. Possessed as she was of high intelligence and huge ambition, she had nevertheless made no advance whatsoever, either professionally or in her personal life. In her years as a nurse she had gone from one workhouse post to another, always seeking improvement and betterment, but with no single engagement bringing her any acceptable degree of satisfaction. And, vitally, her overarching aim, to find security in a satisfactory marriage, had so far, for all her efforts, come to nothing. Her affair with the businessman in Derby having ended with the reporting of his death, she could see, at thirty-three years of age, and with a child still to support, her chances fading by the day, and nothing before her but long years of soul-destroying work in a workhouse infirmary.

With her dissatisfaction growing, matters came to a head with a most extraordinary incident that took place early in December.

As has been observed, things had not been going smoothly following her arrival in the place, and according to Mrs Berry her problems were all due to Dr Patterson. He it was, of course, as the workhouse's medical officer, who had overall control and sway over the medical staff and situation in the place, and it wasn't long before he and his new infirmary nurse were in disagreement.

The Home Office file on Mrs Berry's case reveals a copy of a lengthy letter she wrote on 10 March the following year to Dr John Kershaw, of Sedgely Park, Prestwich. As stated earlier, Dr Kershaw was acquainted with her from earlier years, and his relationship with her would sustain until the end. She had in him, there is no doubt, a true friend.

In her letter to the doctor, she would speak of several conflicts with Dr Patterson, arising, she claimed, from her refusal to carry out some of his requests – one of them to teach midwifery to nurse Lydia Evett. Citing one particular incident, when she had declined to carry out an instruction from the Governor himself, she wrote that Patterson told her that he would have had her suspended for her refusal. 'I felt more pained than I could express,' she wrote, 'and I said, "Dr Patterson, I could not have thought you capable of anything so base and treacherous," and he laughed – a laugh which as I have thought of since has made me shudder, and he said, "You don't know what I could be capable of."' In view of Elizabeth Berry's acknowledged mendaciousness one might wonder if a large pinch of salt might be taken along with her words, but whatever the actuality, early in December there occurred an event that became not only the subject of much gossip, but was also to be reported in the press. Mrs Berry too was later to give her own account of it.

In her letter to Dr Kershaw she writes of the incident, saying:

> I was ill myself with an attack of bronchitis. Dr Patterson prescribed for me. After taking the medicine I had great pain in my head and could not sleep. This sleeplessness continued for three days when he said he would give me a good big draught. Within an hour of taking it I was insane. He again visited same day and gave me chloroform, as he afterwards told Mrs Sanderson would have killed seven strong men. He remained with me the greater part of that night and when he left Mr Fletcher and Mr Minnihan were left in charge.

Others on the scene told a different story of Mrs Berry being 'insane', and a rather more shocking story it was. According to contemporary reports, the dramatic events were brought on by a violent quarrel that erupted between Mrs Berry and another of the senior female employees, most likely to have been Lydia Evett. For Mrs Berry the incident proved to be dynamic. It may be that with her frustration and dissatisfaction near the surface, the quarrel was the catalyst for the horror that was to come. Whatever the case, it set in motion a chain of events that was to end in death.

The *Chronicle* reported on the incident under the heading EXTRAORDINARY BEHAVIOUR AT THE WORKHOUSE. We do not know who was the editor's informant. The account may have come from more than one witness, one of whom was almost certainly Dr Patterson, but whoever the source, it was said to describe a scene 'which will not soon be forgot by those who witnessed it' when, in the female infirmary:

> ... Mrs Berry went into one of the wards where the patients were, and began to slap the poor people on the face as they lay bedfast, while some of those she ill-used by shaking them. The servants under her were naturally much afraid, and called in assistance. It was plainly seen that the woman was suffering from some nervous or brain excitement, and so strange did her conduct become that Dr Patterson was sent for. On his arrival she had become much worse, and it was an extremely difficult matter to conjecture what had come over the nurse. After much toiling with her she became a little quieter, but threatened to kill the first person that came near her, and kept continually calling for a knife so that she could cut their throats. She was walked about in the hope that she would become tired, and after a time was so much improved as to be left by herself. All was not over, however, for in the night she had to be held down by two women, who had the greatest difficulty in performing that unwelcome duty. The next day when she was somewhat better, a draught was given to her with the instructions that she was to take half of it then, and the other half when she went to bed. She did not, however, do that, but took the whole of it at once, and on one of the servants going into her room she flung the glass at her as soon as she got inside. The attack left her as quickly almost as it came on, and when she woke from a sleep, and found a number of persons who had been attending her in her room, she became very indignant and wanted to know what they were doing there. When questioned she would not answer a single

word and not to this day do those who witnessed the affair know what caused the strange attack. During the brief spell of madness she broke several ornaments, and managed to lock herself in the surgery, the door of which had to be broken open.

Mrs Berry's behaviour was nothing if not alarming, and Dr Patterson gave it that she was suffering from a fever due to 'congestion of the brain'.

There was then, it seems, some relative calm for a brief period during which, on 13 December, her sister-in-law Ann Sanderson came to the workhouse for a short visit, bringing with her the young Edith Annie to see her mother. They stayed over until the 15th.

The visit brought no peace for Mrs Berry, however, and as Christmas approached she went on to exhibit more of her brain fever 'indispositions', the outcome of which was that at her request Dr Patterson urged the governor to allow her a few days away from her duties. The Board of Guardians only reluctantly consented, one of them remarking that she had been seen 'knocking about' and that there appeared to be not much the matter with her. Be that as it may, she was given a few days' leave, and so it was that on the morning of Monday 27 December, she left the place. First, it is said – and obviously feeling much improved – she went to a wedding to which she had been invited, and immediately afterwards made her way to Miles Platting and the home of her in-laws, Ann and John Sanderson.

It was there, during her brief stay, that she arranged to bring Edith back again to Oldham for a little holiday, this time extending an invitation to one of Edith's friends, Beatrice Hall, to come along with her for company. And so it was that on 29 December a much-excited Edith and friend Beatrice, in the charge of Mrs Berry, set off by horse-drawn tram to Oldham. They arrived at the workhouse at 6.15.

There is no doubt that the visit promised a very pleasant little break for the two girls, and it began in the most relaxed and carefree way. Edith and Beatrice would eat their meals in Mrs Berry's sitting room and share her comfortable bed at night, while during the day, when Mrs Berry was busy with her nursing duties, they would be free to play about the place or go out to the nearby shops and about the town.

It was the custom that each year the officers of the workhouse held a Christmas/New Year ball. That year it was to take place on Thursday, the day following the girls' arrival, and on that morning Mrs Berry, clearly now completely recovered from her attacks of 'brain fever', set off for Manchester to do some shopping in preparation for the event.

Left to their own devices, Edith and Beatrice went to look around the local shops, where they bought some sweets and biscuits. Later, back at the workhouse, they awaited Mrs Berry's return, and on her arrival ran out into the street to meet her. After helping to carry her parcels back indoors and into her sitting room, they watched as she unpacked the gown that she had bought for the ball, a glamorous, ruby-red affair which, she proudly told them, had cost four guineas (upwards of £450 today). To go with it were silk stockings, a fan and a pair of delicate slippers.

That evening, in all her splendour, Mrs Berry went off to the party, leaving the two girls content to amuse themselves and get to bed. The next day the girls went out to the local Friday market where they bought fish for their tea, and Edith bought a little gift for her beloved Aunt Ann. In the afternoon they went to the local swimming baths where they watched an aquatics display. That evening in Mrs Berry's sitting room they ate their

Edith Annie Berry, from a photograph, c. 1885.

supper, and afterwards went up to the bedroom where they were later joined by Mrs Berry, and where, side by side, once more, the three of them slept the night in Mrs Berry's bed.

It was clear to everyone who had observed Edith since her arrival that she was having a happy time and was delighting in her mother's attentions and affection. At the same time Mrs Berry gave every sign of devotion to her child, frequently being heard referring to her as her 'darling'. Eleven-year-old Edith had had her share of unhappiness in her life, and there can be no reason to doubt that she was greatly enjoying her little holiday in the company of her friend and her usually-absent mother.

Mrs Berry, it would seem, had thought of everything to make her daughter's visit a pleasure, and that Friday night marked for Edith the end of a very happy day. Tragically, it would be the last happy day that she would know.

9

Death in the Workhouse

Elizabeth Berry's bedroom was situated on the first floor of a block situated across a paved yard from the main workhouse building, and there, at about seven o'clock on the morning of Saturday 1 January, she rose from her bed, which she was sharing with Edith and Beatrice, and got ready to start the day. A little while later, with the girls still sleeping, she let herself out of the room and made her way downstairs to the ground floor and there crossed the yard to the main building.

In her sitting room she was served breakfast, after which she began her daily routine, visiting patients in the female wing of the infirmary and then doing any necessary work in the surgery which, most conveniently, was right next door to her sitting room. She and Dr Patterson alone each held a key to the surgery, and it was here where she prepared the bandages, plasters, and whatever ointments and medicines had been prescribed by the doctor. Of all the infirmary's medicinal supplies that were held in the surgery, the most dangerous of the medicines were kept safely locked up in a cupboard to which only Dr Patterson kept a key, though there were many other items not secured in the locked cupboard that could prove perilous to health if wrongly used.

Soon after nine o'clock Mrs Berry's initial duties were finished, and she was back in her sitting room at 9.30 when Edith and Beatrice came in, ready to have their breakfasts. At ten, when the girls' breakfasts were on the table, Edith complained that she felt sick and couldn't eat. Moments later she began to vomit. Alarmingly, her vomiting grew more frequent and soon the vomited matter was seen to be streaked with blood. Something had to be done, and as soon as Dr Patterson arrived at the workhouse shortly after noon Mrs Berry sent for him to come and see the child. He entered the sitting room to find Edith lying on the sofa. She complained of pains over her belly, and Mrs Berry, asked as to the likely cause of the child's illness, said she thought it was due to her having had a heavy supper the night before. She then handed the doctor a towel on which, she said, was some of Edith's vomited matter, and showed him a vessel containing a quantity of matter with blood in it. The doctor thought that the girl might be suffering from an ulcerated stomach, and with this in mind he went next door to the surgery and made up a medicine which he gave to Mrs Berry with directions as to the girl's treatment. Then, after instructing her to put the child to bed, he left.

In spite of the doctor's ministrations Edith continued to vomit and suffer pain, and that afternoon when Beatrice went to see her – she was now lying in Mrs Berry's bed upstairs – Mrs Berry sent her off to fetch the head nurse of the female imbecile ward. She, Sarah Anderson, came without delay, but could do nothing to ease the child's suffering.

That night, at 10.20, having been summoned by Mrs Berry, Dr Patterson came to see Edith again, now in Mrs Berry's bedroom. He found her no better. On asking Mrs Berry whether she had given the child the medicine he had left she replied that she had tried to do so on two occasions, but each time the child had vomited it up. After instructing her to give the child no more of the medicine mixture, he left, saying he would call again the next day.

Next day, Sunday the 2nd, was to bring better news. When Dr Patterson called at noon he was relieved to find Edith's condition considerably improved. The girl's vomiting was less frequent, Mrs Berry told him. She then once more handed him a towel with vomited matter on it. Putting it to his nose he found it had an acidic smell. With Mrs Berry accompanying him, he then went down to the surgery and there set about making up a mixture of creosote* and bicarbonate of soda. Finding the creosote bottle empty, in an act that would come back to haunt him, he made do

---

* There are two kinds of creosote – wood-tar and coal-tar, the wood-tar variety being then used medicinally as an antiseptic, anaesthetic and laxative.

with rinsing it out with a little water and adding the solution to the bicarbonate of soda. After giving Mrs Berry directions on when to administer the medicine, he ordered more creosote to be got from the chemist, and instructed her on how to make up the mixture. That done, he left Mrs Berry's side, saying that she should send him word of Edith's progress.

Although Dr Patterson had expressed optimism when voicing his hopes for Edith's recovery, this was not reflected in the reality, for later that afternoon the child's condition took a turn for the worse. Mrs Berry, expressing great concern at the situation, sent urgently for Sarah Anderson from the female imbecile ward to come and see the girl again, and a little later for the head nurse of the children's ward, Lydia Evett. The two women found Edith vomiting and suffering great pain in the stomach and bowels, but neither was able to do anything to help.

Just after five o'clock Dr Patterson was again sent for, but he did not arrive until about nine o'clock that night. When he did, he was shocked to see the child. Where he had expected to find her further improved, it was to find that in the hours since his last visit her condition had greatly deteriorated. Not only was she in great pain, and vomiting, but now he saw that her lips were red and swollen and there was a blister on her upper lip. When he spoke of it to Mrs Berry, she told him that she had given the child a lemon with some sugar, and she supposed it was the lemon that had caused it. She also said that the child was vomiting very frequently, and was also being purged, the evacuations containing blood. Now alarmed, Dr Patterson said that he wanted to have the opinion of another doctor, and leaving the child's side he at once went to the home of a colleague, Dr Robertson, and asked him to come and see her without delay.

Dr George Robertson – a thirty-seven-year-old Scot with a medical practice nearby – obeyed the urgent summons and accompanied Dr Patterson to the child's bedside. There Mrs Berry told him of Edith's vomiting and purging. Dr Patterson had by now abandoned his initial belief that she was suffering from a stomach ulcer and, unable to account for her condition by any other natural illness, had come to the conclusion that she must have ingested some kind of irritant poison. Dr Robertson concurred, though what poison it might be neither man could say. Anxious to ease the child's suffering, Dr Patterson went down to the surgery and made up a mixture of morphia* and bismuth† and, back in the bedroom, gave a little to the girl. Then, telling Mrs Berry to give the child injections of warm milk and more ice to suck, he and Dr Robertson left. Both were now of the opinion that the child's case was hopeless, and that she was unlikely to survive.

Later that night Mrs Berry was called away to an expectant mother's confinement, leaving the infirmary assistants Ann Dillon and Ellen Thompson to keep vigil at Edith's bedside. Throughout the time they sat with her, she continued to vomit and have diarrhoea.

First thing the next morning Edith's friend Beatrice – having spent the night in the nurse Sarah Anderson's bed – ate her breakfast and prepared to make her way, alone, back to Miles Platting. What had begun as a happy, carefree holiday had ended in the saddest and darkest way. Just before she left the workhouse, about ten o'clock, she went to say goodbye to her friend. She found her very sick indeed. She was never to see her again.

As Beatrice Hall made her way home, Mrs Berry returned to her bedroom where Ann Dillon and Ellen Thompson were sitting at Edith's bedside. A little while later, leaving Edith still in the care of the two assistants, Mrs Berry put on her coat and set out for the post office. There she sent a telegram to her sister-in-law Ann Sanderson:

COME AT ONCE ANNIE IS DYING. E BERRY OLDHAM UNION

Telegrams were notorious for delivering bad news, and it is likely that on receiving it Ann Sanderson felt somewhat alarmed. As she was illiterate, however, she was unable to read its contents and would have needed someone to read it for her – this would probably have been

* Now known as morphine.
† Bismuth is a metal, of which certain components are used in medicine, mainly to treat irritative and painful conditions of the stomach or bowels, on which they have a sedative action. In larger quantities it is a poison, chemically resembling antimony.

one of her young sons, who were home from school for the Christmas holidays. The words of the telegram would, of course, have come as the most tremendous shock, and hearing them she at once hurried to see her husband at his place of work. Together they set out for Oldham.

Arriving at the workhouse, they were taken up to Mrs Berry's bedroom where Ann Sanderson went to the sick child's side and, bending to her, asked, 'Are you poorly, Annie?' 'Yes,' the little girl replied.

Edith had left her aunt and uncle's side in a perfectly healthy state just days before, and one can only imagine how the Sandersons must have felt on finding her now in such a wretched state – seeing blisters on her mouth, observing her vomiting and purging, and hearing her crying out with pain. The little girl had spent much of her short life with the couple, and she had become like a daughter to them.

Ann and John Sanderson stayed by Edith's side through the rest of the day, watching helplessly as her condition continued to worsen. At one time John Sanderson got her to drink a few sips of tea with milk, but as the hours dragged by it became clear to everyone that she was sinking. Dr Patterson called again during the evening, but he was unable to do anything for her. He could see no glimmer of hope for her now.

Later that evening John Sanderson, aware that he could do nothing to help, left the workhouse to rejoin his sons at Miles Platting, leaving his wife to sit with sister-in-law Elizabeth at Edith's bedside.

Close on midnight Mrs Berry, very tired, took off some of her clothes and lay down on the bed at Edith's side, where she quickly dozed off. She was still sleeping an hour later when the silence in the room was broken with Edith suddenly crying out and giving two loud shrieks. Mrs Berry, at once awakened, remarked that a change was taking place.

She got dressed again then and, through the small hours of the morning, as the child's life slowly ebbed away, she and Ann Sanderson sat watching as Edith vomited and writhed in agony, at times clutching at her belly and crying out, 'Oh! Mamma! Mamma!'

As the time passed, the child's vomiting became less frequent and eventually ceased altogether. A little later and she became quiet and calm, her breathing very faint.

Mrs Berry did not remain at her daughter's side. About four in the morning she got up from her chair, telling Ann Sanderson that she could not bear 'to see the lass go'. She went then from the room, and to her bed on the sofa downstairs, leaving her sister-in-law alone with the dying girl.

Outside over the Oldham streets a freezing fog was creeping, wrapping the town in a bitter chill and enclosing the workhouse in its icy shroud. Up in the bedroom Ann Sanderson sat weeping beside the bed in the pale glow of the gaslight, looking down at Edith's pallid cheeks and blistered mouth, and taking in the sounds of her faint, tortured breathing.

Just on five o'clock Edith took her last faltering breath and died.

10

The Doctor's Suspicions

Soon after the coming of dawn, with the morning's pale daylight struggling to pierce the fog, the workhouse came to life and word of Edith's death spread through the building. As soon as the hour was right Mrs Berry sent a messenger to Dr Patterson and he came to the workhouse and to the bedroom where the dead child lay. After a brief examination of the girl's body he covered her face and, after some conversation with Mrs Berry, left the room.

We do not know what passed between them at the meeting, but he made no mention of providing a death certificate, which was required to enable the burial to take place and for the payment of any life insurance monies coming due.

The fact is that the doctor had become more and more convinced that the child had died as the result of ingesting a poison, and he was of the firm belief that it was the child's mother who had administered it. His convictions could not be kept to himself, of course, and after leaving the workhouse he made his way to the Oldham Police Station and there conveyed his suspicions to the borough's Chief Constable, Charles Hodgkinson. At the same time he took with him the towel that he had brought from the child's sickroom. Handing it to Mr Hodgkinson, he asked him to send it to the city analyst for examination.

Back at the workhouse Mrs Berry was growing increasingly anxious to acquire the child's death certificate, and eventually, not having it offered to her by the doctor, she had no choice but to go and ask for it. She took the first opportunity presented when, later that day, Dr Patterson was at work in the surgery. Going into the room, Mrs Berry found him with a patient, with several more waiting to see him. As soon as there came an opportunity she went to him and asked for the certificate, saying that she needed it as she wanted to arrange the funeral. He replied that he couldn't deal with it at that moment, but would see her about it 'presently'.

She was in her sitting room later when the doctor came to her door. Invited in, he told her that he was unable to issue a death certificate as neither he nor Dr Robertson knew what to put on it as regards the cause of death. He then said that he would like her permission to carry out a post-mortem examination of the child's body. If Mrs Berry had been dismayed a moment earlier, these words must have come as something of a shock. After a moment's hesitation, however, she gave her assent. Dr Patterson went on to say – anxious not to arouse her suspicions – that he wanted the post-mortem purely for medical and academic purposes, and that he would confine the examination to the child's abdomen.

After leaving her, the doctor made arrangements for the post-mortem to be performed the next day, 5 January, by himself and Dr Robertson.

It snowed heavily during the night, and next morning Drs Patterson and Robertson braved the snow-deep streets to meet in the workhouse where, together, under the glow of the gas lamps, they made an examination of the girl's remains. Its conclusion, however, left them without satisfactory answers, and they concluded that a complete and thorough autopsy was necessary. To this end a request was made to the District Coroner, with whose permission it was then arranged for a full post-mortem to be carried out the next day, the two doctors working with Dr Thomas Harris of the Manchester Royal Infirmary.

Aware that the doctors had completed the partial autopsy on her child, Mrs Berry was anxious to know of their findings, and, above all, to obtain the much-needed death certificate. So it was that later that Wednesday she went once more to see Dr Patterson. Faced again with her request, he took a rather curious step. In a move that would later bring him some criticism, he agreed to issue a certificate – which he did, stating on it that Edith's death was due to 'acute inflammation of the mucous membrane of the stomach and bowels'.

When Mrs Berry left the doctor she was in a far more satisfied state of mind.

The next morning, Thursday, the Chief Constable, Charles Hodgkinson, accompanied by Inspector Charles Purser, came calling at the workhouse to see Mrs Berry. To their disappointment, however, they found that she was absent from the building.

Unaware of the police's interest in her, Mrs Berry had left the workhouse earlier for Miles Platting. The snow was thick and freezing on the ground and the air bitterly cold, but she was undeterred by the chill. And although she had many things to do, she had the satisfaction of having the child's death certificate in her pocket.

Arriving at the Sandersons' house in Miles Platting, she collected from her sister-in-law the card registering the weekly payments made to the Rational Sick and Burial Association on the policy taken out on Edith's life, and then set off for Manchester to call on the insurance company's representative, Mr Pickford. On their meeting she showed him the card and Edith's death certificate, upon which he paid out to her the £11 that had come due on Edith's death.

While Mrs Berry had been going about her business that morning, the Manchester surgeon Dr Thomas Harris had arrived at the workhouse to join the two Oldham doctors in performing a full post-mortem on the deceased child. Working together, the three made a close examination of the body, in the course of which certain of the dead child's organs were placed in bottles and jars to be delivered to the Manchester city analyst. It was also arranged, following a meeting with the Chief Constable, that an inquest into the child's death would be opened – this to commence the following afternoon.

That night, just after ten o'clock, Mrs Berry was alone in her sitting room when there was a knock at her door. She opened the door to find Mr Lawson standing on the threshold with the police officers Hodgkinson and Purser behind him. After she had been informed as to who the strangers were, she was told by Mr Hodgkinson that he had come to inquire into the circumstances of the death of her daughter.

Edith Annie's death certificate – on which Mrs Berry is stated,
incorrectly, to have been present at the child's death.

In view of the fact that Dr Patterson had issued a death certificate, she must have been extremely surprised to hear the Chief Constable's words. Nevertheless, she replied, 'Very well,' upon which Hodgkinson said that he would like to see the child's body. With that, Mrs Berry put on her coat and led the men out of the building and across the snow-covered yard into the separate block opposite, and there into her bedroom in which lay the child's remains.

Inside, by the pale light of the gas lamp, Mr Hodgkinson moved to the body of the girl, lifted the sheet and looked down at her face. After some questioning of Mrs Berry, he told her that foul play was suspected, that she was suspected of having caused her child's death. At his words she cried out, 'I did nothing of the kind!' and, turning to Mr Lawson, exclaimed, 'Oh, Governor – why should I have killed my darling when I've just doubled my insurance for her in the Prudential?'

Following her outburst, and unmoved, Mr Hodgkinson told her that an inquest into her daughter's death was to be opened the next day, and that she would be required to be present. In the meantime, she was not to leave the premises. She was, in effect, under house arrest.

Immediately following the departure of the police officers, Mrs Berry began to make inquiries into acquiring the services of a solicitor. Clearly, she was very much aware of the gravity of her situation.

Pursuing his investigation, the Chief Constable, with Inspector Purser at his side, was back at the workhouse next morning to look at the child's body again. Pulling back the sheet he once more looked down at the dead girl's face. In the light of the cold, bright day he could see so much more clearly the ugly lesions about her lips. By the gaslight they had appeared red, but now in the daylight he saw them huge and almost black against the pale skin.

In those moments he concluded that there should be a record made of the dead girl's face, and to this end he went off to find a photographer.

11

The Inquest Opens

The inquest was opened at 2 p.m. on that Friday, 7 January, at the Oldham workhouse, before the District Coroner, Mr F. N. Molesworth. Once the jury had been sworn in they were taken to view the body of the child, after which they took their places in the Board Room, where the inquiry was to be conducted.

With little time to pick and choose in her urgent need for legal representation, Mrs Berry had managed to procure the services of Rochdale-born Joseph Whitaker, a thirty-six-year-old solicitor living in Wellington Street, Oldham. He in turn instructed Mr James Cottingham, a respected barrister from Manchester. Both men were already in their places when Mrs Berry, having come from her sitting room nearby, entered the room and took a seat at Mr Whitaker's side. Wearing a black silk dress and a small hat, her hair was styled in the latest fashion, dressed close to her head with the front brushed into what was called a frizette, or Piccadilly fringe.

And so the melancholy proceedings began.

Following the coroner's address to the jury the first witness was called. This was Ann Sanderson, the dead child's aunt, who told the court that Edith, in her usual good health, had left Miles Platting along with her mother on 29 December and that she, the witness, had been with the child when she died on the morning of 4 January.

She was followed by Dr Patterson who stated that on the morning of Saturday 1 January he was asked by Mrs Berry to see her daughter whom he found in her mother's room, lying on the sofa in front of the fire. The girl complained of pains over her stomach, and Mrs Berry told him that about breakfast time the child had begun to vomit, and that the vomit contained a considerable quantity of blood. Initially, he thought the child might be suffering from an ulcer of the stomach, and he prescribed for this. Visiting the child again that evening, he found her no better, but the next morning saw that her condition had improved. That evening, though, he found her much worse, and, forming the opinion that she was not suffering from any ordinary disease, he called on a colleague, Dr Robertson, to come to the workhouse and examine the girl. The next day, Monday, he saw the girl again. She died on the Tuesday morning, and on the Wednesday he and Dr Robertson made a post-mortem examination, in the course of which they found the stomach and intestines very much congested. On Thursday, he and Dr Robertson had assisted Dr Harris in performing a complete post-mortem, at which they had found a spot in the gullet with a black and corroded appearance, and similar but smaller marks all over the lining of the gullet.

At this the coroner asked him: 'What is your opinion as to the cause of death?' to which Dr Patterson replied: 'The corrosion of the gullet, independent of anything else, would be sufficient to cause death.'

'And what is the cause of that?'

'An irritant or corrosive poison had been administered to the child.'

The doctor's words caused a stir in the room, and Mrs Berry was heard to give a little cry. When the room was quiet again, the coroner asked: 'This is your opinion, Doctor?'

'Yes,' Dr Patterson replied. 'It leaves no doubt in my mind.'

Dr Harris would have been called next, but as he had not completed his medical examination following the post-mortem, the coroner announced an adjournment. With this, many of those assembled prepared to leave, but the Chief Constable came forward to say that with regard to the gravity of the situation he wanted Mrs Berry taken to the lock-up at the Town Hall. She, who had outwardly retained some composure, was in no way prepared for this. Deeply shocked, she cried out in protest and appealed tearfully to be allowed to remain at the workhouse. After the coroner had listened to her plea he asked the workhouse master, Mr Lawson, if he would take the responsibility of having her remain on the premises. Mr Lawson said that he would, but only on condition that she was kept under surveillance. With this, Mrs Berry was allowed to return to her room.

Edith's funeral took place the following Monday 10 January. It was a bitterly cold day, and there would have been few people braving the icy, windswept streets. No word of the funeral had been broadcast so no one would have known that the sad little cortege making its way from the workhouse to Chadderton Cemetery carried the coffin of Edith Annie. At the graveside there were just five mourners to witness the burial of the child they had loved. They were Edith's Uncle John and Aunt Ann; her Aunt Jane, sister of her father; and her two cousins, the Sandersons' sons, Herbert and Arthur. As the small, cheap coffin was lowered into the grave there was much bitter weeping. With Mrs Berry unable to be present, but forced to remain at the workhouse, she was truly, as the *Chronicle* had reported, 'not now at full liberty'.

With the resumption of the inquest on Thursday 13 January, Mrs Berry prepared to leave her sitting-room under the watchful eye of Inspector Purser. Before leaving, however, she called in her servant Alice Alcroft and scolded her severely for leaving a small piece of coal on the carpet, and threatened her with immediate punishment on her return. This done, she was escorted to the Board Room again.

There was no lack of curious eyes upon her as she entered and took her seat. The gossip that had been whirling about ensured that she would come in for a good deal of attention, and she was well aware of it, though whatever was going through her mind she gave nothing away. Another Oldham daily, the *Standard,* reporting on the proceedings, said that she was dressed as before, and that 'with the exception of being somewhat pale, she appeared but little distressed'.

The first witness was Dr Patterson, recalled to be questioned as to the availability of the drugs and medicines that were kept in the workhouse.

'There is a dispensary at the infirmary,' he said. 'In my absence Mrs Berry is in charge of it. There is the usual store of drugs there, and the usual sort of cupboard for poisons such as opium, prussic acid, strychnine and that sort of thing. I keep the key of that myself. But not all of the poisons are kept in the cupboard.' He went on to say that on 9 January he had made a list of all the irritant poisons that were *outside* the cupboard on 1 January. 'Mrs Berry had a key of the dispensary,' he said, 'and she would admit a servant, Alice Alcroft, every day to light the fire and clean the room. Also on a cold morning some patients would be allowed in to sit by the fire until I came in and could attend to them. I don't think anyone would be admitted to the dispensary unless either myself or Mrs Berry were there.'

Dr Patterson was followed onto the stand by Dr Harris, who told the court that on 6 January he made a post-mortem of the body of the deceased. 'The body was that of a fairly well-nourished child,' he said, ' – not a robust one,' and then went on to describe the dry patches he had found on and around the girl's mouth. 'Each of these patches felt dry and hard,' he said, 'and was of a brown colour, and quite different both in looks and feel from the surrounding skin, which was of a healthy appearance.' Of his other findings, he said the gullet bore a black and corroded patch, an inch in diameter, and other parts of the gullet presented a number of fine black lines similar to the charred patch. He had found the whole length of the small intestine to be distinctly congested.

He was then asked the question that was on everyone's lips. 'What, in your opinion,' said the coroner, 'was the cause of death?'

'Corrosive poison,' replied Dr Harris. He couldn't state absolutely what the poison was, but he could give an opinion.

'Well, what was it, in your opinion?'

'Sulphuric acid, probably.'

Shock in the courtroom. The coroner took this in, then asked, 'If sulphuric acid had been taken, would it necessarily be found in the stomach or in the analysis?'

'Not at all; it would depend upon the symptoms and the treatment. It is quite possible for it to have been taken and for none to remain in the stomach or the contents of the stomach.'

'Is it merely your opinion that it was sulphuric acid, or are you positive of it?'

'I am positive of it.'

After Dr Harris's sensational testimony he stepped down, and his place was taken by Beatrice Hall, the school-friend of the dead girl.

She gave her address as Vicar Street, Miles Platting, and said she was thirteen and the daughter of John Hall. Questioned, she told the court that she had known Edith for a month, and went to Sunday school with her, and that on 29 December last received an invitation to spend a holiday with her and her mother at the workhouse. 'Mrs Berry fetched us,' she said, 'and we got here about six o'clock in the evening. We all three slept in Mrs Berry's bed, and took our meals in Mrs Berry's sitting room. The day after we arrived we went out and bought some chocolate, and on Friday we went to the market.'

Asked about the events on the Saturday, she said that she got up at nine o'clock and had her breakfast, adding: 'Annie didn't take any because she was ill. She didn't eat or drink anything at that time. Mrs Berry gave her a seidlitz powder* and that and some ice was all I saw her take.' Asked about her movements on the Sunday, she said that she was with Edith for part of the day, and read to her, then in the afternoon left her to go and have tea with the nurse Sarah Anderson. The last time she saw her was about ten o'clock on the Monday morning. 'But I didn't speak to her then,' she said.

Questioned by Mr Cottingham, she said that as well as the chocolate they bought on the Thursday they also bought a pennyworth of biscuits and some coconut chips. Asked whether they had made her sick, she said they had not. 'We bought some fish on the Friday,' she said, 'and had it for tea.' She couldn't remember what they ate for supper. 'So far as I remember Annie and I ate the same things.' Asked about the seidlitz powder that Mrs Berry had given to Edith, she said, 'Mrs Berry gave it to her after she was sick. She brought it in already mixed in a glass.'

Dr Robertson, called next, told the court that he had assisted Dr Patterson in a partial post-mortem examination of the body of the deceased girl, and was present at the full investigation made by Dr Harris on the 6th. As to the cause of the girl's death, he said he agreed with Dr Harris in his opinion that it was due to poisoning with sulphuric acid.

Ellen Thompson, then called, said she was an inmate at the workhouse, and employed as an assistant nurse in the female infirmary. 'On Saturday,' she said, 'I saw the two girls in the corridor, between nine and nine-thirty.

---

* Seidlitz powder: a generic name for a widely sold digestive and laxative aid. To be mixed with water, the powder was composed of tartaric acid, sodium bicarbonate and potassium sodium tartrate.

Edith appeared all right then. I next saw her at eleven when she was ill in Mrs Berry's room. I asked Mrs Berry what was the matter with her, and she said she thought it was a bilious attack. Edith was sick while I was there and vomited blood. I saw her again that night, between ten and eleven. I wanted to sit up with her, but Mrs Berry said she could manage. The next time I saw Edith was between ten and eleven in the morning, and she said she felt a little better. I saw her again about two o'clock. She was in bed asleep, and Beatrice Hall was in bed with her. I noticed a little white blister on her upper lip, and I said to Mrs Berry that the child would be better soon, as the cold I thought she was suffering from was breaking out. Mrs Berry replied that she thought the blister was caused by an orange that Edith had had with some sugar.' The witness said she was with Mrs Berry the next morning, Monday, when she tried to give the child some medicine, but that the child couldn't take it.

Mr Charles Estcourt, the city analyst, was then called and asked whether he had completed his chemical analysis of the body parts delivered to him. When he replied that he had not yet done so, the coroner said the inquest would have to be adjourned again, to allow time for Mr Estcourt to complete his analysis. One of the jurymen spoke up here, saying there was no need to wait for the analyst's report as he thought everyone was agreed that the girl's death was due to poisoning. The coroner replied that it was the duty of the jury to hear *all* the evidence before giving their opinion, and that the inquest would be adjourned for a further week.

Throughout the day Elizabeth Berry had appeared little affected by the evidence that had been presented, and with the coroner's call for an adjournment she must have felt some relief, believing that for a week at least she could retire to the privacy of her rooms and have some respite from her ordeal. It was not to be. She was rising, ready to leave, when Chief Constable Hodgkinson got up to speak. To Mrs Berry's horror, he said that the Guardians were no longer willing to take the responsibility for her remaining at the workhouse, and asked that she be formally arrested on the murder charge. All her self-control vanished at this, and she screamed out, 'I didn't do it! I didn't do it!' and a moment later collapsed headlong on the floor. Warders were immediately at her side. After some minutes she was helped to her feet, and, with difficulty as she struggled, taken from the room. Shortly afterwards, escorted by Inspector

Purser, she was conveyed to the police cell that was to be her home for the rest of the month.

Meanwhile, back at the workhouse, Alice Alcroft, in Mrs Berry's bad books for leaving coal on the carpet, and dreading the threatened dressing down, must have learned with some relief that her mistress would not be coming back.

12

The Wheels Turn

The law is the law, and having been charged with the murder of her daughter, Elizabeth Berry was now required to come before the magistrates in order for them to determine whether there was enough evidence to warrant sending her for trial at the Assizes.

So it was that on Saturday, 15 January, she was brought from her cell to the Oldham Police Court to face the bench, led by the Chief Magistrate, Mr W. Knox. The proceedings were brief. As the medical analyst's report was not yet available, the hearing was adjourned for a week, Mrs Berry being remanded for the period.

Before the magistrates' hearing was due to be resumed, the inquest was set to continue, and shortly after one o'clock on the 20th, Mrs Berry, escorted by Inspector Purser, left her cell at the Town Hall to set out for the workhouse. The cab ride, though short, proved an eventful one. As if there was not drama enough already connected with the proceedings, the prisoner's journey was to be at the centre of a dramatic happening. As the cab drew near the bottom of Barker Street, a child ran out into the road. The cab couldn't be stopped in time, and its splinter bar struck the child on the head. The little one was injured, but fortunately not severely so. A crowd gathered and the crying child was lifted up and carried home. Having no knowledge of the cab's notorious passenger, the solicitous neighbours dispersed and the cab continued on its way.

On Mrs Berry's arrival at the workhouse she met her legal advisers, after which, soon after two o'clock, she was led into the courtroom, taking a seat behind Mr Whitaker. The *Chronicle*'s reporter said 'she looked little the worse for her change from the luxury of her workhouse apartments to the police cell, except that she appeared a little paler'. Her dress was the same as that worn by her the previous week, he said, 'a handsome stamped black silk dolman, trimmed with fur'.

One of the first witnesses was Sarah Anderson, forty, head nurse in the female imbecile ward. She had been called to see Edith on the Saturday between two and three in the afternoon, she said. 'The child was in her mother's room, on the sofa, and seemed to be very unwell. I saw her again next afternoon, Sunday, about a quarter to three. She appeared to be very ill – in fact much worse than on Saturday. I saw her again on Monday, just before eleven o'clock. I noticed a change then, and saw there were blisters on her lips.' She hadn't noticed any blisters or redness on the Saturday.

The next witness was Lydia Evett, the nurse in the workhouse children's hospital. She told the court she had seen Edith on the Sunday about a quarter to five in the afternoon in Mrs Berry's bedroom. 'Mrs Berry said to me, "See what the orange has done to Edith's mouth," and I said to her, "It's very strange," meaning it was strange that an orange should cause such marks.' When she saw her again the next morning, she said, she 'noticed that the red marks around her mouth had blistered'. She ended her deposition by saying that in Mrs Berry's absence from the infirmary she, the witness, had been asked to take on her duties.

Inmate Alice Alcroft came next to give evidence. Described in the *Chronicle* as an 'old woman', she told the court that she worked as 'one of Mrs Berry's servants'. In answer to questions she said that she saw the child Edith Berry on the Saturday morning, when she appeared to be in her usual health, and 'again about twenty minutes later, when Mrs Berry told me to wipe up some vomit'. 'The child vomited while I was there,' she said. 'Mrs Berry sent me to the surgery for some mineral powders. I brought the box of them. She sent me for a glass of water, too.' Here the coroner asked her if she knew what the powders were for, and she replied, 'I believe they're used to make soda water with. They make fizzing drinks.'

'Do you know the name of them? Can you remember what was written on the box?'

'No, I don't know – I can't read.'

Questioned about the children's movements following their arrival at the workhouse, she said, 'They went about where they liked. I remember their going out on Thursday and Friday. They came back with their pockets full of sweets – coconut chips and chocolate. They gave me one or two and wanted me to have more, but I said, "Get off! What does an old woman like me want sweets for?"' There was laughter in the court at this, and when it had died away Mrs Alcroft added, 'Edith was a spirited little thing, and her mother appeared very fond of her.' At this observation Mrs Berry briefly covered her face with her hand. The witness then went on to say that she heard that Edith was ill when Mrs Berry called her to 'wipe up in the room'. 'That was about half-an-hour after I brought them their breakfasts.'

Questioned by the coroner, she said, 'Mrs Berry had her breakfast before the children came down for theirs. When the children came down they talked for a few minutes to some of the inmates in the corridor.'

Mr Cottingham: 'Did you give the children their breakfasts?'

'Yes, and I took the tea in to them.'

'You took the pot and the cups into Mrs Berry's room?'

'Yes.'

'Had you your tea out of the same pot afterwards as you gave the children?'

'Yes.'

'And did you drink some of the tea?'

'Yes. It did me no harm.'

'Rather good, was it, I hope? Stronger and better than you would usually get?'

'Yes.'

This caused some amusement, during which Mrs Berry was seen to laugh also. In the quiet again, a juror asked the witness:

'Had you ever seen the children in the surgery?'

'Yes, I saw them in there once, washing their hands.'

'Was the mother with them in the surgery at the time?'

'I've never see Mrs Berry in the surgery.'

Here the Chief Constable, not satisfied with the witness's answer, spoke up, asking her: 'Did you hear the question?'

Mr Cottingham was having none of this, and he said at once, 'I really must object to a constable of the police acting as an advocate. Any assistance he may give you I do not object to, but I do object to a constable of police interfering with a witness.'

The coroner: 'I hardly think he's interfering with a witness.'

With further exchanges between the witness and Mr Cottingham it was eventually made clear that the witness Alcroft had not seen either of the girls in the surgery with Mrs Berry on that Saturday morning. With this she was allowed to go, and her place was taken by the next witness.

She was Mrs Mary Jane Knight, thirty-four, who told the court that she was an inmate of the workhouse and employed as a servant to Mrs Berry. She said that about 4.30 in the afternoon of Sunday 2 January, Beatrice Hall came for her to sit with the child Edith Berry, and that she stayed with her for about an hour. Asked by a juror whether the child had complained of anything having been given to her, she answered, 'No.' Questioned further, she said, 'I stayed in the room with her until Mrs Berry came back in and told me to go and get my tea. I left Mrs Berry with her.' She went on to say that the next day, Monday, she saw marks about the child's mouth. She was sure they hadn't been there on the Sunday. She then gave the interesting information that she was in the kitchen on Monday afternoon when Mrs Berry sent Beatrice Hall down for an orange.

After the witness was dismissed, Beatrice Hall was recalled. Questioned, she said neither she nor Edith had gone into the surgery before breakfast on the Saturday.

Philip Estcourt, next called, testified to receiving bottles of body parts from Dr Harris, and on 8 January delivering them to his father, Charles Estcourt, the city analyst. Charles Estcourt was the next witness. He told the court that he was a Fellow of the Institute of Chemists, the city analyst of Manchester, and analyst to the boroughs of Oldham, Ashton, Macclesfield, Lancaster, etc. He went on to say that having received the bottles from his son he washed the organs in distilled water and tested the evaporated residue for sulphuric acid. 'I found only a faint trace,' he said, 'the presence of which might be due to natural causes.' He then described how he had further tested the organs for signs of poisonous compounds, metallic or organic, but that none was found. He had found nothing to account for death in any way, he said.

Following Mr Estcourt, Dr Patterson was recalled and, questioned by Mr Cottingham, said that when he first saw the child on the Sunday he prescribed a solution of bicarbonate of soda and creosote. 'But there was no creosote in the bottle,' he said. 'I wanted two drops, but I couldn't get one drop out of it, so I rinsed the bottle out to get a little. So what the child had from me was a mixture of bicarbonate of soda and the washings of a bottle which had contained creosote. That was about twelve o'clock in the day, and I sent an order to the chemist, Mr Goodall, to have the creosote bottle filled. I told Mrs Berry to mix it in a certain way – which I will tell you – '

Mr Cottingham broke in at this, protesting: 'Oh, no! Not unless the coroner wants it.'

Dr Patterson continued: 'The creosote bottle is a 5oz. bottle. In the evening, after consultation with Dr Robertson, we agreed that the patient should have a mixture of bismuth and morphia, and that was made up in the surgery. That was at ten o'clock on Sunday night. I was going to use the creosote to stop the vomiting. I used bismuth afterwards in its place because the creosote hadn't arrived.'

Mr Cottingham: 'What? You sent for it at twelve o'clock to Mr Goodall's and it didn't arrive by ten o'clock that night? It hadn't come in ten hours?'

'No, it came in the morning.'

'You said you substituted bismuth for creosote on Sunday night because the creosote hadn't arrived?'

'I changed from creosote as the patient was worse that Sunday night, and in great pain. The symptoms had changed for the worse. I had told Mrs Berry in the morning before leaving that when the creosote arrived she was to dissolve eight drops in a 12oz. bottle of water, and give the child a tablespoon every two hours.'

The doctor was then asked whether he had told Mrs Berry while the child was alive that he was of the opinion that an irritant poison had been used. He said he hadn't. It was on Monday when he became convinced that an irritant poison was the cause of the child's sickness. 'Dr Robertson agreed with me on every point of the post-mortem examination,' he said, 'and after the examination we were quite certain that the child didn't die from natural causes.' Questioned on the matter of the various bottles that were in the surgery, he said, 'I have given the coroner a list of the bottles that were outside the locked-up cupboard. There were a few of them, on the counter on the left-hand side of the fireplace. They were habitually there, and I won't undertake to say that they were not displaced on the Friday or Saturday.'

On the subject of the child's death certificate, he said he had given it 'in order that the funeral arrangements might be made – and with the cognisance of the Chief Constable'.

Mr Cottingham: 'Do you know the cost of the funeral?'

Patterson: 'Of course not.'

'Did Mrs Berry not tell you that it cost £15 or £18?'

'No.'

'Did she tell you that the child was insured?'

'No, she said it was *not* insured. She said, "I'll have to pay for everything out of my own pocket." I told her not to go and spend a lot of money on the funeral,' he added.

Mr Cottingham: 'While you thought she had poisoned her child you went on giving her friendly advice?'

'That was friendly advice?' said Dr Patterson.

When the doctor had stepped down, Ann Sanderson, the child's aunt, was recalled. Questioned by Mr Cottingham, she said she didn't remember the child ever suffering from vomiting and had never known her to vomit blood. The coroner then asked her: 'Did you ever tell Mrs Berry that when you gave Edith a pill she passed blood sometimes?' Mrs Sanderson replied that she had never told her such a thing.

The witness was released here, and the Chief Constable, Hodgkinson, was called. He told the court that on Tuesday 4 January, Dr Patterson came to his office and gave him a towel that was smeared with blood and which he, the witness, then sent to Mr Estcourt for analysis. He then went on to relate how, in the company of Inspector Purser, he visited Mrs Berry at the workhouse on the Thursday night, and was taken to see the child's body. Mrs Berry told him, he said, that Mrs Sanderson had told her that the child was troubled with constipation, and that when given a pill she always passed blood. She said that when the child came to the workhouse a week ago she was not well, also that no one had given her any medicine but the doctor, 'and *that* she wouldn't take'.

The Chief Constable's next words caused something of a stir. 'I took the cloth from the child's face,' he said, 'and noticing that the mouth was very much broken out, I told her that the doctors suggested there had been foul play – that she had been poisoned. I asked her how she accounted for the eruptions around the mouth, and she said that before the child died her mouth was ulcerated, and she supposed that that was the cause. I said to her, "As a nurse, you must have seen many children after death," and she said, "Yes." I said, "Have you ever seen a mouth like that before?" and she said, "No."' He told her then that she was suspected of having poisoned her daughter at which 'she became very excited, and turned to Mr Lawson and said, "Why should I have killed my darling when I had just doubled my insurance for her benefit in the Prudential." I've made inquiries,' Mr Hodgkinson said, 'and I find that neither she nor the child were insured in the Prudential.'

A juryman then asked whether he had received any report on the towel sent to Mr Estcourt. He replied that he had, and that there was nothing injurious on it. This was then confirmed by Mr Estcourt himself.

Mr Cottingham then asked the Chief Constable, 'Have you heard what was the expense of the funeral?'

'£10, the Master of the Union tells me.'

No further witnesses were called, and the coroner announced that as the inquiry had been twice adjourned he would read out the witnesses' depositions. This he did, and then addressed the jury.

They had heard all of the evidence in the case, he said, and had to consider the cause of the child's death – which he thought had been proved conclusively to have been from the effects of a corrosive poison. They would then have to decide as to how and when the child came by that poison, whether she had taken it inadvertently or whether it had been wilfully administered, and then bring in a 'proper verdict'. And, he said, they must decide purely on the evidence before them, by what he had read to them, and not by anything they had read in the papers. If they found that there was a strong suspicion created against a person or persons, then they must bring in a verdict of wilful murder against that person. He concluded his address, saying, 'If, on the other hand, you consider that the evidence is not strong enough against any person or persons then your only course is to bring in an open verdict, to the effect that there is not sufficient evidence to show how the poison was administered.' He then ordered that the room be cleared to allow the jury to talk the matter over among themselves.

While the fifteen jurymen remained to deliberate, Mrs Berry, waiting in another room, appeared to be low in her spirits. But she was given a cup of tea, and as the time passed she seemed to grow a little easier in her manner. However, just before seven o'clock, when it was announced that the court had reopened, her face turned deathly pale and she said she did not wish to go back in to hear the jury's verdict. The coroner, however, determined otherwise, and she was brought into the room.

When all were assembled the coroner turned to the jury. 'Mr Hanson,' he said, 'you are the foreman upon this jury. Have you agreed upon your verdict?'

The foreman: 'We have, Your Honour. We have agreed that the suspicions point to the death of the deceased having been caused by poison, administered by Elizabeth Berry; and in order that she may be tried at the Assizes, we are unanimous in returning a verdict of wilful murder against her.'*

The coroner then ordered Mrs Berry to stand up, which she did, holding herself very erect. Having cautioned her, he asked her whether she had anything to say. She replied in a clear, calm tone, 'I have not.'

With this she was escorted from the room and conveyed back to her cell.

It had been observed that throughout the investigation she had borne up well, but the events of the day, culminating in the damning verdict of guilty, proved too much for her, and just before entering the police cell she fainted. She was at once attended to by Mrs Warburton, wife of one of the sergeants, and recovered shortly afterwards. However, it was later reported, she 'keenly feels her position'.

---

* With regard to the coroner's inquest having brought in a verdict of guilty against Mrs Berry, this could not happen today. In 1975, following the inquest into the death of Sandra Rivett, at which the jury brought in a verdict of guilty against Lord Lucan, a new bill was passed that banned a coroner's court from naming a putative murderer.

13

The Magistrates' Hearing

Although 20 January saw the end of the inquest, just two days later Elizabeth Berry was due back in the police court to stand for judgement again – this time before the magistrates. However, as the inquest's verdict of wilful murder against her was sufficient to ensure that she was sent for trial, it was argued that it was not now necessary for the magistrates to hear the rest of the case. The matter was much discussed, but eventually it was decided that the hearing, having been opened, must go ahead. So it was that on Saturday 22 January Elizabeth Berry found herself once more in the Oldham Borough police court.

The place was packed. The newspapers, local and national, had been giving great coverage to the case, and when Mrs Berry was escorted into the room everyone was eager to get a glimpse of her. However, if they had hoped to be able to study her for any length of time they were in for a disappointment, for the prosecutor, Mr Mellor, said he couldn't yet proceed as he had only just received instructions to take charge of the case, and wouldn't be ready for a week. At this the Chief Magistrate called an adjournment for a further six days, and the prisoner was taken back to her cell.

It would appear that Mrs Berry's incarceration was less disagreeable than it might have been. The *Chronicle*'s man said of her situation, 'She has not had to complain of the want of any of those little luxuries and liberties which might make a prisoner's confinement less irksome. She has, in fact, been a favoured prisoner, having been allowed to spend much of her time outside her cell, and in the comparatively commodious space which is provided at the Town Hall for the exercise of prisoners.'

If the prisoner did indeed enjoy some degree of comfort in her incarceration, it would have been much diminished if she had known what was taking place outside. As she waited over those six days for the resumption of the hearing, a new development was gaining ground. Shocking and scandalous, it related to a different case entirely, but one that very much concerned the prisoner.

Months before the death of the child Edith Annie, rumours had begun to circulate about that earlier episode in Mrs Berry's past, namely the death of her mother. At first the rumours had got no further than local gossip, but with Mrs Berry being charged with her daughter's murder the rumours had come to the surface. The death of Mrs Finley was now, in the light of the capital charge against the prisoner, being viewed with increasing suspicion – word of which would soon reach the ears of those in authority.

It was almost by chance that there came to be an investigation into Mrs Finley's death. It began, reported the *Chronicle*, early in January when police officers Hodgkinson and Purser started to make inquiries into the death of the child Edith Berry, and in the course of their investigations interviewed Mrs Sanderson, the dead child's aunt. It was during their conversation that Mrs Sanderson happened to mention the death of Mrs Berry's mother, saying that she had died very suddenly at Castleton just the year before. As a result Mr Hodgkinson dispatched one of his officers to Castleton to make inquiries. The detective returned with certain information, including the fact that Mrs Finley had been insured and that her daughter had been the sole beneficiary. A week later, one Detective Lamb was sent to Castleton to inquire further and to interview some of the late woman's neighbours. His investigations quickly led to the Rochdale constabulary taking up the matter, with the result that application was made to the Home Office for permission to exhume Mrs Finley's body. With permission granted, the exhumation was arranged to take place on 3 February – a year to the day from Mrs Berry's arrival at her mother's house in Castleton.

When the magistrates' hearing into the death of Edith Annie Berry was resumed on Thursday 27 January, the general public knew nothing about the investigations into the death of Mrs Berry's mother, nor of the planned exhumation of her remains. All interest was concentrated on the case before the bench. And interest had continued to grow, so much so that long before ten o'clock, when the police court was due to open, a huge crowd, mostly women, and in no way put off by the cold, had gathered at the entrance waiting for admission. The moment the doors were opened they pressed inside, so many that they occupied most of the body of the court and filled the two balconies, places that were used only on rare occasions.

The magistrates made their appearance just after ten, and after spending an hour on preliminary matters, the main business of the day got under way.

After the clerk had called out the prisoner's name, Elizabeth Berry, with every eye upon her, and wearing the same mourning dress that she had worn at the inquest, stepped up into the dock and took the chair that had been set for her. The *Manchester Evening News* observed that 'while unavoidably conscious of the avid interest in her, she sat with an air of unconcerned demeanour', though the man from the *Chronicle* reported that she 'seemed somewhat less at ease than on her earlier appearance in court'.

Before the proceedings proper got under way it was observed that Mr Cottingham, the prisoner's legal representative, had not yet arrived, he being occupied still at the Manchester Assizes. In his absence Mr Whitaker at once announced that he would conduct the case on the prisoner's behalf, and requested that she be allowed to sit near him, in order for him to 'take instructions for the purpose of cross-examination'. Permission was granted, and Mrs Berry left the dock and walked with a light step to the solicitors' bench, there sitting down beside Mr Whitaker.

Mr J.W. Mellor, for the Crown, then addressed the court.

He began by saying that the prisoner, Elizabeth Berry, was charged with causing the death of her daughter, Edith Annie Berry, by administering poison, and it was his duty to lay the facts before the bench, and ask them to say that there was a *prima facie* case upon which they would commit the prisoner to take her trial. 'It is common knowledge,' he continued, 'that at the coroner's inquiry on the 20th instant, a verdict was found that the deceased, Edith Annie Berry, died from poison, and the jury then found against the mother a verdict of wilful murder. She now stands before you upon this charge.'

In a detailed account of the case, he said that Elizabeth Berry had brought her daughter to stay with her at the workhouse, that Edith Annie was in good health until the morning of Saturday, the 1st, when she became unwell and began to vomit. Dr Patterson examined the girl, and soon began to suspect that she was suffering from poison. He got the assistance of Dr Robertson, and after the child's death her body was subjected to a post-mortem examination, and later to analysis. Although no actual traces of any poison were found there were internal appearances which produced a conviction in the minds of the medical men that the girl had died from poison. He closed his address, saying: 'I have desired to open this case very briefly, and I have no desire to give any colour to it. My duty, as the representative of the Crown, is to state fairly the facts of the case, and let the magistrates draw their own inferences, and to satisfy themselves that it is a proper case to be investigated by a jury.'

Of the witnesses called that day, most had testified previously at the inquest and would repeat much of their testimony. There would, however, be others with different stories to tell, and one new witness in particular coming forward with fresh and vital evidence, evidence that would turn out to have the most significant bearing on the case.

The first witness was Ann Sanderson. She told the court: 'Annie came to live with me about six weeks after my brother's death, about August, 1881. I received 3s. a week for her, and she was insured with the Prudential at a penny a week. Mrs Berry paid for the schooling and clothing.' As to the child's health, she said she was only attended once by a doctor, 'and that was fourteen months after her father's death'. Occasionally she gave her a little turkey rhubarb,* magnesia or a Gregory's powder† but never any pills. The child had never been troubled with constipation or had ever passed blood. Following Edith's departure for the workhouse, she said she received a telegram on 3 January, about ten o'clock in the morning. 'My husband and I went to the workhouse,' she said. 'We went into the bedroom, and I went to Annie and kissed her on the cheek, and asked her if she was poorly. She said, "Yes." I saw that her lips were very sore and blistered. I asked Mrs Berry what Annie was suffering from, and she

---

* A herb used in medicine as a laxative, in use from ancient times.
† A laxative powder containing rhubarb, magnesia and ginger. No longer sold.

said it was acute stoppage of the bowels, and that Annie had eaten a heavy supper the night before. My husband gave Annie some tea, cooled with milk, about two o'clock in the afternoon, and afterwards Mrs Berry gave her an injection of cold milk. Annie asked for it. An hour later Mrs Berry gave her a second injection, and I gave her one half-an-hour later. During the time I was with her she seemed to suffer great pain in her belly, crying out, "Mamma, Mamma." Her vomiting continued up to twelve o'clock on the night of the 3rd, and then it ceased absolutely. I stayed with her till her death at five o'clock on the morning of the 4th. Mrs Berry left the bedroom at four o'clock, saying she couldn't bear to see the lass go. Before Annie died she had ease of the pain, and after one o'clock she became very quiet.'

Mrs Sanderson's place was taken by the workhouse inmate Ann Dillon. She had not been called at the inquest, and she had a most interesting incident to relate.

After telling the bench that she had been at the workhouse for three years – having been deserted by her husband – she said that she had been employed as an assistant to Mrs Berry, and that her duty was to help serve their meals to the patients. She had seen the deceased, Edith Annie Berry, on two previous visits to the workhouse, and during the child's last visit had seen her and her friend Beatrice Hall on several occasions over the Thursday and Friday, when they 'were going about the place as merry as possible'. On the Saturday morning, about half-past nine, she said, she saw Edith and Beatrice Hall coming from Mrs Berry's bedroom, though she didn't see where they were going. Then, at quarter-to-ten, she said, she went to the surgery to ask Mrs Berry 'for the dinner note' (sometimes referred to as the 'diet note').

This, it transpired, was something she did every morning. It was her duty to take meals to the patients in the infirmary, and for this purpose she had to find out from Mrs Berry which patients were on 'diet food', which, it appears, was generally sago. With regard to her visit on this particular Saturday morning, however, there would come the most startling revelation – one which cast Mrs Berry's case into a perilous state.

Ann Dillon told the court that when she went into the surgery she saw Edith there alone with her mother. This was in direct contradiction to Beatrice Hall's statement that Edith had not left her side before being taken ill. Said Dillon: 'Mrs Berry was preparing the dinner note when I went in.

Edith said to me: "Are you going out for liberty today, Ann?" and I said, "No, love, it's not my day."'

She went on to say that she was in the surgery for about five minutes, and that the next time she saw the child was in Mrs Berry's sitting room. 'This was about a quarter-to-eleven. I went there to get some cloths. When I went in, Mrs Berry was standing near the door by the sofa, and Edith was leaning against her, vomiting. Mrs Berry said to me, "This child is sick." I didn't see her vomit but there was some on the floor. Mrs Berry had a drinking glass in her hand with something in it, which I thought was magnesia or cream of tartar. She said to Edith, "Drink this, darling." But the child said to her mother: "Oh, no, mamma, I can't." I said to her, "Drink it love, and it'll make you feel better." She couldn't drink it, though.'

Dillon then spoke of seeing the child in the evening between half-past six and seven, in bed in her mother's bedroom. 'She seemed to me a little better than she was in the morning,' she said. 'I saw her vomit twice. The vomit on the first occasion was caught in a bowl. I emptied it away and rinsed it out with cold water.' She had not been instructed to wash the bowl, she said. She went on: 'When I'd been in the room about half-an-hour, Edith, who was always kind and pleasant, asked me to sit down, which, to please her, I did. Ellen Thompson was also in the room, and she left along with me at nine o'clock.'

At this point, 1.15 p.m., the magistrates' clerk called an adjournment until two o'clock, and while a large number then left the courtroom, many members of the public remained in their seats rather than leave and risk losing them for the rest of the day.

When the court reassembled, Ann Dillon was recalled. She stated that on the Saturday night she and Ellen Thompson had offered to sit up with the sick child. 'But Mrs Berry said she could manage.' 'The next time I saw the child was about eleven the next morning, Sunday,' she said. 'That was the last time I saw her alive.'

Ellen Thompson, called next, told the court that she was the wife of William Thompson, who was in Australia, that she was an inmate of the workhouse and had been an assistant to the prisoner in the infirmary. She had seen Mrs Berry, Edith and Beatrice Hall arrive on 29 December, and over the next two days had seen the two girls playing about. 'There was plenty of room for them to knock about,' she said. 'I've got six children of my own. I'm used to looking after children, and as far as I know, the two girls were well.' On the Saturday she had seen them in the corridor about half-past nine, she continued. 'Edith looked well and hearty. I saw them again about eleven o'clock in Mrs Berry's sitting room. Edith was standing up and leaning against her mother's bosom. I saw her vomit three times that I remember. The vomit on the carpet was wiped up by Alice Alcroft with a flannel and water, and afterwards I took a rough cloth and dried it. The second time, Edith vomited into a slop basin. The vomit was streaked with blood and was about a gill* in quantity. At Mrs Berry's orders I poured the vomit down a drain, then washed the slop basin out and took it back to the sitting room. I saw that Edith had been sick again, and two or three minutes later she vomited again.' About two o'clock that afternoon, on Mrs Berry's instructions, she carried the child up to Mrs Berry's bedroom. She saw the child again that night and on two occasions the next day, Sunday, the second time in the afternoon. 'She was in bed and appeared to be asleep,' she said. 'I noticed a small blister on the right-hand side of her lip, and a discolouration on her upper lip. I called Mrs Berry's attention to it. I said, "Do you think that's a cold that's breaking out on Edith's mouth?" and she replied, "I don't know. I think it's an orange she had."'

She went on to say that at 5.15 that afternoon Mrs Berry sent her with a message for Dr Patterson. She was in the bedroom when he arrived, and was there again later when he came back with Dr Robertson, about eleven o'clock. 'After the doctors left I stayed with Edith until seven the next morning, Monday. She was very ill, sick and vomiting almost every ten minutes, with more blood showing as her vomiting went on. She complained of her stomach, and often cried out, "Oh, Mamma, my stomach." Mrs Berry said several times to her, "Yes, darling, Mamma will try to do you good if she can." During the night I said to Mrs Berry that she should give Edith some medicine, but she said, "No, I don't want to punish her. I'll give her some when she's better."'

Ellen Thompson's place on the stand was taken by Dr Harris, who told the court that he had made a post-mortem examination of the body of the child in company with Drs Patterson and Robertson. He described the patches about the child's lips, which, he said, were the remains of

---

* About a quarter of a pint.

blisters. He had made a sketch of the patches, he added, and here passed the sketch to the clerk. He then spoke of his findings on examining some of the internal organs, in particular the corrosion in the oesophagus. After describing the charred patches and the similar lines in the gullet, he repeated his former testimony, saying, 'Judging from the post-mortem appearance, I say that the deceased died from corrosive poisoning.' He was sure of it, he added.

Mr Mellor: 'Is there any known disease which could produce similar appearances?'

'None whatever.'

Asked whether some of the poison would be expected to be found in the body after death, he said that in the case of certain poisons, continued vomiting and purging would eliminate all traces. 'From twenty-four to forty-eight hours would in my opinion be quite sufficient. That would be enough to remove the traces of certain corrosive poisons.'

'Can you,' Mr Mellor asked him, 'from the appearances of the post-mortem examination, fix with *certainty* the nature of the corrosive poison?'

'No.'

After Dr Harris had stepped down, Charles Estcourt, the city analyst, was called. Repeating his earlier testimony he said that in his testing he had found nothing to account for death in any way.

'Do you mean chemically?' Mr Mellor asked.

'Yes.'

'*Pathologically*, did you find anything to account for death?'

'I should say that the black, charred patches I saw would account for death.'

The next witness was Beatrice Hall, who told the court that about half-past nine on the Saturday morning she and Edith had gone down to Mrs Berry's sitting room. Edith didn't eat any breakfast, but complained of being sick. 'Mrs Berry gave her a powder, which she said was a seidlitz powder. She went out of the room and brought the powder in. I can't remember whether Annie went with her, but I think Mrs Berry came back with the powder in a tumbler. On the Sunday I was upstairs with Annie nearly the whole of the day. I was reading to her, and she seemed better than she had been the day before. I slept with her that night. A bed was made up for me in the sitting room downstairs but I didn't sleep on it.' Asked whether she had remained at the workhouse until Edith died, she said, 'No. I went home on the Monday.'

Sarah Anderson, head nurse of the female imbecile ward, told the court that on Saturday, the 1st, shortly after two o'clock, Beatrice Hall had come for her to go and see Mrs Berry's child. In the sitting room she was shown some vomit streaked with blood and was told by Mrs Berry that Edith had become sick just after breakfast. The next day, Sunday, she saw the child again, and then again on Monday, about ten o'clock, when she noticed a blister on her upper lip. 'I said to Mrs Berry, "What has caused that blister?" and Mrs Berry said, "I gave her some lemon and some sugar, and that must have caused it." I saw Edith again in the evening between half-past four and five o'clock, when she seemed worse.'

The final witness of the day was Lydia Evett, nurse in the children's hospital. She said that on the Sunday, having been told that Edith was very ill, she went up to Mrs Berry's bedroom to see her. 'I said to her, "You're starting the new year badly, Edith," and she replied, "Yes." Mrs Berry called my attention to the child's mouth and said, "See what an orange has done to Edith's mouth," and I noticed that her mouth was inflamed and red. Edith vomited very often while I was in the room, and said she had pains in her stomach and chest. To ease the pain, she was poulticed – at her own request. Mary Gibbin brought it and Mrs Berry put it on. It only stayed on for a minute or two. Edith couldn't bear it; it was too hot. That night I delivered a message at the lodge for the doctor to come.'

This ended Lydia Evett's testimony. It was now 6.15, and the hearing was adjourned until ten o'clock next morning.

The *Oldham Standard*, reporting on the day's events at the police court, added a most interesting piece in connection with the matter. The article was headed: RESIGNATION OF MRS BERRY, beneath which was written:

> At a meeting of the Oldham Board of Guardians on Wednesday, the following letter was read from Elizabeth Berry, nurse at the Workhouse, who is now in custody on a charge of having caused the death of her child by administering poison to her: – "Oldham, January 26. Gentlemen – Considering my present unfortunate

position, I hereby tender you my resignation of my appointment as female nurse in the Oldham Union Workhouse. I beg also to inform you that immediately on the release from my difficulty, I shall apply to be reinstated in my appointment."

Mr Schofield moved that the resignation be accepted, and that her salary due, amounting to £2 1s. 6d. be paid. Mr Gartside seconded, and the motion was carried. The question of appointing a successor was raised, and Mr Whitaker moved that Dr Patterson, the medical officer to the Union, make temporary arrangements for the carrying on of the work efficiently. Mr Smith seconded the motion, which was carried.

Mrs Berry's professional career was over.

Mr Cottingham, unable to attend the previous day's hearing, was at the police court well before ten o'clock on Friday morning. There, as on the previous day, the public gallery was tightly packed, with the galleries once more set apart for the female spectators who, as previously, far outnumbered the male.

Just after ten the magistrates came in, and shortly afterwards Elizabeth Berry's name was called. She appeared, 'stepping lightly' to the solicitors' table where she shook hands with Mr Cottingham and took her seat next to Mr Whitaker and his clerk, George Robinson. Dressed again in mourning attire, she also wore a pair of long black gloves, which she removed soon after the proceedings began.

After Mr Mellor had addressed the bench, the first witness of the day, Alice Alcroft, was called. She told the court that she was employed in the workhouse kitchen, which was situated almost opposite Mrs Berry's sitting room, that she had given Edith her supper on the Friday evening and served the two girls their breakfasts the next morning. Half an hour afterwards, she said, she was called into the sitting room to wipe up some vomit, and then sent to fetch a box of mineral powders from the surgery.

After Alcroft came Mary Jane Knight, who said she looked after the lying-in wards at the workhouse, and worked as a servant to Mrs Berry. She had been summoned by Beatrice Hall on the Saturday and found the child lying on the sofa in Mrs Berry's sitting room, and then again on the

Monday afternoon to Mrs Berry's bedroom. On this occasion she noticed blisters on the child's lips. She was in the kitchen on the Sunday morning, she said, 'when Mrs Berry sent down for an orange'. Asked if she was sure it was an orange and not a lemon, she said, 'I'm sure it was an orange. Beatrice Hall went into the store and got it herself.'

Dr Patterson was called next, but just as he was about to step into the witness box Mr Mellor said that the Chief Constable had arrived, and as he was unwell he would like to be allowed to give his evidence next. Permission was given, and Mr Hodgkinson came forward. As he was feeling too ill to stand he gave his evidence seated. In his testimony he told of his going to interview Mrs Berry, of being taken to see the child's body, and of being 'struck with astonishment' on seeing her mouth. The next day, he said, he had photographs taken of the face of the dead child.

Dr Patterson then took the stand, stating that he had been medical officer of the Oldham workhouse for the past twelve years. 'I don't live at the workhouse, but I visit it nearly every day. I don't go on Sundays unless I'm sent for.' He then reiterated his account of being called on the morning of Saturday 1 January to see Mrs Berry's daughter, of prescribing for the child and visiting her again that evening. Calling on her again the next day he found her improved, but that night found her to be much worse. 'Her eyes were sunken in her head and her pulse was almost imperceptible,' he said. 'Her mother told me that during the Sunday she had vomited a great deal and also started to be purged, and that the evacuations contained blood. She told me that the evacuations had been washed away. I also noted the state of the child's mouth – that the edges of the lips were red and swollen. I asked the mother what had caused this inflammation and she replied, "I gave her a piece of lemon with some sugar, and that's what did it."'

Cross-examined by Mr Cottingham, he said he had concluded that between his morning and evening visits an irritant, and probably a corrosive, poison had been administered. 'I told the mother that her daughter was in a very dangerous state, but I didn't mention my suspicions.' He had then brought in Dr Robertson and they had made for the child a mixture containing morphia and bismuth. 'The next morning, Monday,' he said, 'I went to see the child again and found her much worse, and she continued to sink till her death.'

He went on to say that on the Thursday he had assisted Dr Robertson and Dr Harris in making a complete post-mortem. He agreed with Dr Harris in that the child's death was caused by a corrosive poison, but as to the nature of the poison, he didn't know what it was.

'If you suspected poison,' Mr Cottingham said, 'why did you prescribe bismuth?'

'The patient was in great distress,' the doctor replied, 'and I prescribed morphia and bismuth to relieve the pain and allay the vomiting.'

'At the expense of her life?'

'That doesn't follow,' said Patterson. 'It was the most likely thing to help her through.'

'You prescribed to allay the vomiting, and left the poison to do its work?'

'No,' Patterson said at once, 'I will not have that put down.'

'It is what it amounts to,' Mr Cottingham came back, and then, 'What would be the effect of bismuth on the stomach?'

'It would allay the vomiting.'

'Would vomiting have the effect of getting rid of the poison that had not been absorbed?'

'If it was there, yes.'

'Why,' then, Mr Cottingham asked, 'did you not apply yourself to dealing with the poison, and try to get it out of the stomach?' Dr Patterson replied that he and Dr Robertson had agreed that they should relieve the girl's suffering at once, and on that account prescribed morphia and bismuth.

Questioned with regard to his meeting with the Chief Constable, the doctor said that on the Tuesday he gave Mr Hodgkinson a towel that he had received from Mrs Berry and told him that he thought the child had been poisoned. 'And I made the suggestion that Mrs Berry should perhaps be arrested,' he said.

After some further exchanges Mr Cottingham asked the doctor whether he had suggested to anyone that the child, for her protection, should be watched. 'No,' the doctor replied, 'it was too late then.'

This brought Dr Patterson's examination to an end.

The final witness in the hearing was Dr Robertson. He told the court that Dr Patterson had come to him on the Sunday and he had accompanied him to the workhouse to see the sick child. On observing the blisters on the child's mouth, he said, he had asked the mother if she could explain them, and in reply she said she had given her a lemon with some sugar. On asking Mrs Berry to show him the evacuations from the child's bowels, she told him that she had not kept them. 'The child was conscious while I was there,' he said, 'but greatly exhausted.' He formed the opinion that the symptoms were not due to any ordinary disease, but probably arose from some irritant poison, and was further of the opinion that the poison was probably administered by the mouth, in liquid form. He had suspected initially that it was oxalic acid, but came to agree with Dr Harris that it was 'more sulphuric acid than any other acid'. He and Dr Patterson, he said, did not do anything 'to meet the action of the poison' as they did not know what the poison was.

Mr Cottingham had one more question for him: 'Can you say why you did not go back to see the patient again after seeing her on the Sunday?'

Said Dr Robertson: 'I didn't go because I wasn't asked.'

After the doctor had stepped down, Mr Mellor announced that the case for the prosecution was finished, and Mr Cottingham rose, saying to the magistrates that in the event that they had not reached any conclusion following the evidence presented it was his duty to put before them his client's side of the case. The magistrates conferred on this, after which the chairman said the bench would like to hear Mr Cottingham's comments. This was Mr Cottingham's cue, and he was well up to the mark.

'Gentlemen,' he began, 'I can scarcely imagine a more onerous duty which could befall a bench of magistrates. You have before you a gentlewoman of unimpeached character; a woman who has not only held a responsible position in this borough, but who came here with the very best credentials. Upon her character not a shadow of suspicion has ever rested. She is a widow. She had one surviving child. This little girl was beloved by her mother. There has not been a suggestion throughout this case that the mother was ever negligent of her child, or that she was ever forgetful of her duties as a mother.'

After relating how Mrs Berry had brought her child – 'fairly well nourished [but] by no means robust' – to Oldham, and of the child being seized with vomiting on the Saturday morning, he said it was not possible for Mrs Berry to have administered poison to her. Although a witness had attempted to show that Mrs Berry was alone with the child in the surgery that morning, her evidence was contradicted by that of Beatrice Hall, who said her friend had never been out her sight, and also by Alice Alcroft, who was working in the kitchen: 'The door of the kitchen is almost opposite to that of the surgery, so she had ample opportunity of seeing anyone who went in there.' The first time Mrs Berry gave the child anything was *after* she had already started to vomit, and as soon as she realized that her child was ill she sent for the doctor. 'Did you,' he asked, 'ever hear of a mother who poisoned her child and then sent for a doctor at the earliest opportunity?'

He then pointed out that initially Dr Patterson had no suspicions of foul play and had treated the patient for ulceration of the stomach, but that on the Sunday morning, finding her much better, he gave her bicarbonate of soda and the rinsings of a creosote bottle. 'It seems to me peculiar treatment on the part of a doctor to give a patient the *rinsings* from a bottle,' he said. He then went on: 'When the doctor visited that evening he found the symptoms had changed, and he came to the conclusion that an irritant poison had been administered between his visits. Under these circumstances what does he do? Obviously the first thing to be done in such a case is to get rid of the poison, or to neutralize it. Instead of that the child is prescribed bismuth and morphia to relieve the pain, which would have the effect of keeping whatever was in the stomach still there to do its deadly work. Why did Dr Patterson not take active steps to save the child's life? Why did he make no attempt whatsoever to antagonize the poison? And if he believed that the child's mother was guilty of administering poison, why did he not withdraw the child from her custody?'

After saying that the child never complained of anything she had been given, he said he would like to know how the poison could have been administered without her being aware of it. 'Sulphuric acid would surely have burnt her mouth very badly and caused her to complain, wouldn't it?' And, in the event that poison had indeed been administered, how did the prosecution connect Mrs Berry with it? She had never attempted to conceal anything. 'She sent for the doctor promptly. She kept the towels stained with vomit and showed them to him. Is this the way a poisoner behaves?'

He then got to the matter of motive. The imputed motive was the insurance money of £10, which was drawn to pay the funeral expenses. 'Is that a motive?' he said. 'To suggest that a woman in her position should not only have murdered her own child, but to have done it for such a paltry sum of money only goes to show the mare's nest into which the prosecution has fallen.' He appealed to the bench. 'Does the accused look like a murderess?' he asked. 'Are her antecedents such as would lead you to suppose she is capable of this terrible crime? If we send this lady for trial, would a jury of Englishmen convict her? If you have no reasonable belief that they would, and yet you still send her for trial, then I say, with the greatest deference, that you would be guilty of a violation of public duty. But before submitting her to such a trying ordeal you should once again ask yourselves: Is there a single portion of the evidence which points to complicity on the part of the prisoner? And it will not do to say that she was there and had access to the poison. No, the question must be this: Is there any *proof* that she administered it?'

Mr Cottingham was near the end of his address, but he had not quite finished with Dr Patterson. After citing instances of his behaviour, he said, 'I can only suggest to you that the doctor's conduct was very peculiar, and the bench certainly ought not to join him in the suspicions he has thrown out when these suspicions are destitute of any facts.' He concluded by saying, 'I am certain that I have the honour of addressing four humane and intelligent English magistrates, who will not pause to speculate on what further evidence might be obtained if the prisoner were committed for trial, but who will do no more than consider the evidence before them now. Gentlemen, I confidently await your decision.'

With these words Mr Cottingham went back to his seat, and the magistrates rose and left the courtroom to confer and to form their verdict. It was just after four o'clock.

There is no question but that the magistrates had a difficult task before them. Mr Cottingham had done a fine job in defence of Mrs Berry, though it has to be acknowledged that not all of his contentions could stand close scrutiny. The witness Ann Dillon was most certain in her memory of going into the surgery on the Saturday morning and finding Edith in the room with her mother. Mr Cottingham, however, had done his best to cast doubt on her testimony, saying that it was gainsaid by Beatrice Hall and by Alice Alcroft. Beatrice Hall, he said, was sure that Edith had never been out of her sight since they arrived in the sitting room. As for Alice Alcroft, who worked in the kitchen, which was situated opposite the sitting room door, it cannot be supposed for a moment that she had her gaze unswervingly on the door. The woman was not there to observe the comings and goings across the corridor, but to help prepare breakfast for several hundred inmates.

However, although Mrs Berry did indeed have the opportunity to administer poison, there was no evidence that it had happened. She had been seen alone with Edith in the surgery, and she had been seen attempting to give her daughter what she claimed to have been medicine – once a milky-looking liquid in a tumbler, and at another time some mixture which, she said, Dr Patterson had left – but there was nothing to say that those liquids had contained poison. Further, she had shown all the outward signs of being a loving mother, referring to her child as 'my darling' and sending for the doctor as soon as he arrived at the workhouse and, later, seeking the help of the workhouse's resident nursing staff – Lydia Evett of the children's ward, and Sarah Anderson of the female imbecile ward. Further, what motive did she have for murder? Mr Cottingham had stressed that the £10 paid out on Edith's death – most of which had gone on the funeral costs – could not possibly have been sufficient reason for a loving mother to carry out such an horrific act.

Such questions raised by Mr Cottingham must surely have exercised the minds of the magistrates, and there were those who expected them to take considerable time over their deliberations. To the surprise of many in the courtroom, however, they were filing back into the room after only fifteen minutes.

When they had taken their places once more, the chairman of the bench, Mr John Wild, addressed the hushed assembly. 'We have given this case our very careful deliberation,' he said, 'and we have concluded that the evidence, as laid before us, is not sufficient to warrant sending the prisoner for trial.'

After his words there was a moment's silence, and then came an outburst of cheering, with shouts of 'Hear, hear,' and 'Hurrah!' And in the midst of it all the petite, black-clad, bereaved mother sat and hung her head, fighting back tears.

The cheers were proof that Mrs Berry had touched the hearts of some in that assembly, but what was going through her mind? Did she, like many in the room, believe that the magistrates' findings signalled her freedom? Did she, on hearing from all around the demonstrations of support, snatch at a sudden glimpse of hope, and the notion that all was not yet lost?

Indeed, all was not yet lost, and as the hubbub in the room was suppressed, Joseph Whitaker and George Robinson rose to congratulate Mr Cottingham on his great achievement. Mr Cottingham, however, for all his pleasure on hearing the chairman's verdict, was under no illusion. He was well aware of the true situation, which was made clear in the press the following day. Said the *Chronicle*:

> Though the decision of the bench was a dismissal so far as the magisterial proceedings were concerned…the general public, who, as a rule, are not much acquainted with criminal jurisprudence, must not run away with the idea that the accused will be discharged. She still remains in custody, charged on the Coroner's warrant with the wilful murder of her daughter…

Indeed it was so; and while there were many among the spectators that day who believed that Mrs Berry would now be set free, Mr Cottingham knew that his victory marked only the second battle in the war. With the coroner's warrant still out against his client, the magistrates' failure to find a *prima facie* case against her counted for nought. Had the inquest's jury acquitted her beforehand, the magistrates' findings would have seen her set free, but the inquest's verdict took precedence. Therefore there could be no question as regards the outcome: Elizabeth Berry must be sent for trial.

And so there it was: the prisoner was to go to trial with one judgement against her and another in her favour – an unusual situation, to say the least – though it would be as nothing to the most remarkable situation which was shortly to arise.

14

Repercussions

As to how Mrs Berry's situation was generally observed following the outcome of the magistrates' hearing, there were many who set far greater store by the findings of the bench than by a jury whose twelve good men and true were chosen from the public at large. And by this token it was widely believed that the magistrates' findings were the best guide to the outcome of the forthcoming trial, and that the prisoner had an excellent chance of being acquitted.

As we have seen, however, no such sanguine thoughts were shared by her counsel. While Mr Cottingham and Mr Whitaker must have been encouraged by the magistrates' conclusion, they were only too well aware of another dark process at work. This, of course, was the investigation that was taking place into the death of Mrs Finley, and what part in it her daughter might have played. The result of that investigation, they knew, could have the most dynamic effect on their client's future.

While the magistrates had been conducting their inquiry, arrangements were being made for the prisoner's trial. It had previously been assumed that this would take place at the Assizes in Manchester, but this proved not to be practicable and Liverpool was announced as the venue. And the authorities wasted not a minute. The night following the conclusion of the magistrates' hearing would be the last that Mrs Berry would spend in the Oldham police cell. Next morning, Saturday 29 January, carrying just a few belongings, she left the town on the last stage of her journey. The man from the *Chronicle* was there to report on her departure, and also – on a very positive note – to remark on the likelihood of her being given her liberty. Said the paper:

On Saturday morning Mrs Berry, the woman who is charged with causing the death of her daughter by administering poison, left Oldham for Liverpool. She travelled by the 9.28 train from the Central Station, in the charge of Detective Lamb, who, on arriving at Liverpool, handed over his prisoner to the authorities at Walton Prison. As we stated, Mrs Berry stands committed to the Liverpool Assizes under the coroner's warrant...It is however, probable – seeing that the magistrates acquitted her on Friday – that the grand jury will throw out the bill against her, in which case she will be formally liberated. The business at the Liverpool assizes commences on Friday.

For a few days, as Mrs Berry waited anxiously in her cell at Walton prison, there was little or nothing to report on any further developments in the case. Nonetheless, several of the newspapers ensured that the public would not be starved of copy relating to the matter.

Newspaper readers in the free world are fond of having their say through letters to the editors, and the people of Oldham and its surroundings were no different. With the magistrates' hearing at an end there were numerous individuals who were eager to share their thoughts and wisdom in connection with the proceedings. One particular letter to the *Oldham Evening Chronicle* was to cause something of a stir.

Whatever the opinions as to Elizabeth Berry's guilt or innocence, it was generally acknowledged that her counsel had done excellent work on her behalf before the magistrates. In the course of this Mr Cottingham had tried to cast doubt on Dr Patterson's professional abilities as exhibited in the tragedy, and generally gave him a hard ride, at one point going so far as to suggest that it had been in his power to save the girl but that he had neglected to do so. And if the doctor had been rattled on the witness stand by Mr Cottingham's questioning of his fitness in the sad business, his discomfiture wasn't to finish with the ending of the hearing.

On the Wednesday following the closure of the magistrates' inquiry, the *Chronicle* printed a letter from the aforementioned Dr John Kershaw. In giving Mrs Berry his full support, he wasted no time in writing to make it clear that he considered her totally innocent of the charge laid against her and that he regarded Dr Patterson – the man generally acknowledged as having been instrumental in putting her where she was – as the true villain of the piece.

His provocative letter was to become the first in a brief series, which, apart from everything else, suggested that the two doctors, Patterson and Kershaw, were known to one another, and were not perhaps the best of friends.

In his letter, Dr Kershaw brought to the public's attention Dr Patterson's prescribing of creosote in Edith's treatment. This was a matter that had not been fully examined and, even today, as of this writing, there are reports stating, as a matter of fact, that Edith died of creosote poisoning – one writer saying specifically that she died from 'having creosote put in her tea'. If this was a notion held by some at the time, then Dr Kershaw's letter was sure to give the belief some added strength. On 30 January, from his home in Sedgley Park, Prestwich, he wrote to the *Chronicle*, first congratulating the presiding magistrates 'on the sound sense and judgement they [had] shown in exonerating Mrs Berry from the serious charge brought against her by the Medical Officer of the Oldham Workhouse', and then proceeding to take that medical officer to task.

In his attack on Dr Patterson and his abilities, Dr Kershaw wrote that the prescribing of creosote and bicarbonate of soda by the doctor was 'careless and unscientific'. The mixture was much too strong in its proportions, he claimed, and without doubt would have caused the blisters on the girl's mouth. Therefore, he invited his readers to infer, Dr Patterson might well have been ultimately responsible for the girl's death.

Dr Kershaw had not, however, done his homework well. What he appears to have missed – either accidentally or intentionally – is the fact that the creosote ordered from the pharmacist early on Sunday afternoon was not delivered until the next morning, long *after* Edith's mouth was seen to be blistered, and after Dr Patterson and Dr Robertson had been to see her. That night, finding that the creosote had not been delivered, the two doctors had made up instead a mixture of bismuth and morphia. In support of this, Mrs Berry herself was later to say that she had not used any of the creosote that was eventually delivered.

Notwithstanding the facts, however, Dr Kershaw managed to sow seeds of doubt in the public's mind. And having done so, he ended his damning letter: 'With regard to the case in its legal aspect, I have nothing to do, but from motives of humanity, as well as saving the poor woman from the approbation of the uncharitable, I have presumed to place before you a matter which, I believe, has not received that attention which the vital importance of the case has deserved.'

While Dr Kershaw's misplaced and damaging claim may well have chimed with concerns in other minds, support for Dr Patterson was soon to be forthcoming. The following day the *Chronicle* published a letter from an Oldham chemist, Mr C. Granville Wood, an Associate of the Pharmaceutical Society, who wrote saying that he himself had 'made the mixture in the proportions Dr Patterson ordered' and that the solution was 'perfectly in accordance with the laws and rules of accurate dispensing'.

Then, on Friday 4 February, a letter came from Dr Patterson himself. Stung – and not surprisingly – by Dr Kershaw's impugning of his abilities and actions, and not about to take the insults lying down, he wrote:

> Sir, – I cannot think that 'motives of humanity' alone prompted Dr Kershaw to write that letter in the Chronicle of Wednesday evening. Had his objective been to benefit the 'poor woman', I think he could have accomplished it better by observing the usual prudence of silence while the matter is still under judgement. Besides, I understood that Mrs Berry had in Mr Cottingham an experienced and able advocate, to whom Dr Kershaw could have communicated his valuable suggestions, which I will briefly examine.
>
> 1. Dr Kershaw says that my prescription of creosote was unscientific. Only in his ignorance. Let him try to make it, and he will find that the solution is perfect. Not only so, but that a perfect solution of creosote in water can be made of greater strength than that prescribed by me. This statement, No. 1, of Dr Kershaw's is, therefore, untrue.
>
> 2. He suggested that the undissolved creosote in the prescription would blister the lips. There was no undissolved creosote in the prescription, for the mixture ordered was never made. But it would not blister the lips. I painted the edges of my own lips with raw creosote, and could not blister them. Further, I painted the lips of four children same age as deceased, with raw creosote, keeping it on for six minutes in each case. I did not put a blister on any one of the four. Statement No. 2, therefore, is also untrue.

3. Dr Kershaw suggests that I had no suspicion of poisoning till Sunday night. On the contrary, I told Mr Cottingham at the Workhouse enquiry that I suspected poisoning on the Saturday evening. Mr Cottingham took care not to ask me a question on that subject at the Town Hall. Statement No. 3 is, therefore, untrue.

Dr Kershaw magnifies the attention paid to the burning of the lips. It is almost impossible to do this. In conjunction with vomiting and purging of blood, and intense pain in the abdomen during life, and a corroded gullet post-mortem, it told the tale pretty well. And now, in conclusion, how has Dr John Kershaw, 'from motives of humanity' to the 'poor woman,' benefited her by writing such an imprudent letter, made up of absurdities and untruths? Alas, dear Dr John! it has been so with you for many years. The rattle of your relatives' money in your pocket, has, I fear, turned your poor, weak, empty head.

T. PATTERSON.

Dr Patterson's letter is remarkable in several instances – not least for his closing words in which he openly ridicules and insults his older colleague. There is also the matter of his having used four children as guinea pigs in his efforts to prove that raw creosote would not blister an eleven-year-old's lips. Of course, no doctor in Britain would dream of doing such a thing today. Also, exactly what Dr Patterson might have done had he been proved wrong and scarred the children for life, he doesn't say.

In any event, if Dr Patterson hoped that he was having the last word with his sharp reply, he was to be disappointed. Dr Kershaw came smartly back, writing on 6 February:

Sir, – My attention having been drawn to the literary efforts of Thomas Patterson which appeared in your paper of the 4th inst., would, under ordinary circumstances, have provided me with an infinite fund of amusement both in regard to its composition and the veracity, or otherwise, of his statements, were it not for the grave charge now pending, wherein the life of a person is hanging judicially in the balance. The gross vulgarity of his epistle is such that common self-respect and decency forbid me at present entering with him into any correspondence relating to the important matter his *suspicions* give rise to. Otherwise, it would have given me pleasure in the interests of the 'poor woman' to have replied to the alleged 'untruths' in my late letter *in extenso*, and have now only to express my thankfulness that my 'relations' have been kind enough to provide me with sufficient of their 'money' to exempt me from the tender mercies of the learned graduate of *Tulla-na-chree* in his capacity of surgeon to the Oldham paupers. – Yours truly,

JOHN KERSHAW

Along with Dr Kershaw's letter appeared a letter from one Albert Smith who wrote to the *Chronicle*'s editor saying that in his view not only had Dr Patterson acted by the book, but that Dr Kershaw had acted improperly in his criticism of the doctor. His most excellent letter is well worth quoting here. He wrote:

Sir, – In criminal cases of great importance it not infrequently happens that the conflict of medical opinion is very serious, and great issues are involved; but it seldom happens that one medical man will go so far as to impute gross and almost criminal carelessness to another. This is practically what Dr Kershaw has done by publishing the letter contained in your issue of last Wednesday. Unfortunately for himself, he has not taken the necessary precautions to see that his statements are borne out by facts…Dr Kershaw is probably aware that when there is not sufficient of any liquid in a bottle to pour out so as to measure accurately it is the custom to dissolve out of the bottle by rinsing, and then pour all out together. This is what has been done in the case under notice, and I may say that if Dr Kershaw never did anything worse he may be considered a model of precision. But a more serious error follows, in which Dr Kershaw states that the administration of creosote in the above careless and unscientific way would be sufficient to account for the symptoms exhibited by the child. This is distinctly not true. Dr Patterson has since made experiments on the mucous membrane of the lips and mouth, and did not succeed in raising a blister, much less causing the total blackening of the parts touched by the fluid. Further, the effects of poisoning by creosote are (as stated by Garrod*) convulsions and a death-like stupor, which are almost the exact opposite of violent vomiting and purging, from which the poor child suffered. Dr Kershaw should also have remembered that Dr Harris, who is known throughout the kingdom as a specialist in these matters, was in full possession of the facts, but yet found no trace of the effects of an overdose of creosote. I think you will see, Mr Editor, that Dr Kershaw's statements are not in accordance with the facts, and that, in an ill-advised moment, he has tried to prejudge the case by flatly laying it down to carelessness on Dr Patterson's part. It is, in many ways, a pity that such a letter should have seen the light of day. So far from serving the interests of "humanity", it is likely to do the opposite. It is always unwise to discuss such matters whilst they are still before the courts of laws. Each man has a right to his own opinion, but that opinion should not be expressed to the detriment or embarrassment of others. The case remains for a jury to decide. Dr Kershaw should leave it to them to say how and from what cause the child has died. – I am, yours, &c.,

> ALBERT SMITH, A.P.S., M.P.C.
>
> 45, Manchester Street.

This letter from Mr Smith appeared, dispassionately and disinterestedly, to set the case right and, it could be hoped, quell any further debate on the efficacy of Dr Patterson's methods and behaviour. Certainly it would seem to scotch any notion that creosote might have been the cause of Edith Annie's death, although a few weeks later Mrs Berry herself would be making reference to it in a desperate bid to save her life.

Mrs Berry, of course, sitting cut off from the world in her prison cell, would have known nothing of the letters and the insults being traded by Drs Patterson and Kershaw. She was concerned only in learning of the next step in her fate. To this end, on Monday 7 February, the putative witnesses for the prosecution came to Liverpool, summoned to appear before the gentlemen of the grand jury who, after hearing their testimonies, would

* Archibald Garrod (later Sir Archibald Garrod), 1857-1936, a much respected authority on medicine and medical research.

conclude whether or not there was sufficient evidence to commit the prisoner Berry for trial.

She, of course, was hoping against hope that, reflecting the views of the magistrates and of much of the press, the grand jury would throw out the bill and set her at her liberty. To her distress, however, she was soon informed that the grand jury had found a true bill against her, and that preparations for her trial would begin forthwith. As to the date of the event, the *Chronicle* reported on 8 February that it was likely to take place within a week.

15

New Developments

While the Oldham newspapers were airing the conflicting views of the medical and scientific experts with regard to the prescribing of creosote, more dynamic events were taking place outside the newspapers' correspondence columns.

As related previously, following inquiries into Mary Ann Finley's death, application was made for the exhumation of her body. And while there was no official announcement of the application being granted there appeared in the press one or two references to the probability of such an event taking place. As a result, on Monday 31 January two Oldham reporters – one from the *Chronicle* and the other from the *Standard* – went to the Moston Roman Catholic Cemetery to make inquiries.

At the cemetery the Brother Superior, Brother Kleppell, told the two men that he hadn't heard a word about the exhuming of Mrs Finley's body, except what he had read in the papers. Further, he scorned the idea that it was at all likely to happen. There were twelve bodies in the same grave, he said, and the relatives of the others buried there would most certainly object to any disturbance of it.

The grave in question, the *Chronicle*'s reporter noted, was a 'public' or 'inscription' grave, and there had been four bodies put into it before that of Mrs Finley, which meant that seven other bodies would have to be raised before hers could be reached.

Despite Brother Kleppell's claim that there would be no exhumation, on Tuesday two constables arrived to tell him that Mrs Finley's body was indeed to be exhumed, and gave him instructions for the necessary preparations. Next evening, when the two reporters returned to the cemetery they learned from an unhappy Brother Kleppell that the exhumation would take place later that night. It was now after eight o'clock and, intent on getting a story, the men ascertained the whereabouts of the grave and then set out in the dark to find it. The area to search was vast, but they eventually espied a small light at a graveside and, drawing closer, saw some gravediggers at work, with two coffins partly covered with earth standing nearby. One of the men, becoming aware of the reporters' presence, came and asked them their business. When they said they were there to inquire into the exhumation of Mrs Finley's body, they were told that the coffin had not yet been reached, and that it would be some time before the men 'struck it'. With this, the reporters decided to leave the men 'to pursue their gloomy task', and went away.

The next morning, while the gravediggers, by the light of their lanterns, were still hacking away at the heavy, clay-based earth, further away, in Castleton, a different dramatic activity was taking place.

Well before eight o'clock there had gathered in the Blue Pits Inn, situated on the banks of the Rochdale Canal, a jury of fifteen, summoned for the opening of an inquest into Mary Ann Finley's death. They were led by the same Coroner Mr F. N. Molesworth who, just the previous month, had presided over the inquest into the death of Edith Annie Berry. Once the jury had been sworn in, they set off, driven in a three-horse brake, for Moston. In the conveyance along with the coroner was Dr Sharples of Rochdale, Superintendent Tindall of the Rochdale division of the county police, and two of Mrs Finley's erstwhile neighbours, Sarah Wolfenden and Mary Ann Lyons.

In Moston, at nine o'clock, the two Oldham reporters were returning to the cemetery just as the coach containing the inquest party reached the gates. At once the reporters went to the graveside where the men were still working. The *Standard*'s man, reporting in that evening's edition of the paper, told of the unusual event:

> Four labourers, under the supervision of Brother Kleppell, had been at work for some hours at the grave where Mrs Finley was interred,

and…already the six* coffins which had been placed above that of Mrs Finley had been removed. These were placed in a temporary resting place close by, and decently covered with canvas. Owing to the clayey nature of the soil and the quantity of rain which has lately fallen, the work of excavating was very laborious, and could only be accomplished slowly. Soon after the arrival of the visitors from Castleton Mrs Finley's coffin was reached by the workers in the grave, and the name plate detached and handed out. This having been washed was found to bear the following inscription:

MARY ANN FINLEY,

Died 13th February, 1886

Aged 55 years.

Rest in Peace.

The work of raising the coffin was then proceeded with, and was accomplished by the aid of chains and ropes. It was then placed on the sward near to the grave and washed, and the sticky clay and dirt having been removed, it was found to be thoroughly well preserved. Dr Harris, who had travelled from Manchester to make the post-mortem examination of the body of the deceased, was careful to secure a jarful of the soil taken from the grave about 6 inches above where the coffin rested, and he then followed the coffin to the outbuilding near the registrar's office. It had been intended that the examination should be made in this building, but on finding from Brother Kleppell that there would be no objection to such a course, the doctor decided to make the examination in the open air. The coffin was therefore placed on a trestle, and opened to the view of the jury. To allow of better identification some water was poured over the face, and the two females before mentioned were brought forward to look upon the disfigured form of their former acquaintance, and were naturally both very much affected. The face of the deceased woman appeared somewhat swollen, and the body altogether was naturally in an advanced state of decomposition. Having viewed the body the jury were conveyed back to Castleton to the Blue Pits Hotel…Dr Harris concluded his investigation at the

* There were in fact seven coffins above Mrs Finley's.

cemetery shortly after noon, and the result will be communicated to the Coroner and the jury in due course. By order of the Cemetery Board the cemetery is altogether closed to the public today.

On the assembly's return to the Blue Pits Inn the inquest was opened, and Sarah Wolfenden and Mary Ann Lyons testified that the body they had seen at the cemetery was that of Mary Ann Finley. With this the coroner adjourned the proceedings until 7 February. In the meantime Dr Harris would despatch to the county analyst a number of containers holding the viscera of the dead women. When the 7th came, however, the analyst's work was not complete, and as a consequence the proceedings were adjourned for a further week.

When the inquiry resumed on 14 February the newspaper reporters were the first to arrive, followed by the local police, and then, shortly before two o'clock, by Superintendent Tindall of Rochdale. Also present was solicitor Joseph Whitaker, there to watch the proceedings on behalf of Elizabeth Berry. At ten minutes past two the coroner arrived, and the first testimonies were heard.

In what was to be a full day the jurors heard from ten witnesses, some of whom gave evidence that was greatly shocking as they disclosed details of the final days in the life of Elizabeth Berry's mother.

The first witness was twenty-nine-year-old Mrs Mary Ann Lyons of 5 Albion Street, who had previously identified the deceased's body. In her testimony she said that she had known Mrs Finley for eighteen months, seeing her almost every day. 'I was with her on the Friday before her death on the Saturday,' she said. 'I saw her at eight o'clock and ten o'clock that night. She seemed well then, and looked likely to get better. I heard she died at seven o'clock next morning.' She had never expected Mrs Finley to die, she added, 'but we all had suspicions, for on the Friday she looked so likely to get better. I and other neighbours all suspected that something was wrong, but I didn't say anything because I was afraid to. You know, none of them would like to do that.'

The next witness was Mrs Sarah Wolfenden of 11 Back Albion Street, who, like the previous witness, had identified the deceased's body at the cemetery.

The Blue Pits Inn, Castleton, scene of the inquest into the death of Mary Ann Finley. *Photograph: Jack Ireland, c. 1986.*

After saying in her testimony that she knew Mrs Finley well and frequently went into her home, she recalled Mrs Berry's visit on Wednesday 3 February, saying, 'She came to my house because her mother was out – she'd gone to Manchester that morning,' and went on to say that Mrs Finley's state of health was very good on that day, but that on the Wednesday evening, after appearing well all day, she 'was taken poorly'. She added, 'I went to see her and found her in bed. She said she had been very poorly since she had had her tea. I saw her every day until she died. On the Friday night before she died I went to see her about half-past nine. She was in bed then, and said she expected to get better and felt quite well. I left the house about eleven o'clock. I saw her the next morning about seven o'clock or a few minutes before, and she was dying. She was twitching very much all over her body. Every nerve seemed to be at work. Her eyes were closed, and her breast was rising and her tongue was hanging out of her mouth. Her mouth was very dry, as was her tongue, and she appeared to be unconscious. I said to Mrs Berry, "What a change there is," and she said, "Yes, there's a great change." I asked her when the change took place and she said it had taken place at the turn of the night.' After telling the court that she had helped to lay the body out, she was asked about Mrs Berry's calling at her door in Castleton. She said in reply, 'We had some tea, and we were talking about her mother going back to work at the mill, and Mrs Berry said she'd had a dream, and that whenever she dreamed anything to that effect there was usually a death in the family, and she believed this time it would be her mother. She said she had the feeling that she had come to Castleton to bury her mother.'

This ended Mrs Wolfenden's testimony, and her place was taken by Mrs Alice Eaves of 14 Back Albion Street. She told the court that she remembered Mrs Berry coming to stop with Mrs Finley. 'I saw Mrs Finley every day from then until her death,' she said. 'She hadn't been so well the week before, but she had got better of that, and was knocking about until the Tuesday evening. I met her that Tuesday in the afternoon near Mrs Wolfenden's house. She was very poorly then, and at one moment she almost fell. I told her to get home and go to bed, as she looked in such a poor state. I went round that same night and saw her in bed. She was very bad and in a dreadful state. She seemed as if she was in a fit. Her daughter, Mrs Berry, was with her. I went for my husband and fetched him as I thought Mrs Finley was dying. While I was there Mrs Berry took a small bottle off the mantelpiece and gave a spoonful out of it to her mother. Mrs Finley got quieter after this, but she didn't seem to know us. There was a lamp in the room and I held it up to show a little light, but Mrs Berry told me to take it away, saying that she didn't want any light. I offered to stop all night but Mrs Berry said she wasn't frightened and that she could manage by herself. I saw Mrs Finley again the next day and she appeared to be a little better. She was in bed. On the Friday, the day before her death, I went into her house with the agent for the Prudential Society. Mrs Finley wanted one of her policies endorsed and I took him in for that. When I got in, Mrs Berry was washing her mother in bed. I started to talk to Mrs Finley but Mrs Berry said, "Don't talk to her. Her pulse is beating quicker than it should." Mrs Finley told Mrs Berry where the policies were – there were three of them – and Mrs Berry fetched them and the agent took one of them away with him.'

Mrs Eaves then told the court of her last meeting with Mrs Finley. 'That Friday evening I was going past the window of Mrs Finley's house,' she said, 'and she called me in and asked me to give her something to drink. She wanted some beer. She said they had plenty but that her daughter wouldn't let her have any. Mrs Berry wasn't in the house at the time. Mrs Pemberton, Mrs Finley's sister, was there, and she gave Mrs Finley some cake and I gave her a gill of bitter beer. She looked very well at the time and said she felt much better. I went out shortly afterwards and that was the last time I saw her alive. I went into the house a few minutes after she'd died the next morning, and asked to see the body. I didn't see her face as it was covered. Mrs Berry said there had been a great change for the worse in her during the night.'

The next witness was Alice Chorlton who gave her age as twenty-four and said she lived at Five Arches, Spotland Bridge. She told the court that she had lodged with Mrs Finley from 4 July till January 1885. 'After I left Mrs Finley I used to see her nearly every day,' she said. 'I used to call on her on the way home from work. I knew that Mrs Berry came to see her on the Wednesday, 3rd of February last year – it was my birthday. Mrs Finley told me of her visit the next day when she came round to see me. I last saw her on the Friday, the evening before she died, about a quarter-to-six. She was in bed. She called me to her bedside and when I went to her she put her finger to her mouth as much as to say she wanted something to drink. I said to Mrs Berry, "Lizzie, your mother wants something to drink. See – she's just beckoned me for it." Mrs Berry said, "Yes, she's not had her medicine, and she won't take it from me. You try if you can and give her something – she might take it from you." Mrs Berry then poured something out of a bottle into a cup – about a tablespoon. I added some water to it and took it to Mrs Finley's bedside. I raised her head from the pillow, and she drank it straight off, and then she said, "Oh, dear, that is bad! That's worse than poison!" I turned to Mrs Berry and I said, "Lizzie, did you hear what your mother says?" and she said, "Oh, she's always saying that," and she told me to add some more water to the medicine. I went home afterwards, but I called again the same night about half-past ten. Mrs Finley was in bed, asleep. Mrs Berry asked me if I'd like to take some supper with her, but I said I'd be having mine when I got home. I did have a small sup of beer. That was the last time I saw Mrs Finley alive.'

Harriet Dorrick, twenty-seven, residing at 6 Albion Street, was next called, and testified that she knew Mrs Finley very well. In the course of her evidence she said, 'On the Friday, the 5th, I saw Mrs Finley coming down Albion Street. She called to me, and I went over to her and asked her how she was. She said to me, "I don't know." Then she said, "I've got a visitor," and I asked who it was and she said it was her daughter Lizzie. She said, "She's just been giving me some medicine and I feel very sick and queer after it." She'd come out for a walk, she said, to try and shake it off, and held up a jug and said she was on her way to fetch the supper beer. I saw her again the next day, Saturday, and also the following Monday when she introduced me to her daughter, Mrs Berry. At that time Mrs Finley was still looking pretty well. But the next morning, Tuesday, when I went to see her she didn't appear to be very well, and she told me she couldn't eat. While I was there Mrs Berry left the house. She said she was going into Rochdale to get a chicken. That was about eleven o'clock. I was still there when she came back about one o'clock.'

The next witness had also been a neighbour of Mrs Finley. She was Mrs Henrietta Morton, living at 3 Cross Street, Castleton. She said she knew Mrs Finley and used to visit her. 'On the 5th of February Mrs Berry came to my house,' she said, 'and we had tea together, and Mrs Finley came along for her later on to walk home with her. After she had come into the house Mrs Finley sat down and put a hand to her side, and Mrs Berry asked her if she had that pain again. Mrs Finley replied that she had. Mrs Berry told her that she had a prescription that she had taken from a doctor's book, and that she thought it would do her good as it was for lung and heart disease. Mrs Berry asked me if there was a pharmaceutical chemist in Castleton, and I told her I thought not, but that she would get it at Mr Highley's in Rochdale.' She then said that Mrs Berry left her with Mrs Finley, saying she would catch the 6.40 train to Rochdale.

It was no doubt of great interest to the jury then to learn that Mrs Berry had spoken to Mrs Morton also of her prescient dreams. Questioned as to the conversation the witness had had with Mrs Berry when they sat having tea together, Mrs Morton told the court that Mrs Berry said that she had had a dream, and that when she had a dream of that sort there was always a death in the family.

The coroner asked her: 'What was the dream? Did she say what it was?' Mrs Morton replied, 'She told me she dreamed that she went to a new situation, and she was going down one of the wards and noticed that the beds were placed feet to feet. When she got to the bottom of the ward she saw one of the beds reversed and she saw a person lying there. She then saw that it was her mother. She said she asked her mother what was the matter. Her mother didn't speak, but raised herself up on her side and one arm, and Mrs Berry saw marks of blood on her.'

With this remarkable postscript, Mrs Morton was allowed to step down.

The next witness was Mr John Taylor, a chemist of Yorkshire Street, Rochdale, whose evidence was to create something of a stir. He testified:

'On the afternoon of the 9th February last year I remember my late assistant, Fred Butterworth, handing me a slip of paper from a medical man on which was written in Latin: "*Liquor Atropia Sulph.*" I thought it was written by a medical man because it looked so in the handwriting. The translation of it was a solution of sulphate of atropia.* I was in the dispensing room at the time, and I asked my assistant what he, the customer, wanted it for. He said it was a woman in the shop, and when I went into the shop I asked her what she wanted it for. She said she wanted it to drop into the eyes. I hadn't seen her before, and she said in answer to my inquiries that she was an infirmary or workhouse nurse. She said she knew all about the medication and had been using it for some time; that she was accustomed to using it. I asked her if she knew that it was a poison, and she said she did. I told her that I would want her to write her name in the sales book along with her address. She gave me the name: "Ellen Saunders, Freehold, Castleton," and I wrote it in the sales book and she signed the book. I mixed the medication and after she paid me I returned the paper with the Latin prescription to her – which is customary in the trade – and she left the shop.'

Mr Taylor's interesting testimony did not end there. He went on to say that three days later, on the 12th, she was in the shop again. 'She handed me the same slip of paper, and asked for a further supply. I asked what had become of the other as I didn't think it could all have been used in the time for dropping in the eyes, and she answered, "I knocked it over and spilt it." I went into the dispensing room then to prepare the article, leaving the door of the room ajar, and she called out to me, "What will double the quantity be?" I went back and asked her why she wanted so

---

* Now known as atropine.

much of it, and she said if she got double the quantity she wouldn't have to come again so soon. I told her the price and then after she had signed the book I gave her an ounce of the medicine.' Asked to describe the woman, he said she was a little person, between twenty-eight and thirty years of age, and of a dark complexion. He could not, he said, remember how she was dressed.

Mr William Henry Lawson, Master of the Oldham Union Workhouse, was then called. After telling the court that he was familiar with Mrs Berry's handwriting he was handed a letter written by Mrs Berry and then shown the Rochdale chemist's book bearing the two signatures of 'Ellen Saunders'. In his opinion, he said, the signatures were in Mrs Berry's handwriting.

After Mr Lawson came Frederick Wallwork, of the Wesleyan and General Assurance Society, who told the hearing that Mrs Finley had been insured with the society for £100, the premiums paid by Mrs Berry. He was followed by Henry Jackson, an agent for the Prudential Assurance Society, who told the court that Mrs Finley had been insured through his agency for £27 6s. and that on Mrs Finley's death the money was paid to Mrs Berry.

Dr Harris, who had conducted the post-mortem on Mrs Finley's body, was called next, but as his investigations were not complete the inquiry was again adjourned, this time for a fortnight, to be resumed on Monday 28 February.

With the coroner's call for an adjournment the long day's hearing was at an end, and a remarkable day it had been. There had been many testimonies to Mrs Finley's good state of health at the time of Mrs Berry's arrival, and thereafter to her rapid decline and sudden death. There had also been the reports of Mrs Berry's revelations as to her strange dream – the dream which, she said, presaged a death in the family. And not least remarkable was the purchase of a great deal of poison by a woman whose handwriting and physical description were similar to those of Elizabeth Berry.

With regard to this latter, the purchase of the poison, the *Evening Chronicle* made its heading for the report of that day's hearing as 'Mrs Berry's Purchases of Poison'. No newspaper, of course, would dream of printing such a headline today while an inquiry was still in progress. Such a headline might very quickly result in a suit for damages, and possibly jeopardize the inquiry.

In its report of 15 February on the day's hearing of the inquest, the *Chronicle* closed its account by saying that no date had yet been fixed for Mrs Berry's trial in Liverpool, but added that it was expected to be called before the week was out.

The paper then added a line presenting the possibility of a most unusual situation that might arise, saying: 'Should Mrs Berry get acquitted at Liverpool, and the jury which is inquiring into the death of her mother at Castleton return a verdict of wilful murder against her, she will be sent to the next Manchester Assizes for Trial.'

So there it was – a most remarkable situation – one in which if Elizabeth Berry escaped the death penalty at her trial for her daughter's murder, she might well, depending on the outcome of the Castleton inquest, face a second murder trial, this time on a charge of murdering her mother.

16

The Trial Opens

The calendar of indictments for the Liverpool Assizes that spring of 1887 named no fewer than ninety individuals who were to be brought for trial. In addition to the lesser charges, such as theft and assault, were those of a more grave nature, rape, attempted murder and manslaughter. There were three indictments for the ultimate crime, that of wilful murder, of which Elizabeth Berry's was scheduled to be the third, and the last in the calendar.

While she waited in her cell at Walton Gaol, not yet knowing when her trial would begin, she was in constant communication with her solicitor, Joseph Whitaker, who continued to work, unflagging, on her behalf. And Mr Whitaker had a problem. The opening of the inquest on the death of Mary Ann Finley at Castleton had brought further demands on his time and efforts, and he was becoming increasingly concerned over the matter of his fees. He had received some payment from Mrs Berry, but the money was going at an alarming rate. He had represented her from the first day of the inquest into Edith Annie's death, through the petty sessions before the magistrates, and now – though he was not allowed to speak of it to her – he was attending the inquest in Castleton on her behalf. Also, instructed by Mrs Berry, he had in turn instructed counsel for her defence, in the shape of James Cottingham. In addition, the trial was soon to open, at which Mr Cottingham was to be aided by a junior barrister. The costs were mounting.

On his expressing his concerns to Mrs Berry it was agreed that, in the event that she should be unable to meet all his costs, she would turn over to him certain of her possessions, to sell or dispose of as he thought fit. To this end, Mr Whitaker's clerk, George Robinson, travelled to Walton Gaol, where, with Robinson witnessing her signature, Mrs Berry wrote an authorization for Mr Whitaker to take full control of her effects then held at the Oldham workhouse. Addressed to the Clerk of the Guardians of the workhouse, it read:

> I authorize you to hand to Mr Joseph Whitaker Solicitor Oldham 3 pictures and clothes and all other articles and effects belonging to me.
> Elizabeth Berry
> Witness: Geo. H. Robinson
> Feb 16th 1887

She also arranged for Mr Whitaker to be given her watch. On receiving the document, Mr Whitaker put it in his file, to be ready in the event that it was needed.

Elizabeth Berry's trial at the Liverpool Winter Assizes was eventually set to open on 21 February. On that Monday morning, in her cell, she sat waiting for the warders to come for her. While held in the prison she had been kept in ignorance of what was going on in the outside world. Although the inquest's proceedings in Castleton had been widely reported, the rules of the prison denied the prisoner access to all newspapers and also forbade visitors imparting any verbal information on outside events. As things were, however, Mrs Berry's ignorance of any revelations coming from the inquest into her mother's death was probably a good thing for her. She already had quite enough on her plate, and all her thoughts that morning would have been on the ordeal before her and the ensuing verdict on the charge of murdering her daughter.

When at last the time for her departure was due, the officers came for her, and she was escorted across the city to St George's Hall wherein the courtroom was crowded.

Presided over by Mr Justice Hawkins, the trial was the final one in the calendar for the Winter Assizes and scheduled to last for four days. Appearing for the prosecution was Mr William M'Connell, Q.C., a much respected member of the Liverpool Bar, and for the prisoner Mr James Cottingham again, assisted by Mr Henry Byrne. Also among those gathered was coroner Mr Molesworth, who was presently conducting the inquest into Mrs Finley's death; Mr Hesketh Booth, Clerk to the Oldham Magistrates; the Guardians of the Board of the Oldham workhouse and numerous other Oldham officials and workhouse residents. Among the spectators was Dr John Kershaw – he who had written to the *Chronicle* so scathingly of Dr Patterson's methods and behaviour.

Although not all would be heard, twenty-seven witnesses had been called for the prosecution and about nine for the defence. A number of the Oldham witnesses were pauper inmates from the workhouse. Not required to wear the workhouse uniform for their trip to Liverpool, they were allowed their own, personal clothing. Like most of the other witnesses they would be housed in hotels for the duration of their stay.

The principal figures involved in the trial knew well that its outcome was anybody's guess. The guilt and innocence of the prisoner had already been twice tested – and with directly opposing verdicts. The trial would now offer a third hearing of the evidence, after which the jury would decide whether the prisoner was to live or die.

At the solicitors' table Mr Cottingham was very conscious of the task before him. He had done his work well before the magistrates, but the situation now was very different. Since the magistrates' hearing there had been the opening of the inquest into the death of Elizabeth Berry's mother, with evidence which, it could not be denied, reflected disastrously on his client. For just as he himself had read all the newspaper accounts of the sensational proceedings, so he knew that every single member of the jury there in the Liverpool courthouse would also have read them. As a result, when they came to decide on their verdict they would have before them not only the evidence in the Edith Annie Berry poisoning case, but the knowledge that the prisoner was also under the deepest suspicion of having poisoned her mother.

At about ten past eleven Mr Justice Hawkins took his seat, and three minutes later Elizabeth Berry's name was called. She stepped into the dock with a light step, dressed as she had been at Oldham, in her mourning dress, neat little hat, and long black gloves with white cuffs. She stood erect while the charge was read, and in a firm, somewhat loud tone answered,

'Not guilty.' Mr Cottingham had a hurried, low-voiced consultation with her while the jury was being sworn in, and then as he returned to his seat a chair was placed for her, behind which stood one of the female warders.

When at last everyone was in place, Mr M'Connell opened the case for the Crown. The prisoner, he said to the jury, was charged with having caused the death of her child, a female of the age of eleven years and eight months, who had met her death by poisoning. And if the doctors' conclusions were correct, then the question was: Who was it who had administered the poison? It was the view of the prosecution, he said, that it was the prisoner who had done so.

Giving an account of the antecedents of the dead child, he said that since 1881 she had lived with her aunt and uncle at Miles Platting until last 29 December when the prisoner had brought her to the workhouse. The prisoner, in her work as a nurse, had access to the surgery, and although many of the poisonous drugs were locked up, still there were many articles

Elizabeth Berry, artist's impression. It is reported that an artist from the press drew Mrs Berry's likeness as she sat in the dock. Perhaps this is his work, showing her neat little hat and her fashionable frizette.

open in the room which, if misused, would be destructive of life. On the morning of 1 January a woman named Ann Dillon saw the deceased in the surgery with the prisoner. This visit was fixed in the fact that the dinner bill she received that morning was in the prisoner's handwriting. Shortly afterwards the child became ill, and on Tuesday, the 4th, she died. The doctors were of the opinion that the girl had been given poison. A complete examination of the body had been made, but no traces of any poison were found. It was the doctors' belief, however, that the poison had been carried away with the vomit and the purging. Mr M'Connell finished his address saying that he would produce witnesses who would prove the case for the prosecution.

The first witness was Alexander Banks, an architect from Oldham, who produced a plan of the workhouse showing the surgery and its relation to the prisoner's sitting room. Copies of the plans were handed out to the jury. Banks was followed by William Lawson, Master of the workhouse, who, handed a piece of paper, identified it as one of the diet sheets that Mrs Berry prepared each day, which was in her handwriting, and which had been completed on the morning of Saturday 1 January, shortly before Edith Annie had been taken ill.

Ann Sanderson, the dead girl's aunt, was then called. In her examination by Mr Mellor she sometimes spoke in such a low voice that once or twice she was asked to speak up. She told the court that Edith, a 'very lively child', had lived with her and her husband for some years. After Edith's departure for Oldham she had received a letter from her. She produced the letter, and the judge, remarking that it would help 'to complete the history of the case', read it out to the jury.

Written on Friday 31 December, the letter began, 'Dear auntie and uncle,' and went on to tell of the girls arriving safely at the workhouse, and of the Christmas decorations. It wrote also of their seeing the workhouse children 'get their prizes' and of having gone to see the Misses Johnson from Blackpool, swimming, and describing their feats under water. 'It is very frosty indeed since we came,' the letter said. 'Mamma was dressed splendidly for the ball last night. Beatrice and I are enjoying ourselves very much.'

Mrs Sanderson said the letter arrived on the Saturday, and on Monday she received a telegram. The telegram was here given to the judge, who said that it had been handed in at Rochdale Road Post Office, Oldham on Monday 3 January at 8.37. Addressed to Mrs Sanderson, it said: 'Come at once Annie is dying. E. Berry, Oldham Union.'

'I received it a little before ten,' Mrs Sanderson said, 'and we set off at once to Oldham and got there a little before twelve o'clock. My husband was with me. Mrs Berry was in the bedroom with Annie, who was in bed. I said to Annie, "Are you poorly, Annie?" She recognized me and she said, "Yes." Then she said to me, "I've bought you a brooch, Auntie. You'll find it in Mamma's sitting room on the mantelpiece."' Here Mrs Sanderson's frail composure deserted her and she began to weep. 'I found the brooch there,' she sobbed.

When she was calmer, she spoke confirming her earlier testimony that Edith had never suffered from constipation, and as for her passing blood when given pills to counteract it, she had never been given pills of any kind. Questioned on Edith's last hours, she said that at about nine that evening she and Mrs Berry went down to Mrs Berry's sitting room to have some supper, leaving Ellen Thompson with the child. When they returned, Thompson left the room. About twelve o'clock Mrs Berry got undressed and lay down at the child's side, where she fell asleep. Then about one o'clock the child gave two loud shrieks, at which Mrs Berry woke up, saying that a change had taken place. She then got off the bed and got dressed again. Mrs Sanderson went on to say that she herself stayed at the child's bedside until her death at five o'clock in the morning, but that the child's mother left the room at four, saying that she couldn't bear to see the lass go.

Mr Cottingham, cross-examining, was of course anxious to avoid his client being seen in an unsympathetic light, and said to the witness, 'You tell us that Mrs Berry left the room before her daughter died. But the child had been low for many hours before this. Is that not correct?'

'Yes.'

'And is it not a fact that Mrs Berry had hardly been to bed at all during the whole of the time the child was ill?'

'Yes.'

'And is it not true that the doctor on his last visit had ordered her to take some rest?'

'Yes.'

Mr Cottingham, set on establishing that weak bowels had affected other members of the Berry family, said to her, 'Now, regarding the prisoner's husband, Thomas Berry, your late brother – can you tell us how he died?'

'He had a weak inside – weak bowels,' Mrs Sanderson replied, and added that she saw him 'sometimes confined to bed for a day or so'.

'And before he died was he very much emaciated? Very thin?'

'Yes.'

'Edith was not the only child of the marriage, was she?' said Mr Cottingham.

'No. There were two other children. One, a baby, who died at four months.'

'What was the cause of death, do you know?'

'I believe it was from teething.'

'And there was a third child, is that correct?'

'Yes, a boy. He died in 1882.'

'What did he die of?'

'I believe it was from an infection of the head and lungs.'

Mr Cottingham wasn't accepting this, and asked her, 'Did you hear tubercular disease mentioned as the cause of death?'

'No.'

Mr Cottingham held up a piece of paper in front of the witness. 'Then how,' he asked, 'can you account for it getting on this paper?'*

At this, the judge, not happy with Mr Cottingham's approach in this instance, was quickly moved to remark: 'Mr Cottingham, this is very irregular.'

Mr Cottingham may have softened his tone but he continued on the same tack. 'I understand,' he said to the witness, 'that on one occasion when the deceased and the boy came home from Blackpool they were both suffering from sickness and vomiting. Is that correct?'

'Yes,' she replied. 'I didn't see 'em vomit, but they told me they did before they got home. Dr Shaw came to see them.'

---

* Tubercular disease of brain and glands of bowels was given as the cause of death of Harold on his death certificate. It is not surprising that Mrs Sanderson was unable to answer Mr Cottingham's question about it as she could not read.

Having done his best to establish that both the child's father and brother had suffered from weak bowels, Mr Cottingham asked the witness whether she had ever given her any medication. She replied that she gave her Gregory's powder every few months. 'Not because her bowels were irregular, but because her stomach was out of order. She didn't eat very well.'

'Did she ever complain of pain in the stomach?'

'No.'

After Mrs Sanderson had stepped down, the court was adjourned for luncheon. When proceedings were resumed, Edith's friend Beatrice Hall was called.

She told the court that at the workhouse she and Edith played together and had their meals together. On Thursday they went out and bought chocolate and coconut chips and biscuits, and on Friday some fish at the market. 'It was finnan haddock,' she said, and they all three – she, Edith and Mrs Berry – had it for tea.

Continuing, she said that on Saturday morning she and Edith got up about nine o'clock, at which time Edith seemed very well. When they were dressed they went down to Mrs Berry's sitting room for breakfast. 'I ate my breakfast about ten o'clock,' she said. 'Edith didn't have any breakfast because she was sick. After Edith was sick Mrs Berry gave her a powder, and afterwards took her to a closet which was down the corridor. They were gone just for a few minutes.' She went on to say that the doctor came and afterwards Edith was taken up to Mrs Berry's bedroom where she, the witness, stayed with her the whole of the afternoon. That night, she said, a bed was made up for her down in Mrs Berry's bedroom. However, on her telling Edith that she was 'feared' to sleep there alone, Edith slapped the pillow at her side and said, 'Come and sleep here, then.' Beatrice then slept that night in the bed along with Edith and Mrs Berry. 'Edith didn't seem to be any worse in the morning,' she said. 'I asked her if she was any better, and she said she was.' About half-past eight she left her friend to go downstairs and have breakfast and returned to her side about 9.30. She was there when Dr Patterson came about twelve o'clock, and remained there after he had gone until half-past twelve, when she went down to have her dinner, leaving Mrs Berry alone with Edith. She returned to the bedroom about half-past one. There were no marks on Edith's lips then. Questioned further, she said that she stayed with Edith till about four o'clock, reading to her, then went off to have her tea. 'I didn't sleep with Edith that night,' she said. 'They made a bed up for me again in Mrs Berry's sitting room but I was afraid to stay there on my own.' She slept with the nurse Sarah Anderson that night, she added, and went home on Monday morning.

The nursing assistant Ann Dillon went into the witness box next. She spoke of Edith as a 'very merry little girl', and said that at a quarter to ten on the morning of 1 January she went into the surgery and found the child there with Mrs Berry. 'I went into the surgery to get the diet note,' she said, 'as it was my duty to do every day.'

Here Mr Mellor said to the judge: 'Your Lordship has the diet note?'

The Judge: 'Yes.'

The note in question was here passed to the witness, Dillon, who was asked if she recognized the handwriting on it. She said it was the handwriting of the prisoner, and that it was written on the day that she went into the surgery. Continuing, she said she had no conversation with Mrs Berry, except that she told her how many inmates were having liberty that day. It was at that, she said, that Edith said to her, "Ann, are *you* having liberty today?" and I said, "No, love, not today; it's not my day."' Going to Mrs Berry's sitting room about three quarters of an hour later, she said, she found Edith vomiting. 'Mrs Berry was holding a tumbler with something white in it, like magnesia or cream of tartar. As soon as I went in, Mrs Berry said to me, "This girl is sick," and then said to Edith, "Drink this, darling, it'll do you good."'

"Did the child drink it?" Mr M'Connell asked, and Dillon replied, 'No. She said, "Oh, I can't, Mamma."' The next time she saw the deceased was in the prisoner's bedroom that night. She was being sick into a bowl, which she, Dillon, emptied away. 'Edith kept rubbing her stomach and saying, "Oh, my belly."'

Dillon then told the court that she was asked by the Chief Constable to keep a watch on the prisoner. Asked as to any observations she had made, she said that on 11 January, the Tuesday following the child's death, she was in Mrs Berry's bedroom when Mrs Berry began walking up and down, crying. 'I asked her what was the matter, and she said she was crying over it being said that her child had been poisoned. She was saying, "Oh, dear! They think my child has been poisoned."' I said to her,

"Do *you* think she's been poisoned?" and she said, "They say so." I asked her: "Have you given her anything in mistake?" and she said, "No, I never gave her anything, only a seidlitz powder – which you saw me give her." She was in great distress.' Asked whether Mrs Berry knew that the police had instructed her, Dillon, to watch her, Dillon replied that Mrs Berry *did* know it. 'I didn't tell her so,' she said. 'I told her that I would keep her company. She learned that I was watching her from Mr Purser and Mr Lawson.'

The final witness of the day was inmate Ellen Thompson, who testified to seeing Edith on the Saturday, about noon in the prisoner's sitting room, vomiting. While she was there Alice Alcroft came in and wiped up vomit from the carpet. 'I dried the carpet afterwards with a towel. Mrs Berry ordered me to.' She was also ordered to empty and wash out a pail into which the child had vomited. 'When I came back from emptying the pail I found that Edith had vomited into a chamber pot, and this Mrs Berry also told me to take away. About two in the afternoon Mrs Berry ordered me to carry Edith upstairs to the bedroom. I did so, and I put her to bed. I went back up to the bedroom about eleven o'clock that night with Ann Dillon, and the child appeared to be much better. I saw her again on Sunday afternoon, and noticed a small white blister on her upper lip. I could see it plainly and I said something to Mrs Berry about the child having a cold. She said to me, "No, I don't think it's that – I think it's an orange she's had with some sugar."' Continuing, she told how on returning to the bedroom at five-fifteen she saw that the child was very poorly, 'worse than in the morning'. 'She continually moved her head about as she lay there, as if she was in great pain. Mrs Berry asked me to go to the lodge and ask Dr Patterson to come. I took the message, and I next returned to the bedroom after the doctor had been. Mrs Berry said that the doctor was going to call for another physician, and she said she knew the meaning of that. I said, "What is the meaning of that?" and she said, "Well, the child is so weak to begin with, I know she won't recover." After the doctors had gone I sat up with the child along with Mrs Berry. There was a bottle of medicine that Dr Patterson had left and I asked Mrs Berry if she was going to give Edith some, but she said she didn't want to punish her. I said, "The doctor will be angry if he finds you haven't given her any of the medicine," and she said that she would pour some of it away and tell the doctor that Edith had taken it.' During the night, she went on, the child complained of pains in her stomach and was sick several times. 'Mrs Berry gave her an injection as well as some medicine. She gave it in a teaspoon, but it ran out of the side of her mouth. I saw Edith again the next day, Monday, at a quarter to ten at night. Mrs Sanderson was with her. I didn't see her alive again.'

At this stage the court was adjourned for the day.

Soon after the trial was resumed at 10.50 next morning Alice Alcroft, kitchen worker and former servant to Elizabeth Berry, was called into the witness box.

She told the court that just after nine o'clock on the morning of 1 January she had seen Edith and Beatrice coming downstairs. 'I was coming out of the kitchen for some coal for the room,' she said. 'They came across the corridor, and I said to them, "I'll warm you for being late for breakfast," and they laughed and said, "And *we'll* warm *you* when we get out."' She served them their breakfast in the sitting room, she said, and about ten minutes to ten went in again – 'but I'm not sure of the time' – having been called by Mrs Berry to get a bucket and wipe up some vomit from the carpet. At that time Edith was lying on the sofa.

At this point in the proceedings there came an interruption as a telegram was brought in and handed to Mr Mellor, who read it and passed it to Mr Cottingham. It appeared that at the Oldham workhouse there had occurred an outbreak of scarlet fever, made more critical as the medical officer and many of the nursing staff were absent from the place. 'My Lord,' said Mr Cottingham to the judge, 'we have just received a telegram. Some of the witnesses from the workhouse are wanted at home.' After reading the telegram, the judge said that he couldn't allow the request to be granted. 'We'll send the witnesses back as soon as we can,' he said, 'and hope they're not required to return.'

Leaving the scarlet fever sufferers at the workhouse to cope as best they could, it was back to the business of the law, and Mr M'Connell asked Alcroft what Edith and Beatrice had eaten for their supper on the Friday evening. She said they had eaten fish for tea, and for supper cold beef and apple pie. They didn't eat the pie, she said, and she and other inmates had eaten it and the rest of the leftovers. No one had been in the least ill afterwards.

Her place was taken in the witness box by Sarah Anderson of the female imbecile ward, who said that on the Saturday afternoon Beatrice Hall had come for her to see Mrs Berry's daughter. She found the child lying on the sofa in Mrs Berry's sitting room, and some vomit, streaked with blood, in a chamber pot. She saw the child again on Sunday, and on Monday about eleven in the morning, at which time she noticed blisters on the girl's mouth. 'I asked Mrs Berry what was the cause,' she said, 'and she said she had given her a lemon and some sugar.'

Anderson's place was taken by Lydia Evett, who testified to seeing the deceased in the prisoner's bedroom at about half past five on the Sunday. 'She looked very ill,' she said. 'She was vomiting every few minutes, and appeared to be in great pain about the stomach and bowels. She was continually straining, at which times she was lifted out of bed.' Asked about the marks on the child's mouth, she said, 'Shortly after I went into the room Mrs Berry said to me, "See what that orange has done to Edith's mouth," and it was then I noticed that the skin about Edith's lips was red and inflamed.'

After Evett came workhouse inmate Mary Jane Knight who told the court that she saw Edith Annie in Mrs Berry's bedroom on the Sunday afternoon. At that time, she said, the girl was not vomiting, and she saw no marks about her mouth. She saw her again on Monday afternoon about half-past three, and then noticed that Edith's lips were blistered. On the Monday, she said, Beatrice Hall came down to the kitchen for an orange. She then added that at the magistrates' hearing she had testified that Hall had come for the orange on the Sunday. But she had been incorrect; it was on the Monday when Hall came down to the kitchen for it.

Mrs Knight was followed by inmate Ann Partland, who said that about half past five on Sunday 2 January, she was sent for by Mrs Berry to empty a chamber pot of vomit.

This concluded the evidence of the workhouse witnesses, and they were given permission to return to Oldham. When this was done, photographer William Thorpe was called. He told the court that on Friday 7 January, instructed by the Chief Constable, he had taken photographs of the body of the dead child. Copies of the photographs were here passed to the judge and jury.

Detective Inspector Charles Purser, called next, said that on 6 January he had accompanied the Chief Constable when he interviewed the prisoner in her sitting room. Asked if he had taken notes, he said that he had not, 'but the Chief Constable did so'.

It was anticipated that the Chief Constable himself would be called next, but it was announced that he was unable to attend due to having met with an accident five weeks earlier. This was confirmed by Dr Patterson, who said that Mr Hodgkinson was suffering from an injury to the spine, 'caused by a fall during the late frost', and was not in a fit state to travel to Liverpool. The judge, not pleased to hear this, said that if chief constables would instruct their officers to take notes of everything a prisoner said, and ensure that the notes were brought into court, it would save hours of cross-examination.

The next witness was James Pickford, of the Rational Sick and Burial Society who said that on 6 January he had paid Mrs Berry £10, which was the payment due on the death of her child, Edith Berry.

He was followed by Henry Jackson, agent for the Prudential Assurance Company in Rochdale, who offered some most interesting information. He told the court that the prisoner had come to his house in April the previous year, 1886, 'to take out an insurance'. 'She proposed to insure her own life and that of her daughter, Edith Annie, for £100,' he said. 'The insurance was to be mutual. I said I thought it would be a good thing, and that the premiums would be a little over £4.' Asked to explain the term 'mutual', he said it meant that two persons were insured on one policy, and at the death of either of them the survivor would get the premium. He went on to say that Mrs Berry told him that the insurance was for the benefit of her daughter, as she herself anticipated getting married shortly to a gentleman of means in Derby with whom she was keeping company. He was fifty-five years of age and was a builder and contractor. She said also that she would not be staying long in England, as she planned to go to Australia. He said that Mrs Berry was medically examined at Rochdale, as was her daughter Edith Annie at Miles Platting. 'I forwarded her application to the chief office,' he said, 'but the directors declined it on account of the tender age of the daughter.' However, he added, Mrs Berry had had no means of ascertaining whether her application had been accepted or declined as he did not have any correspondence with her. The policy, therefore, had never gone into effect, and Mrs Berry had never paid any premiums on it.

This completed Mr Jackson's testimony, and with his stepping down the court was adjourned for luncheon.

Dwelling briefly on the subject of Mr Jackson's evidence, his statement that the Prudential had declined Mrs Berry's application prompts a question. Both she and Edith had been medically examined, and what Mrs Berry was asking for was quite within the law, so why, one might ask, was the application refused on account 'of the tender age of the daughter'. To this writer's mind, it was refused because the company became suspicious.

Over preceding decades there had been a great number of cases of infanticide and child murder, and very frequently the motive for the crimes was the small insurance pay-outs – known as 'burial money' – that could be realized. There were even a few cases where all the offspring in a family were murdered for what could be gained from life insurance policies.

In an attempt to counteract this grim situation, laws were passed in the mid-1870s to protect vulnerable children, making life insurance pay-outs less tempting for the more penurious, unscrupulous and murderous. For one thing, the new laws decreed that no child below the age of five could be insured for more than £5. Up to the age of ten the maximum sum for a child's insurance was £10. Over the age of ten there was no limit; a child or adult could be insured for any amount.

Mrs Berry, we are told, went to the Prudential applying for a life insurance policy worth £100, which, she told Mr Jackson, was 'for the benefit of her daughter'. This, though, was clearly not quite the truth, for the application was, as we have seen, for a *mutual* policy, whereby either Mrs Berry *or* Edith would collect in the event of the other's death. Had Mrs Berry sought a policy solely for Edith's benefit, then she could have insured her own life solely, naming Edith as the beneficiary. Had this been the case, her application would have been accepted. That said, there can be no doubt that it was the requested insurance on Edith's life that led to the application being refused. In 1886, when Mrs Berry – still lodging in Rochdale following her mother's death – applied for the policy, £100 was a good sum – well over £110,000 in today's terms. As we have seen, the law set no limit on the insured amount for anyone over the age of ten, and here was an application to insure the life of a child who, at ten years old, had just become insurable for a small fortune. It is hardly surprising, then, that the men from the Pru looked at the application with some reservations. And there can be no doubt also that they would have looked into Mrs Berry's record with the company, and seen there the life insurance pay-outs that had been made on the death of her mother and others in her family. So it was, after due consideration, and perhaps not so surprisingly, that they declined to do business.

A question remains: why did the company not inform Mrs Berry of their rejection of her application? Could it have been that they simply could not come up with the right words to cover their suspicions?

Back to the trial.

When proceedings resumed in the courtroom at two o'clock that afternoon Dr Patterson was recalled. He had much to tell the court, and he was to remain in the witness box for some time.

Much of his testimony was as it had been at the previous hearings. In detail he told the court that he had tended the sick girl, initially prescribing for ulceration of the stomach, but later concluding that she was not suffering from any disease with which he was acquainted. Her condition had greatly worsened by Sunday night. He couldn't feel her pulse and her eyes were sunken. Seeing the child's lips red and blistered, he asked the prisoner as to the cause, and she told him that she had given the child an orange with some sugar, and that that must have caused it. 'Later,' he said, 'she told me it had been a lemon.' The child vomited in his presence, he said, and Mrs Berry said that the child was also being purged, that the evacuations contained blood and that the child strained to go on the pot every few minutes.

'I said that the child was dangerously ill,' he said, and concluded that she was suffering from the ingesting of a poison. He called Dr Robertson to see her, and the doctor agreed with him. He saw the girl twice the next day, Monday, and that night gave her an injection of morphia. On Tuesday morning, he said, 'I was called to her bedside and found her dead.'

After some questioning on the matter of the child's death certificate, he caused some surprise by producing a paper which, he said, bore a statement which the prisoner had made. He had told her, he explained, that he wanted from her a history of the whole time of her daughter's illness. He then commenced to read out Mrs Berry's words, but before he had got far the judge stopped him and asked Mr M'Connell whether he had any objection to the statement being read out. Mr M'Connell replied that in his opinion it was immaterial either way. With permission to continue, the doctor resumed the reading of Mrs Berry's statement.

In her written account, dated 8 January, Mrs Berry said that she was out 'on the wards' when she was sent for with a message that her daughter was sick. With regard to the medicines prescribed for the child, she said she had given her nothing but what was prescribed, and as for the creosote mixture prescribed by Dr Patterson, she said: 'I did not mix it and did not give her any of it.' With regard to the blisters about the child's mouth, she said, 'At two o'clock [on the Sunday] I came down to dinner having left Beatrice Hall in charge of the patient. I returned to the room in half an hour. I then noticed the redness about the mouth and she (my daughter) said, "I have had some nice medicine, I have had some chocolate." Later, she said her mouth was sore and I applied some cold cream to it. At her request later in the day I sliced a lemon and gave her a slice with sugar. She complained that this made her mouth smart.'

So, in her own words, Mrs Berry had said that she had never given the child the creosote mixture, and also tried to introduce the notion that while she was away from her daughter's side, someone else had given her medicine of some kind: 'I have had some nice medicine. I have had some chocolate.' As for her statement that she gave Edith some lemon, this is at odds with the account given later in her letter to Dr Kershaw – in which she said that Edith took some medicine, after which '...I gave her an orange with sugar, this was about 2 p.m. on the Sunday. After I went upstairs after tea I gave her another dose and again gave her orange and sugar.'

In addition to the discrepancies above, Mrs Berry also gave differing accounts of becoming aware of Edith's falling sick. While she stated to Dr Patterson that she was out 'on the wards' when she was sent for with a message that Edith was sick, in her letter to Dr Kershaw she writes: '...on coming to my bedroom I looked in to see if the children were up. I saw them leave the room. I went on through the wards then came down, went into sitting room where the children were sat at the table. Edith put her hand on her breast and said I do feel sick, and vomited.'

When Dr Patterson had completed his reading of Mrs Berry's statement, Mr Cottingham got up to cross-examine. At the magistrates' inquiry he had scored considerably in his examination of the doctor, and here he was again, with the doctor once again in the witness box.

He began by asking the doctor when he had first suspected that the child had been poisoned, and Dr Patterson replied that he began to suspect it on the Saturday, before his second visit to the child. It was not from observation but from reflection, he said.

'And when you found the child better on the Sunday morning were you still of the opinion that she had had poison?'

'I had a suspicion,' the doctor said.

'Did you,' Mr Cottingham asked, 'do anything when you left the child on Sunday at twelve o'clock?'

'No. I said to the mother that the child was so much better and that she must send me a message as to how she was.'

Mr Cottingham now tried to sow some seeds of doubt as to the doctor's judgement and procedures. 'Isn't it rather an alarming thing,' he said, 'when a doctor goes away under those circumstances, to get a message unexpectedly to come back at once?'

'Yes,' Dr Patterson agreed, 'it was a strange thing.'

'You say you got the message at seven o'clock?'

'Yes.'

'Then how is it that you did not go at once?'

'I had one or two urgent matters to attend to.'

'What were they?'

'First of all, I had to stay during the surgery hours at my own house. Secondly, all my people had gone to church, and I had no one to leave in the house until they came back.'

'So you wouldn't go to visit a patient after receiving a request from the mother because you had no one to leave in the house?'

Here the judge came in. 'He gave a double reason,' he said. 'First he had no one to leave in the house, and then he says he had his patients to attend to.'

Mr Cottingham then asked the doctor as to the time he eventually got to see the patient. Dr Patterson replied: 'I got to the workhouse at a quarter to nine, but I didn't see the child until nine-thirty as I had several urgent cases in other parts of the house to attend to first. I had to go into the lunatic asylum for one thing.'

'Why did you not postpone your visit to that part of the house where the lunatics are, and go to the child?'

'Because I didn't consider that the case was then a case of urgency.'

Questioning the doctor on his suspicions that the child had been given poison, Mr Cottingham asked: 'Why did you not prescribe some antidote, or some alleviative, or some treatment of the poison to the girl?'

'I *did* prescribe an alleviative – morphia,' said the doctor. 'I did not prescribe an antidote for two reasons. First, I didn't know what the poison was, and secondly, an antidote for a corrosive poison is useless after the lapse of an hour from the time that the poison has been taken.'

The judge: 'Do you mean to say it is *impossible* to save life after the lapse of an hour, or that the chances are against it?'

Dr Patterson: 'If I knew what corrosive it was, I should give the patient a chance, but if I did not it would be unsafe to prescribe. There were new symptoms set in on the Sunday, including purging and blistering of the mouth.'

Mr Cottingham: 'Did you tell her mother that she was suffering from poison which had been administered to her?'

'I didn't think it wise to do so.'

'You suspected the child was being poisoned, and that the mother was poisoning her. Why then did you leave the child in the care of her mother – the whole of Sunday night?'

'Because the child was fatally ill, and it would have done no good whatever to have left her in the charge of anyone else.'

Mr Cottingham pressed him. 'Well, you left this woman, whom you suspected of giving poison to her child, alone with the child, and near to the surgery – that is, in close proximity to it?'

'Yes, I did so, but I locked the bismuth in the cupboard.'

Turning to another line of questioning, Mr Cottingham asked, 'When you handed over to Dr Harris the intestines for a post-mortem did you tell him of your suspicions?'

'Very likely I did, but I am not sure.'

With this, Mr Cottingham announced that he had no further questions, but before any new witness could be called, he asked the judge if he would put a question to the doctor; he wanted His Lordship to ask if the chocolate and coconut chips the deceased had eaten on the Friday would do her any harm.

His Lordship made no attempt to hide his irritation at this, and asked, 'What are coconut chips?' Told by Cottingham that they were 'parts of a coconut', he said, 'I don't see what it has to do with it.'

'I would be interested to find out what quantity of these the child ate, and who saw her eating them,' Mr Cottingham said.

'Well, it seems a very vague and useless question to me,' said the judge, 'but if you insist, I will put the question.' Then, to Dr Patterson: 'Would coconut chips have produced the appearance you saw?'

'No.'

'Would fish?'

'No, not sound fish.'

'Was there anything about the symptoms that would lead you to believe that they might have been produced by eating coconut chips or chocolate?'

'Decidedly not.'

'Or cakes, or anything of such character?'

'No.'

With this exchange Dr Patterson was allowed to step down.

As the Chief Constable of Oldham, Charles Hodgkinson, was unable to attend due to his injury, Mr M'Connell requested that his deposition be read out, which was duly done. In his deposition Mr Hodgkinson stated that he went to see the prisoner on 6 January to inquire into the death of her daughter, that the prisoner had told him that the child was in the habit of being constipated, and that when she was in that state her aunt had given her a pill. On his telling her that the doctors suspected foul play, she had said to the Governor of the workhouse, 'Oh! Governor, why should I kill my darling! I, who have just doubled my insurance on her?' The statement continued: 'I told her that she was charged with having administered poison to her daughter, and she replied, "I did nothing of the kind."'

After the reading of the statement Ann Sanderson was recalled and stated that Edith Annie had never suffered from constipation and had never been given pills of any kind.

Following Mrs Sanderson the last of the crown's witnesses of the day, Dr Robertson, was called. He was to spend some considerable time on the stand. In his testimony he stated that on the night of 2 January he was asked by Dr Patterson to see the child Edith Berry where she lay in bed. 'She was greatly exhausted, but conscious,' he said. 'Her pulse was very quick and heated...The tongue was coated white all over...I have never seen such a tongue.' He described also the 'peculiar condition' of the mouth, the blisters and the redness. On asking Mrs Berry for an explanation for it, he said she told him that she had given the child a lemon with some sugar.

Following the child's death, he went on, he and Dr Patterson performed a post-mortem examination, and the next day he was present when Dr Harris and Dr Patterson made a further examination of the girl's body.

Asked what he thought had been the cause of the child's death, he replied: 'Corrosive poison.'

'From the post-mortem alone?' asked the judge.

'No, my Lord,' said the doctor. 'From the symptoms during life as well as the post-mortem appearance. The symptoms I saw were not consistent with any form of ordinary disease. The signs and marks I saw pointed to death from corrosive poisoning.'

Under cross-examination by Mr Cottingham – which was lengthy and very thorough – Dr Robertson said that at first he had suggested that the poison might be oxalic acid, but since the post-mortem he had not come to any absolute conclusion, though in his opinion it was sulphuric acid, which had been suggested by Dr Harris. He had never in his career, he said, had a case of oxalic or sulphuric acid poisoning.

Shortly after this testimony Mr Justice Hawkins announced that the court would be adjourned for the day.

17

The Verdict

Wednesday 23 February: the third day of the trial. Soon after its opening at 10.35 a.m. Dr Robertson was recalled by the prosecution.

Telling of his visit with Dr Patterson to the sick child, he said he asked to see the child's vomit, and Mrs Berry handed him a towel on which was fresh-coloured blood in an excessively tenacious condition. 'I have never seen mucus like that,' he said. 'I asked to see the evacuations of the bowels, but she said they hadn't been kept. I asked her when the redness of the child's lip had commenced but she didn't reply, though Dr Patterson said, in her presence, that the redness hadn't been there on his Sunday morning's visit.' Concluding his testimony, he said that Mrs Berry told him that her daughter had become much worse after being seen by Dr Patterson.

In a surprising move, it had been the prosecution's intention to bring into the witness box John Taylor, the Rochdale chemist who, in February of the previous year, had sold quantities of atropia to the woman calling herself Ellen Saunders shortly before the death of the prisoner's mother. But it was announced that he was not well enough to attend, and into court came his medical doctor, Dr Edward March, who said that Taylor was suffering from 'excitement of the brain'. 'I last saw him this morning,' he said. 'He is bordering on acute mania, and is not in a fit state to travel from Rochdale to Liverpool. If he were to travel now it might result in an attack of mania. He has to be watched day by day.' However, he did then admit that his patient was capable of travelling, and was sane, and therefore would be able to understand any questions put to him. With this, there came deliberation over whether Taylor's deposition given at Rochdale could be presented in evidence. However, due to the fact that Mrs Berry had not been present at the Rochdale inquest when Taylor had testified, the judge decided that the chemist's deposition could not be admitted.

As to the prosecution's purpose in wanting to bring the chemist into the witness box, it must be a matter for speculation. Any evidence he could give did not on the surface relate to the matter of Edith Annie's death, but to that of Mrs Berry's mother, Mary Ann Finley. It is perhaps likely, then, that he had been called in the hope that he would identify the prisoner at the bar as the woman who had bought the poison atropia from him on two occasions. This being the case, it is a great pity that he did not show up, for had such an identification taken place it would have proved a considerable coup for the prosecution – not to mention providing one of the most dramatic episodes in the whole affair.

After Dr March had stepped down, Dr Thomas Harris was called to the stand, and the subject was brought back directly to that of the murdered child. In his testimony he spoke of the dried patches about the dead girl's lips, and after looking at a photograph of her face, produced a drawing he had made, saying, 'I made a rough sketch to show the relative size of the patches.' The photograph and the sketch were here handed to the jury, with the doctor adding: 'Those marks I've described are not consistent with the idea that they have been caused by a lemon and sugar. And they are not consistent with the idea that the patient has been suffering from *herpes labialis* [commonly known as a cold sore].' After describing the congested condition of the gullet and the black, corroded, charred patch on it he was asked by Mr Mellor: 'What would you say was the cause of death?' and replied that he believed it was caused by the ingestion of a corrosive poison, 'probably sulphuric acid'.

'Would it alter your opinion if you were told that on analysis no traces of poison could be discovered?' Mr Mellor asked.

'Not at all,' the doctor replied, repeating his assertion that through vomiting and purging the traces of a corrosive poison could be worked out of the system within twenty-four hours.

Mr Cottingham, for the defence, asked the doctor if a corrosive poison, swallowed, would leave marks in the mouth where the poison had come in contact with the surface. Dr Harris replied, 'Not necessarily.

**Edith Annie on her death bed, a newspaper illustration
from one of the photographs taken shortly after her death,
showing the blisters around her mouth.**

It would in all probability produce changes in the mouth, but usually sulphuric acid does not produce charring in the mouth.'

Mr Cottingham then referred to the doctor's post-mortem report noting that a 'cheesy nodule' had been found in the child's right lung, and suggested that she had suffered from tuberculosis. Dr Harris would have none of it; the child had *not* been tubercular, he said. Asked how the poison could have been administered without her complaining, the doctor replied that he didn't know. As to *how* it was administered, he said that the marks about the mouth indicated that it 'was administered in a fluid form, and that there had probably been some accident in its administration'.

Mr Cottingham: 'Could the appearances on the mouth be produced by creosote?'

'In my opinion it could not.'

City analyst Charles Estcourt then took the stand to testify that in the parts passed to him he had found no poisonous matter, organic or inorganic. In his opinion the charred patch on the gullet would have been caused by sulphuric acid. When examining the gullet, he said, he had not tested it for any matter other than sulphuric acid.

After Mr Estcourt, Henry Jackson of the Prudential Insurance Society was called back to identify the signature of the prisoner on the insurance policies taken out with his company. Following this, the court was adjourned until the next morning.

The trial had been running for three days now, a rather longer time than some had anticipated, and so far only the witnesses for the prosecution had been heard. The jurors were growing weary, and as the spectators left the courtroom one of the jurors approached the judge to ask how much longer it was likely to take. When the judge said that he could not hazard a guess, the juror remarked on their protracted confinement in their hotel, and their being unable to get any fresh air or exercise. The judge sympathized, and said he would arrange for them to be taken for a drive the next day before the court was resumed.

His Lordship was true to his word, and after breakfast the following morning the jurors were taken on a carriage ride through the city, taking in some of the sights of interest in the bracing February chill, after which they were conveyed to St George's Hall for the resumption of the trial.

There in the courtroom at 10.45, when all were assembled, the judge took his seat, and the first witness of the day was called. This was Dr Patterson, recalled to be questioned about the poisons kept in the surgery. He said that there had been a large number of them in the surgery on New Year's Day, and that on 9 January he had prepared a list of them. Handed the list by the Clerk, he confirmed that it named all the poisons in the surgery on 1 January that had been lying loose on the counter, and that all of them were irritants or corrosive poisons.

His Lordship: 'Among them was there sulphuric acid?'

'There was, my Lord. Not the strongest, though there was sulphuric acid there.' (Dr Patterson's list of the poisons kept in the surgery outside the locked cupboard is among the Home Office papers on the case. His paper is headed 'Corrosives & Irritants not locked up in Surgery on January 1st 1887', and lists twenty-five poisons. Sulphuric acid is noted twice.)

Dr Patterson's evidence concluded the case for the prosecution, and it was then the turn of the counsel for the defence.

Their first witness was William Thompson, from Manchester, an experienced analytical chemist. Questioned by Mr Byrne, he said that in his opinion if sulphuric acid had been administered by the girl's mouth he should have expected to find marks in the throat and mouth similar to those on the lips, and to find traces of the acid for weeks afterwards in the gullet. Strong sulphuric acid, if applied to the skin, he said, would cause great pain for a while, and if swallowed would cause intense pain on those parts with which it came in contact. His opinion was founded upon experiments he had made. Sulphuric acid would produce vomiting, and if such ejected matter came in contact with a carpet, many of the colours would be destroyed. If the carpet was woollen he would expect to find the acid in combination with the wool. A towel vomited on would be destroyed unless it was a very large one.

Cross-examined by Mr M'Connell, he said that sixteen years earlier he had examined the viscera of a person who had died from sulphuric acid poisoning, and as far as he could remember the whole of the tissues of the gullet were marked by the acid. Shown a photograph of the dead child's face with the marks about the mouth, he said, 'Looking at the photo, I should assume that the poison was administered by drinking.' He went on to say that if a person had lived for a few days after taking a corrosive poison, and vomited frequently, he would still have expected to find traces in the body after death. This he had concluded from experiments made with sulphuric acid upon some animal flesh, and upon his own hand.

He was then handed Dr Patterson's list, after which he was asked by the judge, 'Would you say that some of the poisons on this list of Dr Patterson's would produce the same corrosive effect?'

'Yes, they would.'

On the properties of creosote, the witness said that it would not char, and a single drop would make not make any impression upon the skin.

Mr Thompson's testimony at an end, he was allowed to step down. The time was 12.25. It had been understood that counsel for Mrs Berry had brought a number of witnesses to the courthouse to give evidence, but to the great surprise of the prosecution, Mr Cottingham announced that he would be calling no more.

And so it now fell to him to present the defence's case. The last time he had made such an address had been before the magistrates, and he had succeeded in having the case against his client dismissed. Now, facing the jury in the Liverpool courtroom, he was well aware of the task before him. This time his client's life hung in the balance.

He began by speaking of the gravity of the offence for which the prisoner was on trial. In the history of the ages, he said, murder by poisoning was looked upon as the most diabolical, as it not only involved the crime of murder and great cruelty, but was by its nature premeditated and cold-blooded. 'And you must remember,' he said, 'that Mrs Berry is not only charged with poisoning a fellow creature, but also with causing the death of her child.'

After saying that there had been shown no motive for such a crime, he suggested that Dr Patterson had never acted as if the child had been given poison in the first place. The doctor had prescribed for ulceration of the stomach, but later claimed to have suspected poisoning – and that the child's mother had administered it. 'But if he really believed that the child was being poisoned,' he said, 'how could he leave the mother in charge of all the poisonous medicines at her disposal and not take any precautions to prevent the life of the child being further tampered with?' For all the work of the doctors, they had not been able to prove that the child had indeed been poisoned, let alone say what the poison was, and the whole course of the doctors' conduct 'was antagonistic to the hypothesis that poison was administered by *anybody*, much less the prisoner'. As for the post-mortem, it was not until the doctors had held their examination that they came to the conclusion that poison had been administered, yet they would not say what the poison was. 'Is it not a matter of surprise that none of these men should have hit upon the real cause of death?' he said. 'They all three agreed that sulphuric acid was probably the poison used, but they were *not certain.*'

He then tried to cast doubt on the contention that sulphuric acid could have been administered by the girl's mouth. Sulphuric acid would have had an immediate effect on the lips, he said, and on all other parts of the body with which it came into contact. Further, while the chemist Mr Thompson had said positively that he should expect to find traces of sulphuric acid after death, Mr Estcourt's findings showed nothing that might not be found after death from natural causes. Had the jury, he asked, ever heard of a case of criminal poisoning where poison in some form or other had not been found on analysis? All of this, he said, led him to posit the concept that the whole of the child's sickness was not as much in the way of poisoning as the result of acute inflammation of the bowels.

After an adjournment for lunch Mr Cottingham went on to develop his theme, that the girl's symptoms were *not* those of having received repeated doses of poison, but from natural causes, insisting that she had not been a healthy child, but had in fact been 'a tubercular subject'. It was important, he said, to look into her history. 'Her father died after a few years' illness, of emaciation, and of her two brothers, one died from dentition, and the next brother, older than the girl, was brought home ill from Blackpool with the little girl herself, both suffering from an affection of the stomach and bowels. The boy died, and the girl recovered.' He then suggested that the coconut chips the girl had eaten, 'which were exceedingly indigestible', might have caused her illness.

His Lordship: 'Do you say that as an expert?'

'No, my Lord,' Mr Cottingham replied, 'only from common sense; and I say, with the greatest respect, I am not giving evidence.'

Having politely put his Lordship in his place, Mr Cottingham went on to ask how the child could have taken sulphuric acid without complaining. It was a poison 'which would pass down the throat like liquid fire', he said, 'yet she made no complaint of pain in her throat until near her death…It is physically impossible that she could have disguised the pain – pain that would make her scream to swallow the acid.'

After suggesting that some of the girl's symptoms might have been due to one or other of the medicines that Dr Patterson had prescribed, he said to the jury, 'Supposing you had it proved beyond doubt that the child's death *was* the result of the ingestion of sulphuric acid, there must remain the question: Did that woman – the prisoner, whose conduct had always been that of an affectionate, solicitous mother, administer it?' It had not been possible for her to have administered poison, he said. Beatrice Hall never left her friend's side that morning, and Alice Alcroft would very likely have seen the child going into the surgery with her mother. As for Ann Dillon's testimony that she had seen Edith and Mrs Berry in the surgery at 9.45, there was no evidence to support this.

Coming again to motive, he suggested that the only possible motive anyone could cite must be greed, but how could that be attributed, 'when all that was gained was one small insurance pay-out – which had been consumed by the cost of the funeral?' As for the proposed £100 insurance on the child sought by Mrs Berry, it was not accepted and no premium was paid in respect of such insurance. So, he asked, 'What motive could transform a mother into a monster so horrid, so detestable, that a crowd of common criminals would move aside to allow her to pass with a shudder of reprehension? I cannot conceive of a woman so detestable, so much a monster, as to accomplish the death of her own child under such circumstances.'

He had one final question for the jury. 'If that poor child could return from the grave,' he said, 'would she come to judgement as an accuser and in vengeance upon her mother, or would she come to judgement as a ministering angel proclaiming the innocence of a mother who had always been so solicitous and so anxious for her welfare?'

The ending of Mr Cottingham's address brought a burst of applause, which was swiftly silenced. It was three o'clock. Now Mr M'Connell rose to speak for the Crown.

It was his duty, he said to the jury, having laid the evidence before them, to make his remarks upon the issues raised by his learned friend and then leave the matter of the decision to them. The first of the issues was whether the death of the deceased was caused by poison and, next, whether that poison was administered knowingly by the prisoner. Mr Cottingham, he said, had challenged the prosecution to show motive for the alleged crime, but while no motive could be commensurate for a case like that before them, neither was it the duty of the prosecution to *prove* motive.

On the subject of evidence, he pointed out that they had the evidence of Dr Patterson and Dr Robertson, in addition to the symptoms which were seen during life, and the appearances after death. And if they did not believe the evidence of those two medical men they should remember that it was followed up by that of Dr Harris. 'You will have to ask yourselves,' he said, 'if Dr Harris was right when he said that death was *not* the result of natural causes, but the result of a corrosive or irritant poison. And if that is so, the question arises as to *who administered the poison.*'

He came then to the matter of opportunity. 'If it is proved,' he said, 'that the prisoner had sufficient opportunity to have administered it, I think it must weigh with you...It must also enter into your consideration whether, if there was poison administered, and if on *two* occasions, the poison was the same both times. As to the first occasion there is no direct evidence, but there is *circumstantial* evidence. The prisoner was seen in the surgery with the deceased at a quarter to ten on the Saturday morning, and shortly after that the child was taken ill.' There was plenty of opportunity for the mother to administer to the child *anything*, the child believing that it was administered for her good, and the whole circumstances – the appearance of the blister on the mouth, and the continued vomiting – showed that something deleterious had been administered. As to what the deleterious agent was, the only person who had constant access to the deceased was the prisoner, and all throughout, neither the vomit nor the other matter was preserved. 'I say,' he said, 'that with her proper motherly feelings she *ought* to have preserved them, in order to see what was actually the matter with her child, and send for alleviatives. The prisoner had full access to the whole of the drugs and poison in the infirmary, and she knew, to a great extent, their use.' Having looked at all the facts, he had to ask the jury to say whether it was made out that the child had come by her death by poison. 'And if you think it made out,' he said, 'that the prisoner's was the hand that knowingly administered the drug, then it is for you to say so. I ask you to give it your most serious and careful consideration, and unless you have reasonable doubt you are bound by your oath to do your duty.'

With these words Mr M'Connell rested the case for the prosecution. The time was 3.25, and it now came to the judge to begin his summing up.

After saying that he would not enter into the details of the case, Mr Justice Hawkins said that they had now arrived almost at the last stage of the 'painful and unfortunate case'. In a reference to the criticism made of Dr Patterson, he said they were not there to try the doctor, but the prisoner at the bar. 'If the prisoner is guilty,' he said, 'a more foul and abominable crime could not be committed by man or woman, and if you are satisfied from the evidence that she committed it, no one could deserve punishment more.' The first question that the jury had to answer was whether the child had died from the effects of a corrosive poison, and if they found that she had, the next was whether the prisoner had wilfully administered it. If they found both questions answered in the affirmative, then she was guilty of the crime.

Going into the history of the case, he spoke of the child coming with her mother and her friend to spend a few days at the workhouse and then being taken ill, which illness, according to the prisoner, was an acute stoppage of the bowels due to her having eaten a hearty supper the night before. 'Is there any evidence that there was any hearty supper?' he asked. 'I must confess that I have seen none.'

In order to prove that the child had died from poison, he said, they must look at the evidence of the medical gentlemen, Drs Patterson, Robertson and Harris, and consider whether their accounts agreed with their own view of things. Following the post-mortem, which revealed on the gullet a black, corroded patch and streaks of corrosion, Dr Harris said he saw no trace of death from natural causes, and concluded that the child had died from the administration of a corrosive poison, and Drs Patterson and Robertson agreed. 'If you can see any reason to doubt the doctors' evidence, you must give the benefit of the doubt to the prisoner. But if, adopting the view of the medical gentlemen, you come to the conclusion that the poor girl *did* die of poison administered to her, then you have to ask yourselves whether the prisoner administered it.' He then said that if poison had been administered then it must have been by the mother. It was never suggested that anybody else would have given it. The prisoner was with the girl for the greater part of that Saturday morning. Another question was whether the marks around the girl's mouth were a result of corrosive poison, and whether they were caused by the prisoner. 'The child herself couldn't do it,' he said. 'She was on her back, and couldn't stir. And no one suggested that little Beatrice or any of the women were so cruelly minded as to take the poor little thing's life.'

Speaking of motive, he said, 'It has been said that the prisoner had no motive. But it is quite impossible to expect to find adequate motive for a diabolical crime like this. Though in some cases there would appear to be no motive, you must depend upon it that in all great crimes committed by people in their senses there is *always* a motive.' Referring to the financial position of the prisoner, he said that a proposal for the mutual assurance of her and the deceased for £100 had been refused, but the prisoner had not been aware of that fact, or, at all events, had not been informed of the refusal.

He then referred to the testimony of the Chief Constable to whom the prisoner said that the child was in the habit of being constipated, and was ailing at the time she came to the workhouse. Mrs Sanderson, however, had denied the truth of those assertions, he said, and asked, 'Why attribute to Mrs Sanderson something she did not say? And why did the prisoner want to make people believe that the child was ill when she left Mrs Sanderson's charge?'

The only two questions the jury had to take into consideration, he said, drawing now to a close, were whether the child died from poison – it did not matter whether irritant or not – and, if they came to that conclusion, whether that poison was knowingly administered by the prisoner. It all came down to that. 'It is now for you to do your duty,' he said. 'The matter is a serious one. It deeply concerns not only the prisoner, but also the interests of justice. If the prisoner is innocent, or you think the evidence does not satisfy you as to her guilt, she is entitled to be acquitted. But if the evidence before you satisfies you that the dreadful crime imputed to the prisoner was committed by her, then the interests of justice demand that you say so in your verdict.' He added, as a final instruction, 'Do not let your verdict be the result of either passion, or prejudice, or sympathy.'

Mr Justice Hawkins had finished.

In the silence following the judge's final words the jury remained in the box for a minute or two and then rose and left. Following their departure the warders escorted the prisoner from the dock, after which the judge himself withdrew.

It was now almost 5.45. Over the two hours of the judge's address there were those in the courtroom who had grown weary, allowing their attention to wander. But this had most certainly not been the case with the prisoner. She had remained alert for every minute since her entrance that morning. Said the *Chronicle*: 'The prisoner throughout the day maintained the quietest demeanour, never appearing restless, but always sitting in the same posture, occasionally with her right hand ungloved, for the purpose of taking whatever notes of the evidence she thought might be useful to her counsel.' Also, it was noted, she had appeared to be little affected by the constant attention she received from the spectators. 'She did not,' said the *Chronicle*, 'throughout the whole of the trial, seem to realize that she was under the gaze of hundreds of curious eyes. Always the same, morning, noon and afternoon, there she sat, leaning back in her chair, one hand crossing the other or sometimes clasping the wrist of the other.'

And her composure had been evident still during the last hours of her trial. All during that Thursday afternoon she had closely watched the proceedings. At times she had showed signs of restlessness, but she had not moved a muscle even when the judge, in his summing up, came to the strongest and most damning part of the prosecution. Here it was observed that instead of looking before her, as she had done hitherto, she looked downwards, gazing fixedly at her gloves. Her composure was so impressive, the *Chronicle*'s man added, that, 'one Assize Court official said that of the thirty persons he had seen put upon their trial on the capital charge, he never had seen such a "cool customer" as Mrs Berry was'.

Mrs Berry's composure was soon to be put to the greatest test.

The jury did not take long about their task. After only ten minutes the judge received word that they had reached a verdict, and he returned at once to the bench. And with the jury in their places again, the prisoner was brought back into the court, walking with a steady step to the chair that had been provided, and taking her seat. The female warder, who had followed her, stationed herself immediately behind the prisoner's chair. She was followed by the governor of the prison, it being the usual practice for him to be present in the dock when sentence was being passed.

All now were assembled, and there was perfect silence in the courtroom.

'Gentlemen of the jury,' said the Clerk of the Assize, addressing the jury in the hush, 'have you agreed upon your verdict?'

'We have,' said the jury's foreman.

'Do you find the prisoner guilty of wilful murder or not guilty?'

The foreman: 'Guilty.'

A murmur of sensation ran through the court, and Mrs Berry, hearing the foreman's single, damning word, threw her head back and lifted her hands in what appeared to be a gesture of despair. In the same moment the female warder stepped forward and placed a hand on her shoulder. The Clerk then spoke again, this time directly addressing the prisoner. 'Prisoner at the bar,' he said, 'have you anything to say why the court should not proceed to pass sentence of death upon you, according to the law?'

At the question Mrs Berry rose from her seat and took a step forward. Then, with the court hearing her voice clearly for the first time in the four days of the trial, she replied in a firm, though somewhat emotional tone, 'I may be *found* guilty, but the whole world cannot *make* me guilty.' She stepped back and resumed her seat, and all eyes then turned to His Lordship as the black cap was placed upon his wig.

'Elizabeth Berry,' he said solemnly, 'the law of this country knows but one punishment for the crime of murder. The crime of which the jury have just now found you guilty – a murder so cold-blooded, so merciless and so cruel, in causing a poor little child, whom you gave birth to, to suffer so much pain, and so much agony, and whose sufferings you have witnessed so callously – passes all belief. The law for your crime demands of me that I should pass upon you the sentence of death, and in doing so I beseech you, during the few days that remain to you here upon this earth, to endeavour to forget this world and all its belongings, and prepare yourself to meet the Almighty God, from whom alone you can hope for pardon of your great sin. The sentence of the court upon you is that you be taken to the place from whence you came, and from thence to a lawful place of execution, that there you be hung by your neck till you be dead, and that when you are dead your body be buried in the precincts of the prison within the walls of which you shall be confined until you are executed. And may the Lord God Almighty have mercy on your soul.'

The *Chronicle* reported that following the judge's words the prisoner, attended by the female warder, and appearing 'unmoved, walked out of the dock and down the steps unassisted'. She was then led away to the cells.

The trial was over, and it remained only for the judge to thank the jury, to which he added his regret that he could not award them some compensation for their patience and attention. What he could do, however, he said, would be to see that they were not called upon to serve for the next four years.

The Assizes then were formally closed.

18

After the Trial

Immediately following the closing of the trial several of the country's newspapers offered up their comments on the business. The *Manchester Guardian* wrote:

> …That a woman should deliberately inflict upon her young child a lingering and agonising death; that she should stand by with an impassive countenance whilst her victim slowly succumbed to the effects of the poison she had administered, and that this atrocity should have been perpetrated for the sake of a paltry sum of money – ought not to be believed except upon the clearest and most convincing evidence. Unhappily such evidence was forthcoming, and the jury which tried Elizabeth Berry had no hesitation whatever in pronouncing her guilty of the foul crime laid to her charge. Most unfortunately for the fair fame of this country, it has been found again and again that women are ready to assume the role of the secret poisoner from the greed of gain. The grave had hardly closed over the woman Britland – who had without doubt poisoned several persons, two of them her nearest relatives – when this terrible crime at Oldham was perpetrated. The case becomes more horrible when we remember that even now an inquiry is pending as to the death of the convict Berry's own mother, whom she is suspected, with very good reason, of having poisoned.

From the London *Evening News*:

To most people it would seem incredible that a mother should under any circumstances be willing to put her own daughter to a painful death. But when we come to the question of motive we seem to sink to the very deepest depth of shame and horror. That a sane woman should deliberately, and in cold blood, murder her own daughter for an utterly paltry consideration like a small insurance on the child's life, would be altogether incredible if it were not so clearly established. Unfortunately, there is a terrible suspicion present in the public mind that these awful poisoning cases are much more frequent than the comparatively rare discoveries of them would suggest. Students of these terrible records will also find that in the vast majority of cases the criminals are women, whilst their victims are trusting, affectionate, and helpless dependents.

The London *Evening Mail* was not so sure that greed was the motive:

The crime of which [Elizabeth Berry] has been convicted is one of the most terrible that can be conceived. According to the evidence, she administered a deadly poison to her child and calmly and dispassionately stood by her bedside for hours while she felt all the agonies of the most cruel and lingering death. Here was the mother, actuated with the worst passions of brutality, determined at all hazard to get rid of her child, and to be free from any encumbrance, and on the other side was the confiding and innocent girl, who had come full of life and joy to the Workhouse, to spend the holiday with the only person in the world upon whom she could look with the deepest esteem and pleasure. The motive for the crime has not been made very clear at the trial at Liverpool. The deceased girl was insured for £10, and the accused was entitled to that amount in the event of death. The deceased also cost her mother about £13 a year for maintenance, but as she was eleven years of age, there was a possibility that she would soon be able to labour in some vocation, and thus partly, if not completely, relieve her mother of any responsibility as regards expenditure. Probably there is some motive for the crime which has not yet been revealed.

There can be no doubt that the verdict found against Elizabeth Berry was the correct one. For all Mr Cottingham's brilliance and passion, he had found scarcely anything to put forward in the way of her defence. Mrs Berry could not, herself, speak out. It was not until the Criminal Evidence Act of 1898 that defendants would be given the opportunity to speak in their defence. One wonders, though, what she could possibly have said to rebut the charge against her, and of her behaviour in the business.

True, while Edith Annie was lying ill her mother had called in other nurses in the workhouse to come to the sick child – this in spite of the fact that the girl was already being tended by Dr Patterson – but this was done to give the impression that the anxious mother was doing all she could. She no doubt believed that such actions would be construed in her favour – giving a picture of a desperate mother who would stop at nothing in her efforts to save her child. Such 'efforts', though, come over as transparently bogus, while the cold cruelty behind them is almost inconceivable.

The evidence against her, although circumstantial, was damning. Witness her many lies. As to the cause of the child's illness, she said that the night before being taken ill Edith had eaten a heavy supper of cheese and apple pie. It is common knowledge that eating cooked cheese before bedtime might well have a negative impact on digestion, and this was what she hoped would help to explain her daughter's illness. Alice Alcroft, however, made it clear that the meal had consisted of beef, potatoes and apple pie. Witness also how Mrs Berry lied when trying to account for the blisters on the child's lips. She had given the girl an orange with some sugar, she said, and in support of this even had Beatrice Hall go down to the kitchen the following day for an orange. Later, having decided that the acidity of an orange might not be seen as sufficient to cause harm, she changed her story, saying that she had given the girl some lemon.

What went through Mrs Berry's mind on being found guilty of her daughter's murder we shall never know. She was, of course, desperately hoping to be cleared of the charge, as she had been by the magistrates, but hearing the judge's summing up, she must have feared the worst.

What, though, in the event that the jury had acquitted her? Did she believe that she would then be set at liberty? If so she was much mistaken. A verdict of not guilty at the Assizes would not have seen the end of her troubles, and her most perilous predicament was alluded to in the *Chronicle* immediately following her trial's conclusion. In an article drawing attention to the fact that the inquest into her mother's death at Castleton was yet to be completed, it said:

> Had the jury at Liverpool not found the prisoner guilty she would have been arrested at the Assizes on suspicion of poisoning her mother. An officer was in waiting at the Assize Court with a warrant for her re-apprehension.

Quite unaware of what was being written and spoken about her in the world outside the walls of the gaol, Elizabeth Berry, now in the condemned cell, was putting her mind to some of the practicalities associated with her bleak position. And in this regard she sent word to the prison governor asking him to write to Mr Whitaker's clerk, George Robinson, with a request that he be allowed to attend her at the prison at the earliest opportunity. She wished, she told the governor, to speak urgently to the clerk about arranging her affairs.

Twenty-seven-year-old Altrincham-born George Henry Robinson was the son of an Oldham schoolmaster. Employed as Mr Whitaker's clerk from his early twenties, he had been involved with Mrs Berry's case from the day of her arrest and had had much communication with her ever since. He had visited her frequently when she had been confined in Oldham, and afterwards, with her removal to Walton Gaol.

Acceding to the condemned prisoner's request, the governor wrote at once to Mr Robinson. In the meantime, Robinson's employer, Mr Whitaker, was given permission to call on his client on the day following her conviction. Arriving at the prison and conducted to her cell, he met her in the presence of her warders. In the course of the meeting Mrs Berry urged him to petition the authorities with a view to having her sentence commuted, to which he replied that he already had the matter in hand.

It is likely that when they parted he left her encouraged in the hope that all was not lost. Though notwithstanding any words of hope he may have given her, he was well aware that, just three days hence, the inquest into the death of her mother was to be resumed, and that its outcome could have the most profound effect on any plea for mercy that he or anyone else might make on her behalf.

The day after Mr Whitaker's visit to the prison, his clerk, George Robinson, having received the governor's letter just that morning, made his way to Walton to see Mrs Berry. On the way he must surely have wondered how he would find her in her most desperate plight. With the press now giving their attention to her in her new position of condemned woman, there had appeared in the papers various reports on her mental and physical state. Going by some accounts, she had fallen into the deepest despair, the *Chronicle* reporting that '...she broke down immediately on being sentenced, and continued to sink lower by the hour'.

Whatever George Robinson might have read about her condition, he was to witness the change in her at first hand.

On his arrival at the prison at eleven o'clock he was conducted to the female wing and there to a spacious room intersected with slate partitions arranged to form two compartments. Within each compartment was a counter and an aperture looking through a screen of wire netting into the other part of the room. Taking a seat at the counter in one of the compartments, he waited, and after several minutes heard sounds of the unlocking of doors and the clanking of keys. He then saw the prisoner appear, escorted by two female warders.

In spite of what he had read in the papers, he was in no way prepared for the dynamic change in Mrs Berry since last seeing her in the courtroom. Gone were the elegant clothes that she had worn in the dock, the black silk dress, the gloves, the little hat perched behind the teased fringe of her dark hair. She was dressed now in the prison garb of a blue serge dress with white collar, and with her hair with its fashionable frizette now covered by a white cap. It was not just the sight of her in prison clothes that shocked him, though, but also the change in her physical appearance. Her once rather ruddy colour seemed now to have quite gone. Pale and very weary, she looked, he thought, like a dying woman.

But the wretched convict's appearance was not to be the only shock he received in those early moments of his visit. As she drew nearer to him she had only time to say, 'Good morning,' to him, and then to his horror fainted and fell heavily, striking the back of her head on the flags. While she lay unconscious, tended by one of the warders, the other dashed off, returning soon afterwards with two of the gaol's doctors and the matron.

Peering through the grill, George Robinson watched as the doctors bent over her, trying to revive her. She remained senseless, however, and soon the warders were lifting her prostrate form and carrying her away out of sight. Facing the empty room again, Robinson remained in his chair, not knowing what to do, only waiting and hoping that she would soon recover and be able to see him. It was not to be. He was still sitting there some two hours later when an officer came and advised him to leave, suggesting that he return that evening, at which time, it was hoped, the prisoner would have recovered.

Taking the advice, Robinson left the prison. When he returned at seven o'clock he was told that Mrs Berry had remained unconscious for more than three hours. At one point the doctors had thought that she might actually expire, and in their treatment had given her an injection and opened a vein. To his relief, however, he was informed that she was now well enough to see him.

Taking his seat in the dimly-lit visitors' room as before, he again waited, peering through the coarse wire grille into the other part of the room. After a while the door facing him was unlocked and opened and Mrs Berry appeared once more, again attended by two female warders. Seeing him, she at once came forward.

The *Chronicle*, reporting on Robinson's meeting with the convict, remarked of the warders, and their duties:

> …They watch over her night and day. She is watched so closely that if she desired she could not by any possibility hasten her fixed end. She is not even allowed to touch a pin except in the presence of one of the wardresses. No, the prisoner does not receive any of those attentions which, when at Oldham, helped to make her confinement more bearable. There is, for instance, no policeman going out on the very feminine errand of borrowing a pair of curling tongs for her use, as was the case when she was at Oldham.

Now, as Mrs Berry came forward, Robinson saw again the great change in her, noting her weary manner, her step no longer light and sprightly as he had seen it in the past.

Reaching the partition she put her hand through the grating and shook hands with him. She then sat down, and they began to converse. As they talked she spoke of her trial, remarking bitterly that the summing up of the judge had been harsh, and then complained also of one of the witnesses – though she would give no name. As for the verdict, she said it had not come as a surprise, and went on to say that she was expecting no reprieve and was quite prepared to meet the penalty given out. She was, she said, now diverting her attention from all worldly affairs, and simply preparing to meet her Judge. She did not want any visitors, but wished to prepare for her fate in solitude. As Robinson sat listening to her sorrowful voice he began to think that she might voice some confession to her crime. It was not to be. At no time during their meeting did she make any reference to her guilt.

It was some minutes into their melancholy conversation when Mrs Berry turned to the purpose of her request for his visit, which was the disposal of her belongings. These, it appeared, were some items of furniture that were kept at the home of the Sandersons at Miles Platting, and certain other effects which were being held at the Oldham workhouse. These latter, her personal belongings, were made up of clothes, pictures, photographs, books, pieces of jewellery and various other items, which were, she told him, along with her furniture, all that she now possessed in the world. She had no money at all now, she said. At the start of her trial she had had almost £50 in the bank, but all of it had gone to pay Mr Whitaker for his services.

Notwithstanding that she had already given authorization for Joseph Whitaker to be granted possession of her effects, she now commenced to give George Robinson directions as to how her goods should be disposed of, naming certain beneficiaries and the articles they should be given. And clearly she found the business a very emotional one, for several times Robinson had to pause in his note-taking as she gave way to bitter weeping. With her elbow resting on the small counter, she put her face down into her palm and sobbed, while he, not unmoved, could only murmur sympathetic words and wait for her to recover some composure.

It must have made a dramatic and melancholy scene. The only light in the room came from a single candle that was kept on the prisoner's side of the grille and which she sometimes took up and held in her hand.

And all the while as the drama was played out the two wardresses stood by, grim and silent, observing all, while at the same time the single male warder broke the quiet with his measured footfalls as he paced to and fro in the passage that linked the two halves of the room.

At last, nearing the end of her instructions to the clerk, Mrs Berry came to the main item. It was her wish, she said, that certain of her effects be sold in order to pay for a stone which she wished to have erected on her daughter's grave.

With that the painful interview was over, and Mr Robinson, with a promise soon to return for her final instructions, took his leave.

As he walked away he turned and looked back, and saw her still sitting there by the pale light of the candle, watching his departure.

19

The Inquest at Castleton Concludes

While George Robinson went about his business, Elizabeth Berry herself could do nothing but try to accept the enormity of her situation. And her situation was even bleaker than she was aware. While she languished in her cell, counting the days and praying that the Home Secretary would eventually be moved to grant her a reprieve, the men of the press were eagerly looking forward to the coming Monday where, in Castleton, the inquest into the death of her mother was to be resumed.

The *Chronicle* reported that 'although it may appear incredible, we are informed that [Mrs Berry] knows nothing whatever of the exhumation of her mother, and of the inquest held upon Mrs Finley's body'.

In the event that Mrs Berry did indeed know nothing of the matter – though it would have been in the prison authorities' interests to deny that she did – she would most certainly learn about it in time.

Before her trial at Liverpool the inquest into the death of her mother had, not surprisingly, opened to the greatest fascination. And following its adjournment Mrs Berry had been found guilty of a most diabolical murder, ensuring that when the inquest was resumed it would get the closest attention. If Elizabeth Berry could poison her own innocent child, then what else was she capable of? The public would soon find out.

The inquest into Mrs Finley's death was resumed at two o'clock on Monday 28 February, and when the jurors were in place the first witness was called. He was Mr George Shaw of Cobden Road, Chesterfield, employed as Clerk to the Guardians of the Poor for the Chesterfield Union Workhouse.

His testimony told the remarkable story of Elizabeth Berry's brief employment at the workhouse the previous year when, having commenced her duties as nurse on 1 February, she abruptly left at 11.30 the next morning, giving her reason for leaving as the condition of her mother who, she said, was seriously ill. He went on to say that he received a letter from her on 5 February, sent from Castleton, Rochdale, in which she wrote: 'Sir, – My mother is sinking very fast, so that it will be impossible for me to leave her. Will you please present the enclosed to your board at their next meeting.' The 'enclosed' was a letter tendering her resignation. Dated February 3rd, 1886, it said, 'Herewith I resign my office as nurse in your Workhouse. Owing to my mother's dangerous state of health it is impossible for me to leave her. Yours truly, Elizabeth Berry.'

Dr Frank Paul, Lecturer on Medical Jurisprudence at the University College, Liverpool, was called next to testify, and said that he had made analysis of the body parts delivered to him following the post-mortem on Mrs Finley's body. He had found no mineral poison present, but he had extracted a substance from the stomach and intestines which he believed to be atropia, a substance extracted from the deadly nightshade. It was impossible to say how much atropia there was in the body, as it was a drug that would disappear in the course of time. 'A very small quantity would be fatal,' he said. Asked as to the effect of it on the system, he said that the most marked symptom was dilation of the pupils of the eyes. 'You have perhaps been to a chemist's,' he said, 'and had something dropped into your eyes. That would be atropia. It doesn't act on the system the same way as an irritant, like a mineral poison; it acts on the nerves, and causes death through the nervous system.'

Dr Paul's place was taken by Dr William Sharples, who was in practice at Castleton. After telling the court that he had assisted in the post-mortem of Mrs Finley, he said that he had attended her early in the previous year when she had suffered from bleeding of the nose. She had recovered from this by the end of January, but he was called to see her on 6 February by her daughter, Mrs Berry. Mrs Finley complained to him of sleeplessness, he said, for which he gave her sedatives, and attended her from time to time up to the 12th, the day before her death. She had some symptoms of paralysis on that day, and also complained of thirst. On the subject of the patient's death, he said, 'When I left her on the Friday night I thought she was rather seriously ill, but I didn't expect her immediate death. But the next morning, Saturday, Mrs Berry came and told me that the woman was dead, that she had had several convulsive attacks during the night, and that she died in a convulsion.' He added that after discussion with Mrs Berry he gave her a certificate saying that death was due to cerebral haemorrhage and coma. 'I gave the certificate from what Mrs Berry told me,' he said, 'and from what I saw of the deceased during her illness. I was considerably puzzled about the case, but I thought that that was, to the best of my judgement, the cause of death.' He went on to say that while attending Mrs Finley he noticed the pupils of her eyes several times, and on the last day of her illness saw that they were largely dilated and unequal. He said also that at one time he saw her in a kind of convulsion or fit, which he regarded as a symptom of brain disorder. 'Her face was flushed, the pulse quick and irregular, and she had some tremulous motion of the muscles all over her.' He hadn't noticed the condition of her pupils at the time, he said. 'It was impossible to examine them. When I tried to examine her eyes she pushed me away. The next time I saw her after this she exhibited symptoms of paralysis. And she looked as if she had had too much spirits. She was excited, and had the appearance of a person intoxicated.'

Questioned as to the cause of her death, he said, 'Having made the post-mortem I am of the opinion that she did *not* die from cerebral haemorrhage, but from atropia poisoning. I say this from what I have seen lately, and from the symptoms of the deceased during the last two or three days. Of course, I only saw the dilation of the eyes once, but the other symptoms I saw towards the end of her illness were consistent with poisoning by atropia. The reason I gave the certificate was because I saw no reasonable doubt that the cause of death was not a natural one.'

After Dr Sharples had stepped down, Dr Paul was recalled. He said that all the symptoms spoken of by Dr Sharples were quite consistent with poisoning by atropia, and as for Dr Sharples finding Mrs Finley in an excited state and apparently intoxicated shortly before her death, there were few poisons that caused such an excited state as atropia. 'Persons under its influence are generally flushed, and excited and delirious.'

Next called was Dr Thomas Harris, who had conducted the post-mortem examination of Mrs Finley's remains at the Moston Cemetery. After saying that the body was very much decomposed – 'the hands nearly separated from the arms by maceration' – he said he had found no evidence of any sufficient disease that could account for death. As to the symptoms described by Dr Sharples, he said that they were not only *consistent* with poisoning by atropia, but '*suspicious* of atropia poisoning'. One of the strongest symptoms mentioned, he pointed out, was the excited state of the patient, and added, 'Poisoning by atropia may be mistaken for *delirium tremens*.'

The coroner: 'The three chief characteristics of atropia poisoning are dilation of the pupils of the eyes, extreme thirst, and convulsions?'

'Yes, with delirium, very often terminating by coma.'

After saying that convulsions in a woman of Mrs Finley's age were distinctly uncommon, Dr Harris was allowed to step down, and Sarah Pemberton, of Burslem, Staffordshire was called.

She had much of interest to tell. She was, she said, a widow, and the sister of the late Mary Ann Finley, and came to Castleton on Thursday 11 February, having been summoned by a telegram from Mrs Berry. The telegram had since been destroyed, but she could remember its contents. It had said: 'Mrs Walsh* is dangerously ill. If you wish to see her come at once. E. Berry.' On receiving the telegram, she said, she left her home immediately, reaching Castleton about five o'clock that afternoon. Arriving in Back Albion Street, she said she had found her sister better than she had expected.

She went on to say that she stayed at the house till her sister's death on the 13th, Saturday. She never gave her sister any medicine, she said, and saw no one but Mrs Berry give her anything. On the evening of the day she arrived, Mrs Berry left the house saying she had to go into Rochdale, and was away nearly two hours. That night Mrs Berry made up a bed for her mother downstairs while she herself slept upstairs in her mother's bedroom. She, the witness, sat up all night with her sister.

On Friday morning, she went on, Mrs Berry told her that she believed that her mother was sinking fast. 'This,' said Mrs Pemberton, 'came as a surprise to me, and I said to her, "I don't think so. I think she's better than she was yesterday."' Later that day, she continued, Mrs Berry's young daughter, Edith – then ten years of age – came to visit her grandmother,

---

* Walsh is the spelling as given in the *Chronicle*'s report.

having travelled by herself from Miles Platting. She left after tea and Mrs Berry went to see her off on the train to Manchester. Soon after returning from the station, Mrs Berry went out once more, saying she was going to Rochdale again. She returned after about an hour. 'She'd brought with her some jelly,' the witness said, 'and gave my sister some, but after tasting it my sister pushed it away, saying, "Take it away! I don't like it."' Asked as to Mrs Finley's general appearance that evening, Mrs Pemberton said she seemed very cheerful and much better, and even spoke of coming to stay with her in Burslem when she felt strong enough for the journey. Asked if she knew what sort of medicine had come from the doctor, she replied that she only knew that it was medicine. 'Mrs Berry always gave her the medicine, and as she was a nurse I didn't interfere. I thought she knew more than I did how to nurse her mother.' That Friday night, she continued, Mrs Berry began to examine her mother's eyes. 'She did it a great deal, pulling her eyelids about, and my sister protested, saying, "What are you doing with my eyes?"' Mrs Berry said that her mother had an affection of the brain. 'I wanted to stay up with my sister on the Friday night, but Mrs Berry wouldn't allow it. She insisted on me going to bed.' Asked if she knew of the reason for this, she replied, 'No doubt she did it out of kindness.'

Having found her sister not nearly as sick as she had anticipated, Mrs Pemberton said she told Mrs Berry on the Friday evening that she would leave the next day to return home. She was to sleep in her sister's bed upstairs that night, and when she went up to bed about midnight she left her sister 'feeling not too bad'. Then, somewhere between four and five the next morning she was awakened by the sound of Mrs Berry opening the bedroom door. On asking what was the matter, she was told that during the night there had been a great change for the worse, and that her sister was now gravely ill. Hurrying downstairs, she found her sister lying on her back twitching and trembling all over. 'Her face was of a livid colour and her eyes were closed,' she said. 'She never opened them again before she died.' Asked whether she thought her sister had died a natural death, she said she thought she had – but she had had no reason to think otherwise.

This brought Mrs Pemberton's testimony to a close, and her place was taken by Mr Joseph Chadderton of Eccles, district manager for the Wesleyan and General Assurance Society. He told the hearing that Mrs Finley was insured in his office for £100 and that Mrs Berry came to him on 23 March to claim the money. He was somewhat surprised to find her there so soon after her mother's death, and told her that she couldn't be paid as under the terms of the policy, payment wasn't due for another three months. On hearing this she said she needed the money urgently. 'She couldn't wait,' he said. 'She had to have it at once as she was about to leave the country. She said she was going to Australia, as nurse-companion to an invalid who was going for the good of her health. She mentioned the ship, but I quite forgot the name. She said she wanted the money at once, so I let her have it. We paid her £100 less 16s. 8d. – the amount of interest on paying the money before it was due.' Asked by whom the policy had been taken out, he replied that Mrs Finley had taken out the insurance against herself in December 1882, and later assigned it to Mrs Berry.

After Mr Chadderton came Mr George Coombes, of Moss Side, Manchester, clerk to the Rational Sick and Burial Society, Manchester. He said Mrs Finley was insured in the office for £13 4s., which was paid out to Mrs Berry on 15 February 1886. The policy had been taken out by Mrs Berry. Mrs Finley knew of the insurance and had paid the premiums of 2d. a week.

The next witness called was 'letter carrier' William Taylor of Freehold, Castleton. His brief testimony would give most interesting evidence to the inquiry with regard to the name of Ellen Saunders that was written in the Rochdale chemist's poison register by the woman who had purchased quantities of sulphate of atropia. Asked whether he knew of any person named Ellen Saunders living in the Freehold district of Castleton, he replied that in the last seven or eight years in all his work he had not come across anyone with that name, 'and had such a person resided at Freehold,' he said, 'I should have known her – I am quite sure of that.' He had also made inquiries, he said, and failed to get any information of such a person having resided at Freehold.

Mr Taylor was the final witness, and after his dismissal the coroner read over to the jury the evidence they had heard. He then told them that they must decide whether there had been any foul play in the case, and in doing so must take into consideration the doctors' medical evidence. If they were of the opinion that Mrs Finley died from natural causes they must bring in a verdict to that effect, but if they believed there was foul play and that she was poisoned, then they must, if possible, say who administered the poison. He pointed out that when Mrs Finley was taken ill, there were only two other people stopping in the house – Mrs Pemberton and Mrs Berry. 'You have had Mrs Pemberton before you,' he said, 'and you have heard her give her evidence in a very straightforward and proper manner. I think there can be no suspicion against her.' The jury, he said, must look at the facts and say whether they create such strong suspicion against Mrs Berry that the case should be sent for further investigation. 'Then what you have also to decide,' he added, 'is whether the woman Ellen Saunders was the same person as Mrs Berry. The fact that atropia has been found in the body of the deceased makes it, in my opinion, very suspicious, but I feel certain the jury will give every consideration to the evidence, and find a true and proper verdict upon it.'

At the conclusion of the coroner's address, the court was cleared to allow the jurors to confer and reach a verdict. Twenty-five minutes later the assembly was allowed back in. When all were seated the coroner asked the jury whether they had reached a verdict. 'Yes, sir,' the foreman replied. 'We are unanimously of opinion that Mrs Berry is guilty of murder.'

The coroner: '*Wilful* murder, I suppose?'

The foreman: 'Yes.'

With this the inquiry was closed.

Looking at the testimonies of the witnesses, there can be no doubt that the jury was correct in its finding that day. When Elizabeth Berry set off for Castleton on 3 February, she went with the sole intention of killing her mother, her intention springing from her own impecunious situation and her mother's illness with her nose-bleeds.

A glance at Mrs Berry's successive periods of employment in the various workhouses, and it becomes clear that none of them could be termed in any way successful. None had brought her satisfaction. Nevertheless, they offered the only real means of earning a livelihood, leaving her no option but to accept such work.

Records show that she was very much in two minds when it came to committing herself to employment at the Oldham workhouse, and this might also have been the case with the post offered the previous year at Chesterton. Further, it is likely that she took the Chesterton position with some desperation, for when she began her first day's work there she had been unemployed for over three months, and would have been very low in funds. However, after just one day in the job, she had had enough, and was anxious for a way out of the situation.

So it was that the following morning she informed the Clerk to the Guardians that she had received a letter from her mother saying that she was dangerously ill, and would have to go to her. Two days later she followed her departure with her resignation, due, she said, to her mother's increasingly dangerous condition and need of her. There was, of course, no truth in it. Although her mother had been suffering from the nose-bleeds, she had no life-threatening illness. What her mother did have, however, were several valuable life insurance policies, and all in her daughter's favour.

The fact that Mrs Finley had been so recently under the care of a doctor was a godsend to Mrs Berry in her plan, and it is likely that it strengthened her resolve. And for a time her plan worked. Although there was unease among some of the neighbours over the circumstances of Mrs Finley's death, Dr Sharples himself was not suspicious. He was aware that his patient was being cared for by her daughter who was a qualified nurse, and not only that, but Mrs Berry would have known exactly what to say to him to allay any unease that might have arisen. He had no reason, therefore, to mistrust her. Indeed, so persuasive was she that, as we have seen, when he was writing out the death certificate, he wrote, at her suggestion, that 'coma' was a contributory factor in Mrs Finley's death.

The calendar of Mrs Finley's murder is not difficult to see.

On arriving in Castleton on the Wednesday Mrs Berry at once makes inquiries as to where she can find a pharmaceutical chemist, and from him, on the Thursday or Friday, she buys some deleterious preparation. Friday evening, and Mrs Finley goes out to 'fetch the supper beer' and tells Harriet Dorrick that she has just been given some medicine by her daughter and feels 'very sick and queer after it'. The next day Mrs Berry sends for Dr Sharples, telling him that her mother is not well and cannot sleep, so establishing in the doctor's mind the 'fact' that her mother is once again ill.

On Tuesday the 9th Mrs Berry goes into Rochdale and from the chemist John Taylor buys a quantity of atropia, signing the poison book in the name of Ellen Saunders. Back in Castleton she gives some 'medicine' to her mother, after which Mrs Finley is seen by Alice Eaves to be very ill. Mrs Pemberton, summoned with urgency, arrives on the Thursday, and is surprised and relieved to find her sister in a better condition than she had feared.

On Friday the agent for the Prudential comes to the house – summoned to endorse one of Mrs Finley's life insurance policies. On the same day, Mrs Berry once more visits Mr Taylor's chemist shop, and under the name of Ellen Saunders buys more atropia, this time double the amount.

The poison works. Although Mrs Pemberton and the neighbours find Mrs Finley appearing fairly well all through that Friday, by 7.15 the next morning she is found to be dying.

Mrs Berry benefited from four life insurance policies on her mother's death, the total sum realized being something in the region of £150 to £200 (between £165,000 and £220,000 in today's money), to which was added whatever cash could be raised through the disposal of her mother's effects. It was also revealed that Mrs Berry was in such a hurry to collect the £100 due from the Wesleyan and General that she spun a story about having to leave on a ship bound for Australia, and was prepared to sacrifice 16s. 8d. in interest fees.

When there came the opportunity to bring about her mother's death to her own great advantage, Mrs Berry grasped it with both hands, and with a single-mindedness that would be remarkable in anyone's book.

20

'A Very Small Heart'

In her cell, Elizabeth Berry remained in ignorance of what was happening beyond the prison walls, but with her trial concluding with a verdict of guilty, and followed by the same verdict at the inquest into her mother's death, she continued to be the news of the day – her guilt, and her situation, prompting wide coverage in the press.

In the course of her life she had moved about a good deal and made many acquaintances. Some had come to know her well, and among them were those who were eager to impart their recollections. Where once such stories might have been disseminated only in whispers, however, they now appeared in the newspapers for the world to see. And of course the editors were glad of all the information they could get – and the more scandalous the better.

Numerous reports were concerned with Mrs Berry's earlier life, with remarks on her pride and ambition. And the negative views didn't vary much in tone. To many who had been acquainted with her she was seen as aloof, 'inordinately fond of fashionable clothes and outward display', to be ashamed of her working-class beginnings, and eager to give the impression that she was of a higher station in life. Acknowledged also now as a liar, it was revealed that she had not only tried to elevate her father's social position, but also her mother's, as was alluded to in a piece in the *Chronicle* following an interview with Mr Lawson, of the Oldham workhouse. After citing her intelligence and positive qualities as a nurse, the *Chronicle*'s report went on:

She made a deep impression upon the people at the workhouse, and naturally they feel her position very acutely. At the same time, it is only fair to state that there were persons there who couldn't 'read' her, and regarded her as a mystery, as they thought her high-flown notions were entirely out of keeping with the position she occupied. She endeavoured to impress those she spoke to with the idea that she did not belong to 'common working folk'. Her mother's death she often alluded to, but she told a far different tale to that which was the outcome of the inquest. Instead of her mother being a weaver, and dying in comparatively poor circumstances, her explanation was the reverse, for she boasted that she inherited a fortune of £1,500. But, alas! How often it is proved that truth is stranger than fiction?

Her mother's situation was also touched upon in a letter from an unnamed correspondent to the *Chronicle,* obviously one who had known her:

Mrs Finley was a very kind mother, and stinted herself to assist her daughter to appear in a style beyond the requirements of her position, yet on one occasion, when Mrs Berry visited her mother at Rochdale, and when the old woman, who was out of work, had pawned some of her clothing to procure extras for tea, she had the effrontery to display the sum of £11, all of which she replaced in her pocket and gave her mother nothing.

With journalists from the *Standard* and the *Chronicle* going out of their way to find stories relating to the convict's past, their work took them into several districts where she had lived at one time or another. They found no shortage of anecdotes. And through them it becomes clear, at all times, that however she might have been viewed, she had never been disregarded. Always, it seemed, she had provoked comment.

Some reports published related to her time at the Oldham workhouse. So another unnamed contributor wrote to the *Chronicle*:

When Mrs Berry cared to do so she could make herself very agreeable, as she possessed a very good voice, and sang and played the piano fairly well. As a conversationalist she was very entertaining, and her company was much sought...It was also said that she was fond of reading to some of the patients who took her fancy, but at other times she was more inclined to keep away from them.

But such comments were about as positive as could be found. Generally she was shown as demanding, fastidious and, as we have seen, frequently abusive. An account of her violent and aggressive behaviour, and of Dr Patterson being sent for and diagnosing 'brain fever', has already been given (see pp. 54–6). It is a most interesting account, and there can be little reason to question its veracity. For one thing, it describes the doctor playing a major part in the incident, and as we have seen how quick he was to correct any perceived misreporting of him, there can be little doubt that had the *Chronicle* used his name in vain he would have been on to the editor like a shot.

Mrs Berry's episode of 'brain fever' drew another letter to the paper, clearly from one owning some medical expertise and knowledge of Mrs Berry. It is almost certain to have come from Dr Patterson. The anonymous correspondent wrote:

[Mrs Berry's] strange conduct...was due to an attack of hysteria which she had some weeks before Christmas. The attack was brought on by a violent quarrel with one of the female officers of the House. The 'swoon' into which she falls when wound up to a high pitch of excitement is another hysterical manifestation. When about to be arrested after the inquest at the Workhouse she fell heavily, from the above cause, on the back of her head on the boardroom floor. She had a similar heavy fall on the flags of the police cells at the Town Hall, and, again, it seems, at Liverpool. Her cool and quite brilliant deceptive qualities, such as she exhibits, are always seen to greatest advantage in hysterical women. Females of this type are great liars and dissemblers, almost without apparent motive or effort. In many of them also there is a complete loss of the moral sense. Without any exhibition of feeling they commit cruelties and crimes at which people shudder. It is not quite fair to the female sex to think of Mrs Berry as an ordinary woman, but as a person of low or perverted nervous organisation, possessed certainly of much ability and intelligence, but whose ambition and love of display and finery, associated with too little self-control, led her to the committal of at least two most inhuman and unnatural crimes.

One piece in the *Chronicle* followed an interview with Ellen Thompson, the workhouse inmate assigned as a servant to Mrs Berry, who gave evidence at her trial. Published under the title: THE CONDEMNED WOMAN AND HER HUSBAND'S PHOTOGRAPHS, it said:

It was well known amongst the Workhouse officials that on the mantelpiece of Mrs Berry's sitting room in the Oldham Union were two photographs. One of them was that of her late husband, Thomas Berry, the other, she said, was that of a gentleman she often spoke of. She was constantly admiring the latter photograph, and often spoke of the 'chance' which she had missed. Occasionally she would go on to say that the gentleman lived at Derby, and was exceedingly well to do. She said she would have been his third wife had he not died. The fact of his death she often deplored, as she said it had prevented her from getting into the 'highest society' and living in ease and luxury. At the time when Mrs Berry was in the charge of the police at the Workhouse the photos were in their usual place. Ellen Thompson was attending to Mrs Berry, and one night she noticed her carrying something under her gown [and later] noticed something lying on the floor near Berry's dress. She picked it up, and found it to be the photos of Thomas Berry and the Derby gentleman before referred to, which had been crumpled up. Thompson put them on the mantelpiece, where Mrs Berry found them the next morning. The photos no sooner caught her eye than, with a kind of smile of triumph, she threw them into the fire, and stood by until the last fragment disappeared. Her reason for so acting cannot be divined, but apparently she had no desire of the photos falling into other persons' hands.

A further report related to the brief period while Mrs Berry was under house arrest at the workhouse. Said the *Chronicle*:

When Mrs Berry was under the charge of the police she attempted to act pretty much as she did when she enjoyed her own liberty. She was particularly hard on the doctor, who, she repeatedly said, would have to suffer for it along with Ellen Thompson and the others who were attending on her at the time. She was just as particular about the tidiness of her room as she was before; and would continually have someone trotting about for the curling tongs or something else. A person more scrupulously clean could not be met with than the misguided woman Berry, for like the rooms of the other lady attendants, hers were the picture of tidiness...

Another contributor from the Oldham workhouse reported:

She did not care about any mention being made of her deceased relatives, but seemed to deeply lament the death of the child Harold, whom she frequently said would have been of great assistance to her. She never said anything about the death of the other child, who was younger than poor Edith, and who died when only a few months old. Whenever the conversation at all turned towards her mother, Mrs Berry was always noticed to get rather uneasy and did her utmost to change the subject in another direction. She was known to a great many persons outside the workhouse, and was never more at home than when she was in company.

One very interesting report resulted from one of the *Chronicle*'s men managing to track down William Finley, who was staying at the Blue Bell Inn at Royton. On 9 January the journalist interviewed him for a piece published in the paper's edition of the 12th, some parts of which have already been presented in this book. The reporter speaks of Finley as 'an old man', saying of him: 'He is rather over middle height, not over well dressed, but attired as you would expect a travelling pedlar to be, and wears a beard which has turned grey very early, for he is still in his fifties.'

Since 1880, Finley told him, he had been travelling about the country eking out a living as a pedlar, adding the remark that 'he would be better off had he not seen so many empty gill pots'. It was not before three weeks earlier, he said, while he was in Manchester, that he had learned of his wife's exhumation, at which he 'was thunder-struck', and at once came down to Royton, where he intended to stay 'to see it out'. Asked about his stepdaughter Elizabeth, he said, 'She was very fond of reading novels of any sort, and she was pretty good at history. …She was always proud [and] wanted to be a bit above the other girls in the mill.' Of the death of his wife Mary Ann, he said, 'She had been dead eight months before I heard of it. I was then coming from Rushton to Blackburn, and met a friend, who told me that she was dead.' The reporter then asked him what he thought of 'the two crimes', to which Finley replied that he thought that Mrs Berry was guilty of both, 'and more than that if it was found out'. And he added, 'An Oldham doctor who knew her told me the other day that she was one of the cleverest women he ever knew, but she had a very small heart.' As for Elizabeth's feelings for *him*, he said, 'She never liked me; in fact, I'll tell you what, if I'd lived in the same house as her much longer I should have been a goner. That's my opinion, and there's many a thousand thinks so besides.'

Going on to canvass the feelings of some of Mrs Berry's erstwhile neighbours, the *Chronicle*'s man duly reported:

> The excitement in Albion street, Jackson Street, Saville Street and the numerous other small thoroughfares in that part of Miles Platting continues as great as when Mrs Berry and her suspected poisoning of her own child first became the subject of unpleasant rumour, afterwards to be verified with startling distinction. The feeling against the woman in the localities named is exceedingly strong, and if she was let loose, and her former neighbours could have their sweet will of her, there would be no necessity for the services of her namesake, Berry, the public executioner.

So much, then, for the opinion of the public. Such as it was, it did not bode well for any public petition for clemency.

21

The Earlier Deaths

As public opinion had shown, there was great support for Elizabeth Berry's capital sentence. Not only that, but there was increasing gossip regarding the deaths of other members of her family, namely her husband and young son Harold. In spite of the gossip and the speculation, however, no official inquiries were made into their deaths. This is not surprising, of course. The putative suspect was already in prison awaiting execution, so even in the event that more deaths were laid at her door, her sentence could not be made any more severe. Also, the business of post-mortems and inquests was a costly one – added to which the earlier deaths had taken place years before, and the bodies' advanced decomposition would have greatly reduced any chances of a satisfactory autopsy procedure.

In the matter of suspicion, however, it is of interest to look a little more closely at the circumstances of the earlier deaths that occurred in Elizabeth Berry's immediate family. We have already seen that an inquest jury found her guilty of the wilful murder of her mother, but what of those who had died before?

At the start of Mrs Berry's trial the judge made reference to her having had two children, a boy and a girl. As we have seen, however, there had in fact been three, one dying in infancy. With regard to this infant, who was never named, reports in the press simply referred to the child as male – witness Mr Cottingham (see p. 151) in his reference to Edith Annie's 'two brothers'. However, I could find no information on this second son, and the lengthiest searches for a record of his birth and death in the General Record Office turned up nothing. How to explain it? And then came the solution to the mystery – showing that Mr Cottingham, in this instance, had not so thoroughly done his homework. There had not been two brothers, there was no second son. There among the papers that make up the Home Office file is a brief statement from Ann Sanderson, where she says: 'There had been a third child, a girl which died three years before the father of teething.'

And there was the answer. And so it was that some few facts were gleaned relating to the brief life of the Berrys' third child, the infant Elizabeth Jane Berry, born 13 June 1877, died 26 October 1877.

Elizabeth Jane's death certificate also cleared up another mystery. The statement that the baby died of teething, or dentition, as it was more properly known, appears to have been accepted as fact; it was given as such in the newspapers, and also by Ann Sanderson at Elizabeth Berry's trial.

A baby's teething is, of course, a natural part of its development, and while the resulting discomfort often leads to fretfulness and parents' sleepless nights, it is hard to believe that it could be accepted as being instrumental in a child's death. Back in earlier times, however, this appears to have been the case. The very high incidence of infant mortality in early Victorian times so commonly coincided with the occurrence of a baby's teething that the two phenomena became linked, and became so strongly accepted that in 1842 'teething' was registered as the cause of death in 7.3% of infants up to the age of three who died in London.

Not surprisingly, then, when 'teething' was given out in court as the cause of death of the Berrys' youngest, it was accepted by all, the death being regarded as just one more infant fatality in the calendar. There was not, though, as it turned out, any truth in it.

The baby Elizabeth Jane's death was pronounced and certified by one Dr I.A. Palanque. With no mention at all of teething, he gave the cause as 'Dysentery and convulsions'.

It should be noted that 'convulsions' as a cause of death is something of a catch-all term commonly used in earlier times. It is used for the phenomenon of rapidly alternating contractions and relaxations of the muscles, often accompanied by unconsciousness. Although 'convulsions' was frequently given as a cause of death, it is in fact a *symptom* of an illness. Many illnesses can bring on convulsions, among them whooping cough, pneumonia, infection, encephalitis and damage to the brain. In the case of Elizabeth Jane, her convulsions and dysentery could well have been symptoms of arsenic poisoning. Indeed, they are classically symptomatic of it.

Arsenic, the favourite weapon of poison in Georgian and Victorian times, was very easy to come by, as was strychnine, both approved means of dealing with rats and mice. And just how commonly available were such deadly poisons in the eradication of vermin is illustrated in the following small article that appeared in the *Chronicle* of 2 February 1887 under the heading POISONED BY MOUSE POWDER:

> An inquest has been held by the Egremont Coroner on the body of John Braden, six years old, who died from eating mouse power. The poison was placed underneath the table in the parlour, and when the deceased came home from school he ate some of it with fatal results. The Coroner said the parents had shown gross carelessness in placing poison where five children had access to it. A verdict of 'Accidental poisoning' was returned.

The mouse powder concerned was likely to have contained arsenic or strychnine, or a mixture of both, and the boy's death would have been agonizing. The jury's acceptance of the given account of how the boy came to die appears to show that the parents seem not to have been held in any great suspicion. The sad case goes to show once again that murder by means of a commonly-bought mouse powder could, in some circumstances, be relatively easy to get away with – and, as we have seen, perhaps provoke nothing more than a stern ticking off from the coroner.

In the case of Elizabeth Jane, although her death was officially put down to dysentery and convulsions, Mrs Berry had family and friends believe that it was due to a different cause entirely – to teething. Clearly, she lied.

It is perhaps significant that in all the many reports relating to Elizabeth Berry's various statements about her life I have been unable to find any single reference made by her to her daughter Elizabeth Jane – not in any regard whatsoever, be it the baby's birth, life or death. It is as if the child never existed. Further, it is interesting to note that the informant of the baby's death to the registrar was Thomas, her father, who was with her when she died.

As we have seen, the next member of the family to die was Thomas himself. And following Mrs Berry's conviction it was revealed that his death, at the time it happened, gave rise to comment, some of the erstwhile neighbours concurring that he 'died with startling suddenness', and was 'buried with equal quickness'.

He was only thirty-four on his death in July 1881. The *Manchester Times* reported that he 'died somewhat suddenly, after having been at a social party'. His death certificate gives the cause of death as 'Aortic Regurgitation. Haemorrhoids 2 years Diarrhoea'. According to his widow, who was present at his death, and who registered it two days later, he had been in poor health for some two years. Ann Sanderson, at Elizabeth Berry's trial, said that her brother had weak bowels, and that she 'saw him sometimes confined to bed for a day or so'.

It must be said that the view of Thomas as having been weak and ill for years was not generally shared. The *Sunderland Daily Echo & Shipping Gazette* stated that those who knew him well at Miles Platting 'deny that he was a delicate man whilst employed there as a railway official', and in support of this statement was the fact that he was passed by an insurance doctor 'as a thoroughly healthy subject, and accordingly insured without any problem'. Also, at no time, it appears, until the very last, was he much out of work. And it must be acknowledged that if he had been unable to work for any lengthy period there would have been *no money* coming into the house, and this is not for one moment an imaginable scenario where Elizabeth Berry is concerned. Further against any such notion is the fact that throughout the Berrys' short marriage they were regularly moving house in favour of betterment. And such moves did not come cheaply.

The cause of death as given on Thomas's death certificate is interesting. 'Aortic regurgitation' is a term used to indicate a condition in which, as the result of valvular disease, the blood does not entirely pass on from the auricles of the heart to the ventricles, or from the ventricles into the arteries. As a result, a certain amount of blood leaks past it, or 'regurgitates' back into the cavity from which it has been driven. It is not a disease which in 1881 would have been easy to diagnose, and as no autopsy was carried out on Thomas's body there was no way of verifying it. As for his having suffered from diarrhoea and haemorrhoids for two years, this also is remarkable in that it should be regarded as contributing to the death of such a young person. Haemorrhoids are a likely consequence of severe and chronic diarrhoea, and diarrhoea is known to be a consequence of persistent poisoning by certain agents, typically arsenic. To my mind, all the known facts point to the supposition that Thomas was poisoned by his wife.

And what of the Berrys' son? There is no doubt in my mind that he was Elizabeth Berry's third victim.

Harold Berry died at eight years of age at 68 Albion Street, Miles Platting, on 27 September 1882, a year after the death of his father, and following a visit to Blackpool. In the early part of that September Mrs Berry came from her work at the Wellington workhouse and went to Miles Platting where the children were living with the Sandersons. On arrival she packed up some of the children's belongings and, keeping them away from school, took them off to the coast. A week later, on the 18th, they returned to Miles Platting with the children suffering sickness and vomiting. Mrs Berry blamed their illness on their having slept in damp sheets at the lodging house. The sheets in question, she said, were still drying out on the clothes line when they arrived at the place. A Miles Platting practitioner, Dr Shaw, 'an old man', as Mrs Sanderson described him, was called to the children after their return, but Harold's condition continued to deteriorate.

He died ten days after his arrival back in Albion Street. His death certificate states that he had been ill for fourteen days, and gives the cause of death as 'tubercular disease of membrane of brain and glands of bowels'. It is not easy to accept that a seemingly healthy boy who a fortnight earlier had been enjoying the delights of the seaside should succumb with such suddenness to tuberculosis, or to accept Mrs Berry's claim that his illness was brought on as the result of sleeping in damp sheets at the lodging house. One might ask the question as to why, if he was suffering so severely from tuberculosis, his mother took him away in the first place, and also, if indeed the sheets were damp, then what was a loving mother thinking of in putting her precious children to sleep in them?

If one regards Harold's death with suspicion, a possible scenario presents itself – in which Harold and Edith are given poison by their mother on the journey back from Blackpool, probably in a drink. As a result, by the time they arrive at Albion Street they are showing signs of sickness. Said Ann Sanderson in a sworn testimony: 'I didn't see 'em vomit, but they told me they did before they got home.' If they had been given the poison too early they would not have been able to travel, and it is essential that Mrs Berry gets them back to Miles Platting.

Once there, Dr Shaw is sent for, and on arrival finds Harold very sick but Edith less so. (Ann Sanderson: 'She was sick but soon got better.') Questioning Mrs Berry as to the likely cause of the children's illness, the doctor is told that they were taken ill while on holiday. If, as is very likely, she says that the children were attended by a doctor in Blackpool, Dr Shaw would have no way of verifying her claim. The children, being only eight and seven years of age, would not, of course, be likely to contribute any information to the doctor. He, then, has no option but to accept the story and, faced with an apparently distraught mother, takes her at her word. It must be borne in mind of course that Mrs Berry was an experienced nurse – which fact the doctor would have appreciated. Further, as a nurse in a workhouse she had seen the deaths of many children, so was well versed in what information was required for the completion of a death certificate.

Did Elizabeth Berry intend to kill only Harold, or did she hope to kill both of her children? I have no doubt that she knew exactly what she was doing, and that she set out to destroy only the boy – which outcome would well suit the scenario that she had in mind.

It is a most interesting fact also that when it came to the moment of the boy's death his mother was nowhere to be seen. When little Harold died it was his aunt Ann Sanderson who sent for the doctor, who came to the house and pronounced him dead. Whether the doctor ever inquired as to the whereabouts of the boy's mother at such a crucial time we shall never know. And just as it was she, Ann Sanderson, who had stayed at Harold's side, so it is her mark, a cross in lieu of a signature, that appears on his death certificate, signifying that she was a witness at the moment of his death.

Just as Elizabeth Berry left Harold's side before he died, so she had done in the case of baby Elizabeth Jane. She would do so again in the case of Edith. And surely it must be observed that no normal mother would ever have dreamt of doing such a thing. To be faced with the imminent death of a most precious child, a mother's heart would keep her there, close at her child's side. This was not the case with Elizabeth Berry. When it came to Edith's last hours, her mother actually lay on the bed at her side and slept. Then, when the child was even closer to death, she chose to leave her, and go to sleep in her sitting room.

I do not think there can be any doubt that Elizabeth Berry was rightly convicted of the murder of her daughter Edith, and that she was also guilty of the murder of her mother. Where the deaths of her husband, son and baby daughter were concerned, it seems very likely that in each case the attending doctor had the wool pulled over his eyes. Certainly in the view of this writer, Mrs Berry got away with murder. All three, the baby Elizabeth Jane, husband Thomas, and finally her son Harold, suffered extreme diarrhoea in the days leading to their deaths, which phenomenon was in each case noted by the certifying doctor as a contributory cause of death – and which is also a symptom of arsenical poisoning. It is my belief that they died from being poisoned – almost certainly with arsenic. I believe also that the ease with which Elizabeth Jane was dispatched contributed to the deaths of those who came after.

Assuming that arsenic was employed in the first three murders, one might wonder why Mrs Finley was despatched with atropia. A likely answer is that Mrs Berry had become wary of using arsenic again, for the simple reason that it had become an increasingly used and easily detected poison, and she feared that it might lead to her discovery. As an experienced nurse, her knowledge had widened, and perhaps she thought that atropia, a far more rarely used agent, would be less likely to be suspected or so easily diagnosed. Therefore a change was due.

When it came to the murder of Edith, there was a further change in Mrs Berry's *modus operandi*. At the trial the judge spoke of Edith being poisoned on the Saturday morning and again on the Sunday afternoon, and raised the question as to whether the same poison had been administered on both occasions. It is a good question. The first poison, administered shortly after nine forty-five on Saturday morning, led to stomach pains and vomiting, the vomited matter containing blood. But it was not until the following afternoon that the bloody purging began and blisters were seen about the child's mouth. Judging by the difference in the child's symptoms, I think we must accept that there was a second poison given, and that it was the corrosive poison, sulphuric or oxalic acid, as claimed by the doctors. And the reason for switching to a different poison? Mrs Berry's perception that the first administered was not having the required effect. On being told on the Sunday that Edith looked likely to recover, Mrs Berry discarded the first poison and switched to the corrosive poison – and this, as she determined, proved deadly.

There is a matter of interest also with regard to the towels which Mrs Berry gave to the doctors. She gave one to Dr Patterson which, he said, had blood on it and gave off an acidic smell. Then, when Dr Robertson called on the Monday night and asked Mrs Berry if she had kept the evacuations from the girl's bowels, she replied that she had not, and gave him a towel with much 'tenacious matter' on it ('I have never seen mucus like that,' he said). We are told that both towels were analysed for poison but that nothing of a suspicious nature was found. The question arises, then, as to whether all the blood and mucus came from Edith Annie. Elizabeth Berry was a cunning and clever woman, and was well enough read to have known that material excreted by a suspected victim of poison was almost certain to be analysed in an effort to determine whether poison had been administered. Although the faecal matter excreted by Edith had been washed away, and so was not available to the doctors, Mrs Berry was more than ready to offer up towels which, she said, were soiled with Edith's vomit. How was it, then, that analysis of the towels revealed no controversial matter? I believe that the answer is not difficult to find. As head nurse in the infirmary, Mrs Berry had under her care dozens of sick inmates, several of whom could have provided quantities of bloody mucus, which matter could have been used to adulterate the towels in Edith's sickroom.

Mrs Berry's reasons for carrying out the killings have been touched on beforehand in this book. There can be no doubt that her all-consuming motive was her determination to move on and to elevate her social position, and to this end her husband and children were obstacles. It is true that she collected varying amounts of insurance pay-outs with their deaths – and she was glad of them – but what is more significant is the fact that, once she was earning, so much of her salary went on the upkeep and schooling of Harold and Edith. I do believe that this was a factor in their murders. With so much of her wages taken up with the children's care she had very little to spend on herself – and she was a woman who was fond of fine clothes and jewellery, items which she would have considered assets in her search for a wealthy husband.

And how did she decide to turn to murder in the first place?

The murder of Elizabeth Jane is perhaps telling. Elizabeth did not want the child and she soon took steps to dispose of it. This was not the end of the matter, though. With the arrival of the baby, her third, she had seen the writing on the wall. She and Thomas were a fertile couple, and with no reliable means of birth control she could see before her a succession of births – and with this a consequent descent into poverty. This was not to be contemplated, so she took steps. With the new baby success-fully disposed of, and no questions asked, she then turned her attention to her husband. And so Thomas was made ill, in very small doses at first, ensuring that he would never again be in a condition to claim his marital rights. There would be no more children. Not only that, but she was soon to decide that she would be better off with him out of the way altogether.

As for her mother, as noted previously, Elizabeth Berry held her in no affection. Added to this, there were the insurance policies out on her life, and Elizabeth was in need of money. Further, by the time she set out to kill her mother she was practised in the art, and knew that she could do it.

It appears to be a not-uncommon phenomenon in the careers of serial poisoners that they develop a taste for it. This becomes evident in the most casual study of our criminal history, which is littered with such cases. And it would appear that the serial poisoners had one thing in common, a particular quality that enabled them to go about their deadly work untouched by conscience, or any sense of compassion for their victims. They were invariably possessed of an ice-cold detachment that allowed them to administer the cruellest of poisons even to their nearest and dearest, those trusting and loving individuals who should have been the most beloved and protected.

Observing this, it is hard to avoid the idea that a certain amount of pleasure and satisfaction must have played a part as Mrs Berry admin-istered the poisons and carefully monitored the effects. The need for power is a very positive quality in some personalities, and there have been numerous serial killers in which this quality appears to have been evident. From earlier days names such as Mary Ann Cotton and William Palmer come to mind, and from more recent times those of Dr Harold Shipman and hospital nurses Beverley Allitt and, this very year, Victorino Chua.

I am convinced that this was the case with Elizabeth Berry as she demonstrated the most cruel callousness when poisoning her family, on each occasion coolly observing how the deadly poisons took effect. In the case of her mother she calmly examined her eyes to see whether the pupils were dilating, checking that the atropia was doing its work. The same happened with little Edith. Her mother watched her suffer the most intense agony, and through it all addressed her as 'my darling,' and feigned the deepest affection. Clearly, once Elizabeth Berry had set out on her task, no amount of the suffering that she witnessed could stop her. She had come to find a certain pleasure in the execution of her power, and in doing so was blind to everything but her own wants.

It is perhaps no wonder, then, that on being formally arrested for the murder of her child she screamed and fainted away on the police court floor. So single-minded and self-confident had she become in her murderous projects that, blinkered to all but her own desires, the possibility of being found out had never realistically occurred to her. When it came, then, the discovery of her guilt, it was something for which she was totally unprepared.

22

'How Great the Fall'

In more modern times, when a murderer was condemned to die, it might follow that several weeks would elapse before the penalty was carried out. Appeals launched against the sentence had to be constructed, heard and considered. It all took time. But back in Georgian and Victorian days there was little in the way of legal procedure to delay the final act. Once the death sentence had been passed there was usually only a short time left to the condemned felon between the conviction and the scaffold.

This was the situation for Elizabeth Berry at the time of her conviction. On Thursday 3 March, a week after the trial's end, she was informed that she was to hang on the 14th. Her wretchedness was deepened further when the chaplain came and told her that he could see no hope of a reprieve.

According to the female warder who spent much time with the prisoner, Elizabeth Berry slept badly following the devastating news. She, Miss Clarke, wrote to the governor:

> The prisoner, Elizabeth Berry, passed a restless night. Shortly after six o'clock the following morning while I was reading a portion of Scripture to her she asked me to stop, saying she preferred talking to me – with apparent anguish of mind she said, 'Oh, Miss Clarke, you do not know my mind, I cannot bear the burden of it. I have suffered awful trepidations during the night.'
>
> She commented upon the Clergyman who had visited her the day previously having told her that he did not think there was any hope of her life being spared (here she wept) then further said, 'As

I have been lying here I have been thinking that perhaps after all I might be guilty. I had suffered so much with my head, I cannot account for many things that have happened.'

Over Mrs Berry's first days in the condemned cell she had said she wished to see no one, but as the precious days passed she was glad to have visitors, among them her sister- and brother-in-law, Ann and John Sanderson. It was stated by the *Chronicle* that Mrs Berry wrote urging them 'to visit her in her deep affliction', and that they went to the gaol wherein 'a most sorrowful interview took place'. The *Manchester Evening News,* however, stated that Mrs Sanderson was received 'in anything but a kindly spirit'. If this was so, perhaps it was due to the fact that Mrs Sanderson's testimony at the trial had been so telling. Perhaps Mrs Berry had been hoping for support from her sister-in-law, but had perceived that support to be in short supply.

Another request for a visit went to Mrs Berry's aunt, Sarah Pemberton. While Mrs Berry had been before the magistrates in Oldham, Mrs Pemberton had travelled from Burslem to see her, only to have her niece refuse a meeting. Later, when Mrs Pemberton was in Castleton for the inquest into her sister's death, she received a telegram from Mrs Berry asking her to come and see her. Mrs Pemberton, however, was so distressed by the inquest proceedings that she could not face seeing her niece, and no further meeting between them ever occurred.

Through all the hours spent in her cell at Walton on the Hill, Mrs Berry did not, of course, give up hope of escaping the extreme penalty, and she prayed that the Home Secretary would look benevolently on the petition that was being drawn up by her solicitor, Joseph Whitaker.

As for Mr Whitaker himself, he had an additional, very pressing matter on his mind.

On learning of what had earlier passed at the meeting at the gaol between Mrs Berry and his clerk, he was much dismayed. Notwithstanding that Mrs Berry had given written authorization for him, Whitaker, to take possession of her effects, here she was giving quite different instructions for the disposal of her goods – and she had still not fully reimbursed him for all the costs he had incurred, and was still incurring, on her behalf.

Learning of this very disagreeable state of affairs, it is highly likely that Mr Whitaker instructed his clerk to make no move in the matter.

Walton Gaol, c. 1900.

Following, he wrote to the Guardians of the Oldham workhouse, pointing out that under the law a condemned person's goods were no longer forfeit to the Crown, and that, as the prisoner owed him money, her goods held at the workhouse should be given to him to dispose of. In support of his request, he had Mrs Berry's written authorization.

The Clerk to the Guardians replied that they would make inquiries as to the intentions and desires of the prisoner, and that a senior member of the board would be writing to Mrs Berry to solicit her wishes on the matter. This they did, and consequently wrote to Mr Whitaker with the disappointing and surprising news that Mrs Berry refused his request.

The matter could not rest there, of course, and Mr Whitaker then wrote to the Oldham magistrates, asking to be appointed curator of Mrs Berry's worldly goods, arguing that they, the magistrates, had the power under the Act of Parliament to appoint him. He pointed out that Mrs Berry was a debtor to him in respect of all the work he had done, and in order to reimburse him for money out of pocket she should leave her belongings to him.

On receiving his letter, the magistrates were uncertain as to what to do, and extricated themselves from the quandary by advising Mr Whitaker to make his application to the Home Office. Which he did. Addressing his letter to the Right Honourable Charles Matthews, M.P., Secretary of State, he wrote from his home at 1 St Peter Street, Oldham on 3 March:

Sir,

Regina v Berry

This prisoner Elizabeth Berry who is now in Walton Gaol under sentence of death for poisoning her daughter was represented by myself as her solicitor three days on the Inquest and two days before the magistrates. I instructed Counsel at her request, and when the prisoner was committed to the Assizes the case occupied four days. Two Counsel were engaged, and my costs of course were very large. The prisoner had little money, and I am now a considerable sum out of pocket. The prisoner gave me an authority (a copy of which I enclose) to the Governor of the Oldham Workhouse to hand to me certain articles which he had possession of and belonging to her. He however refuses at present to part with them.

I have this morning made an application to the Magistrates of the Borough of Oldham and they said I had better apply to you and that you would no doubt appoint me administrator. The prisoner has no near relatives, [except] her aunt who is the only one with whom the prisoner is at all intimate and who has handed me her consent to my being appointed an administrator of her effects. I therefore humbly apply to your Lordship to appoint me as such administrator.

I shall be glad to hear from you early, by return if possible, as the estate may be squandered, no one being legally responsible for it.

I am,

Your obedient Servant

Joseph Whitaker.

Prisoner's Solicitor

And, no doubt impatiently, Mr Whitaker then waited.

While Mr Whitaker was pursuing his own interests in the business, the press continued to concern itself with the prisoner's situation as she passed her final days in the condemned cell. The *Manchester Evening News* spoke of her turning increasingly for comfort to her religious faith, saying, 'As an adherent of the Church of England, she is regularly seen by the gaol chaplain, to whose ministrations she seems to pay great attention, while fully realizing her fearful position.' They also reported on some of the visitors Mrs Berry received, among whom were two officers from the Oldham workhouse, Mr Fletcher and Mr Minahan. Having received a request from her to go and see her, the two men set off on Saturday 5 March for Walton Gaol, arriving there shortly after noon. There they were met by the prison matron, who informed them that they would be taken to see the prisoner in her cell, where a male and female warden would be present at all times. Further, they would be permitted to shake hands with the prisoner only after they had shown that their hands were empty, and on no account must they impart any information concerning any goings-on in the outside world that had occurred since the beginning of her incarceration.

The two men were then conducted to Mrs Berry's cell, where she stood waiting. All three were much moved at the reunion, it was said, in particular Mrs Berry, who wept 'scalding tears'. She wore a brown dress and chequered apron, and looked somewhat paler and thinner than when the men had last seen her. Also, she had lost the 'frizette' which had been a characteristic of her appearance, her hair now being combed straight out in front, and made into two long plaits behind, unfastened and hanging loose.

The men were somewhat pleasantly surprised, however, at the cell in which she was housed, it being far more comfortable than they had anticipated. Furnished with a single bed with a coloured counterpane, it had a small table to one side, and in the centre of the room a larger table on which were tracts and papers and a number of books, among them a Bible and prayer book.

When the three had taken seats – Mrs Berry in an armchair on the other side of the bed – she told them that the prison officials had been very kind to her, and that she was feeling considerably better than she had been at the beginning of her incarceration. Indicating a number of letters that lay on the bed, she said she had received a great many, both from friends and from people she didn't know, 'all of them,' she said, 'sympathising with me in my great distress and sore calamity, and from which I have received great comfort. In fact I don't deserve the sympathy that has been shown to me; it has been so great, so real, and so true.'

She went on then to speak of her trial, expressing herself satisfied with all the witnesses with one exception – though not naming the particular person. She also voiced satisfaction with her solicitor's work, saying that no one could have had done more or served her better than Mr Whitaker and his clerk, Mr Robinson. Asked by Mr Fletcher if she had expected the verdict that was returned at the trial, she said not until the Thursday morning, when, on scanning the faces of the jury, she read her fate in their looks. To the surprise of her two visitors, she then brought up the subject of her dead child and, referring to the claims that she had killed her for the small insurance pay-out, said, 'How can people invent such a paltry motive for so great a crime?'

Mr Minahan then asked her whether she held any hope of a reprieve being granted, and she replied, 'Very little. I'm preparing for the worst, and getting ready for the end. I don't say I'm ready at the present moment to go with the executioner to the scaffold, but I can say I have no fear of it.' She added, 'The things of this world are rapidly passing from me, and each friend's face I see for the last time is one more ordeal gone through. I look upon the transition from this world as stepping into a train from which I shall alight very shortly in a far more beautiful place.' As she finished speaking, the prison clock struck two, and she said, 'I listen to the striking of that clock and almost count the hours upon it, and I know, one morning, very shortly, that I shall hear it strike seven for the last time. But I'm not dismayed, and I hope to have sufficient strength to bear it.'

Rising from her chair, she moved to the table and, taking up one of the books, said, 'I feel as Longfellow describes resignation in his beautiful poem of that name.' Opening the book she then commenced to read aloud Longfellow's poem, 'Resignation'.

> There is no flock, however watched and tended,
> But one dead lamb is there!
> There is no fireside, howsoe'er defended,
> But has one vacant chair!

She went on to read to the men the complete poem.

For those unfamiliar with the work I quote it here in full, as I think it is pertinent to her situation in relation to her dead child. Those familiar with it, however, might care to skip to the end.

The poem continues:

The air is full of farewells to the dying,
And mournings for the dead;
The heart of Rachel, for her children crying,
Will not be comforted!

Let us be patient! These severe afflictions
Not from the ground arise,
But oftentimes celestial benedictions
Assume this dark disguise.

We see but dimly through the mists and vapours,
Amid the earthly damps
What seem to us but sad, funereal tapers
May be heaven's distant lamps.

There is no death! What seems so is transition;
This life of mortal breath
Is but a suburb of the life elysian,
Whose portal we call Death.

She is not dead, – the child of our affection, –
But gone unto that school
Where she no longer needs our poor protection,
And Christ himself doth rule.

In that great cloister's stillness and seclusion,
By guardian angels led,
Safe from temptation, safe from sin's pollution,
She lives, whom we call dead.

Day after day we think what she is doing
In those bright realms of air;
Year after year, her tender steps pursuing,
Behold her grown more fair.

Thus do we walk with her, and keep unbroken
The bond which nature gives,
Thinking that our remembrance, though unspoken,
May reach her where she lives.

Not as a child shall we again behold her;
For when with raptures wild
In our embraces we again enfold her,
She will not be a child;

But a fair maiden, in her Father's mansion,
Clothed with celestial grace;
And beautiful with all the soul's expansion
Shall we behold her face.

And though at times impetuous with emotion
And anguish long suppressed,
The swelling heart heaves moaning like the ocean,
That cannot be at rest, –

We will be patient, and assuage the feeling
We may not wholly stay;
By silence sanctifying, not concealing,
The grief that must have way.

There was complete silence as she read, and even the two warders, it was said, were moved by her reading. Putting the book aside she then read extracts from some of the letters she had received, saying afterwards: 'I have much sweet thoughts in these letters, and I remember last Easter Sunday the pleasant day I spent with my friends – and now I know that I shall spend *next* Easter Sunday in a far better place.'

Speaking briefly of her time at the workhouse, she said, 'I was very proud of my position, proud of my ability, but how great the fall.'

She then said that she had given a few close friends each a small present, and that if her visitors would like something of hers she would be pleased to give it to them. The men then were offered a choice among some of her possessions, at which each named a small article that he would like, after which she said she would instruct her solicitor to hand it over to them when he had obtained possession of her belongings.

Mr Fletcher, when he could get a word in, asked her if she had heard of the verdict with regard to the inquest on her mother's death. This caused the warder to raise his hand warningly, however, and the man fell silent. Even so, Mrs Berry replied to his question, saying that she knew of nothing beyond the exhumation of her mother's body, and, clearly blaming the authorities for the proceedings and presenting herself as one wronged, said, 'They weren't even content to let her remains lie in peace, but must needs bring *that* charge against me.'

Conscious of the warden's warning, Mr Fletcher forbore to tell her the inquest's verdict but said, making it clear what the verdict was, 'Mrs Berry, I must tell you candidly, there is no possible hope of a reprieve for you.'

For a moment she was silent, then she said, 'I suppose there are all sorts of rumours current about me, but I am perfectly indifferent to them.'

Said Mr Fletcher, 'I am not at liberty to tell you anything concerning what is said about you.'

From then on the conversation stayed on safer ground. She spoke of the food she ate – 'a strengthening diet, mostly jellies' – and then of the previous visitors she had received, adding that she didn't expect to receive many more in the time left to her, but rather wished to spend her time alone.

At last the two men rose to leave. She shook hands with them, saying, 'Goodbye, and God bless you,' and they left her.

On their way out of the prison they met her solicitor, Mr Whitaker, who had come to pay her a visit.

Joseph Whitaker was later to speak to a journalist from the *Manchester Evening News* of his meeting with Mrs Berry that day. His visit had not been arranged, he said, but he had called in the hope of seeing her, and after receiving word that she would like to see him was conducted to her cell. There she rose from her seat and shook hands warmly with him, 'at first so overcome with emotion', he said, 'that she seemed almost unable to speak'.

She soon regained her composure, however, and as they talked she spoke of the many letters she had received, and read some of them aloud to him 'in a most affecting way'. Afterwards she spoke of her child, Edith, and said, 'Oh, Mr Whitaker, do you know that beautiful poem by Longfellow, "Resignation"? That expresses my feelings as regards poor Edith.' With that, just as she had done an hour before, she took the book of Longfellow's poems from the table, and read aloud the poem from beginning to end. She read it, Mr Whitaker said, 'with an amount of feeling that was awe-inspiring'. Afterwards she drew his attention to the line: 'There is no death; what seems so is transition,' saying that she wished to have those words engraved on Edith's gravestone. She appeared, he said, quite resigned to her fate. 'I have little to live for,' she said to him. 'Those whom I loved have already gone. I look upon death now as a five minutes' journey by train, and when I get out of the train at the other station the first one to meet me on the platform will be my daughter Edith.'

We do not know, but it is very likely that during Mr Whitaker's meeting with her that day he spoke on the subject of her debt to him. It would not have been an easy matter to broach, but time was running out. The visit was, by his own decision, the last he would make, so he did not foresee another such face-to-face opportunity. It is possible that she initiated the subject. Only hours earlier she had offered to Mr Fletcher and Mr Minahan each a keepsake, which, she said, they might receive as soon as Mr Whitaker could obtain possession of her belongings – so it is not unlikely that she should have brought up the subject with Mr Whitaker while she had the opportunity. And, of course, he would not have been pleased to hear that she had already embarked on the business of giving her possessions away. What might have passed between them on the matter, however, we do not know.

It was probably a rather difficult two hours for the solicitor, but at last came the time for his departure. Mrs Berry thanked him for his endeavours on her behalf, and they said their last goodbyes. They were never to meet again.

Following Mr Whitaker's leaving, Mrs Berry was visited by her brother-in-law John Sanderson, who had been waiting for the solicitor to leave. What transpired during his meeting with her is not recorded. Perhaps she regaled him also with a moving reading of 'Resignation'. If so, it would be the third time that day that the warders who were present in her cell were so entertained.

So very conscious of the little time left before her, Mrs Berry had requested to be allowed to petition the Home Secretary for clemency. Her request was granted, and on 7 March she took up pen and ink to complete the official petition form. Beneath the penned entries inserted of her *Name, Sentence, Date appointed for Execution*, etc., is the printed text:

To the Right Honourable Her Majesty's Principal Secretary of State for the Home Department.

The Petition of the above named prisoner

HUMBLY SHEWETH –

[after which she wrote, her grammatical errors here intact]:

– that the allegations by the prosecution that my child Edith Annie Berry died by poison is in my opinion insufficient.

Other relatives of mine have died from tuberculosis and their illnesses have generally commenced very suddenly. My boy Harold died of tuberculosis and his illness commenced very suddenly.

That no poison was administered to my knowledge. The circumstantial evidence of the prosecution even if the child did die of poison is contradictory. That Beatrice Hall one of the witnesses was in the sitting room on the Saturday morning from 9.30 until the child was taken to bed in the afternoon. Therefore the evidence of Ann Dillon is incorrect as to seeing me in the surgery at 10.30. I done all I could for my child that would lead to her recovery. The medicines I gave her was those prescribed by Dr Patterson. I had only just recovered myself from a severe illness and Dr Patterson can testify that during that illness, that is from the 13th to the 18th of December 1886, I was insane. The anxiety of my child's illness on the 2nd of January 1887 again affected my head. And I was very ill during that night.

I humbly beg you will take these points into consideration and as it is Her Majesty's Jubilee Year I earnestly pray that she will graciously look upon me in my distress.

I am your humble servant,

Elizabeth Berry

The first page of Elizabeth Berry's petition to the Home Secretary.

On the same day, the prison matron wrote to inform the governor: 'Sir, I beg to report that Elizabeth Berry states she is not pregnant.'

There had been a rumour going round that Mrs Berry was pregnant. This, if true, would have delayed her execution until after the infant's birth, just as pregnancy had delayed the trial of poisoner Mary Ann Cotton in 1873. In the case of Elizabeth Berry, however, the rumours were soon scotched, the matron being informed by one of Mrs Berry's warders: 'Madam, I beg to state that Elizabeth Berry's monthly courses were on while down at the Assize Court.'

Notwithstanding any words that Mr Whitaker and Mrs Berry might have exchanged on the subject of his fees, it was soon to be made known that she had become dead set against him selling off her goods and keeping the proceeds – this in spite of her earlier expressions of appreciation of his work on her behalf. On 7 March, shortly after writing her petition to the Home Secretary, she wrote to Mr J. Mellor, Clerk to the Board of Guardians of the workhouse, making clear her wishes. She wrote:

Dear Sir,

I presume you are aware of the terrible doom that awaits me, and in the short time that is left to me there are several matters I wish to arrange. You will know that my clothing, together with other articles, are still at the workhouse. These things Mr Whitaker wishes me to give to him, on the plea that he has not been sufficiently paid for my defence. Mr Whitaker has received from me £64; in addition to this sum he has my watch and chain, which are valued at £14. I mention this that you may understand what I shall speak of presently – that is, the disposal of the articles which are at the workhouse. I have left every article that belongs to me to Mr George H. Robinson, to dispose of according to my instructions. He has promised to erect a stone over the grave of my darling. And for which I feel exceedingly grateful; and I appeal to you, as a guardian, to put a request before the board, and that is, that no one be allowed to remove a single article belonging to me from the workhouse except Mr G.H. Robinson.

And a word with regard to myself. I am very sad, but at peace and in full submission to God. None but He knows what I have suffered through death. None but He could still my agony under this crushing blow. I think I must have loved my dear ones amiss, since God, either in His mercy or His jealously, has removed them.

Believing that this request will receive your kind consideration, I am,

Yours sincerely,

E. Berry.

Two days later Mrs Berry wrote also to the prison governor stating that she wanted Mr George Robinson, 'who has promised to erect a stone over my child's grave', to be the administrator of her property, and 'not Joseph Whitaker'. Of Mr Whitaker she wrote:

> …I have not had a bill of costs from him. Mr Whitaker speaks of the sale of my clothing &c as bringing a large sum at present on account of the public interest in this case, which is to my mind to say the least of the matter very revolting.
>
> I have no creditors.

The matter, which was classed as 'pressing', proceeded swiftly. Mr Robinson received a series of telegrams from the Home Office asking him to take on the office of administrator of the convict's effects, and he wrote back at once, accepting, with a request for directions as to 'the mode' in which he should carry out the administration. He believed the property was small, he said. He ended his letter saying: 'I believe there are no debts, unless Mrs Berry's solicitor has a claim for costs.'

There, for the time being, the matter rested.

As we have seen, in her letter to the Oldham Board of Guardians, Elizabeth Berry made reference in her closing words to the deaths of those nearest and dearest to her, writing of those deaths: 'None but He knows what I have suffered through death. None but He could still my agony under this crushing blow. I think I must have loved my dear ones amiss, since God, either in His mercy or His jealousy, has removed them.'

Her articulate letter was published in the papers for all the world to see, and there must undoubtedly have been many who, on reading it, were moved by her seductive words, her allusions to God having taken from her those 'dear ones' whom, she, said, she 'must have loved amiss'. And among those readers perhaps there were some who were moved to pity, accepting her presentation of herself as a devoted and loving mother, wife and daughter. And while that may have been so, it is certain that there were many more who regarded her plaintive words as just another bogus display of innocence and grief.

23

Final Days

Notwithstanding Mr Whitaker's frustration and disappointment with regard to his claim to his not having been sufficiently reimbursed for his work, he nevertheless continued with his efforts on Elizabeth Berry's behalf. Among those efforts were those in the preparation of the petition to save her life. And he soon had it complete. However, although he had told her that it was 'extensively signed by gentlemen of position in the town', he had not remarked on the general belief that it was unlikely to meet with any success. The petition in question is preserved in the Home Office file on the case. It is a large document, of parchment, with twenty-seven signatories pleading for clemency, prominent among them Dr John Kershaw.

The fact is that while the petition was being signed by those 'gentlemen of position' it was stated in the papers that no steps had been taken by any members of the public with regard to getting up any similar petition. Views on Mrs Berry's case had been canvassed, revealing a strong feeling that there should be no interfering in the capital sentence. There was no question in the minds of the public at large but that she fully deserved the punishment that the law had ordained. And if there had been some who for a time thought that this attractive little woman was incapable of the unspeakable cruelty of which she had been convicted, they would have had second thoughts on reading of the inquest into the death of her mother. Faced with the evidence of her guilt in that other cold and calculating murder, it would hardly be surprising if any lingering feelings of doubt and sympathy evaporated.

Notwithstanding, Mr Whitaker sent the petition off to the Home Secretary on the 9 March and received an acknowledgement from Whitehall the very next day, saying that the application would be 'fully considered'.

There were no reasonable grounds presented on which Mrs Berry's death sentence was likely to be commuted, and she must have been aware of this. Had she been found to have been insane at the time of the murder of her daughter then she would not have been given a death sentence, and it was possibly with this in mind that she made the oblique reference to insanity in her petition, and also touched on it far more directly when speaking to the wardress, Miss Clarke, in her cell: 'As I have been lying here I have been thinking that perhaps after all I might be guilty. I had suffered so much with my head, I cannot account for many things that have happened.'

Whatever questions might have been raised about her sanity, however, she nevertheless continued to protest her innocence, declaring to more than one of her visitors that if her daughter had been poisoned it had not been at *her* hands, but by the medicine administered by the doctors.

And it was Dr Patterson, of course, who came in for her greatest opprobrium.

Although she had once made it very clear that she had never given any creosote mixture to her sick child, she later changed her story. A memorandum from one of the prisoner's wardresses on 4 March stated:

After receiving a letter from Mr Robinson the prisoner said, Yes, if I had studied myself and not others, I should not be here now. It was to save Dr Patterson [that] I told a lie. When I was asked if I gave [my child] a dose of the creosote I said 'No,' but God knows I had.

So she now blamed Dr Patterson for her daughter's death. And she still had not finished with him, as was made clear during a meeting with another of her visitors.

This visitor, whom Mrs Berry received in her cell, and quite unexpectedly, was one Joseph Emmett, of Hollinwood. Speaking to the *Chronicle* of his visit, he said he had known Mrs Berry as Lizzie Welch when, in her teens, she had worked near him at a local mill. He spoke of her there 'as a very quiet person who did her best to isolate herself from the other workpeople employed near her', adding, 'She was at times gay and giddy, but at others just the reverse, and her temper, even in those younger days, could never be depended upon.' He had met her again, he said, by chance, in 1884, when returning from Blackpool and meeting her and her daughter Edith on a train – both, he recalled, looking well and happy. Now, two and a half years later, reading about her in the newspapers, he had set off for Walton Gaol, hoping for a meeting. There, following a long wait after his arrival, he was given permission to see her, with the official conducting him giving him the interesting instruction: 'Follow me, and don't let's have any nonsense with her; we've had quite sufficient.'

Escorted to her cell, he said he was warmly received, but was amazed at the change in her, finding her 'aged terribly', and in her prison garb looking 'the picture of misery'. As they spoke they recalled happier times, he said, but when their conversation turned to her present situation her composure faltered. She didn't respond when he mentioned her mother, and when he spoke of her trial she complained that the judge had been against her. As for the crime of which she had been convicted, she told him that she had had no reason to poison her child, having had some £70 in the bank at the time.

Rising after an hour to take his leave, he asked her if there was anything he could do for her. She replied that he might put some flowers on Edith's grave.

Mr Emmett was to give his story not only to the *Chronicle*, but also to the *Oldham Evening Express*, and to that paper he told a little more. Under the heading *The Oldham Poisoning Case*, and the sub-heading *A Startling Assertion*, it told of his visit to see the prisoner in the condemned cell and of his first sight of her: 'Mrs Berry was arrayed in an uncomfortable-looking prison dress, several sizes too large,' he said, 'and her hair, instead of the usual curly appearance, was quite limp and straight.' At one point in their conversation, he said, she spoke of the petition whereby Mr Whitaker was seeking to obtain a reprieve for her, at which he had 'advised her not to build up her hopes too much on this account'. She said she did not do so. The *Express* article further reported:

> …Presently Mrs Berry turned the conversation to the trial at Liverpool Assizes, and proceeded to discuss the evidence, together with several incidents occurring there. She said she noticed the judge did not

favour her from the beginning, though she seemed inclined to think that he should have done so. 'But,' said her visitor, 'Mr Cottingham did his very best on your behalf,' to which Mrs Berry did not answer. She severely criticised the evidence of Dr Patterson, and…early impressed upon him [Emmett] that she was quite innocent of the crime of which she had been found guilty. In explanation of this assertion she said, 'If the dear child has been poisoned at all, the poison was given by me as medicine by Dr Patterson's orders.' She further told her visitor, whilst alluding to Dr Patterson, that that gentleman's conduct and actions were not in the slightest such as to lead anyone to suppose that he thought the child seriously ill. 'What do you think?' she said to Mr Emmett, 'On one of the nights when the child was ill, he asked me if I would go to the theatre with him.'

Not content with criticizing Dr Patterson's medical expertise, she was now calling into question his morals. This, of course, was a red rag to a bull, and the doctor immediately wrote to the paper's editor:

Sir, – The trial of Madame Berry has been no very easy matter for me. For a medical man to make a statement to the authorities that involved a charge of murder against a mother, and a woman whose character, as far as known here, was good up to that time, was a proceeding requiring prudence and caution. In this lengthened trial one thing always sustained me. It was this – with the nurses at the Workhouse I have always been on terms of friendship, but never on terms of familiarity with any of them. In my dealings with Madame Berry, whom I soon found to be untruthful and a person of low morals, I was especially guarded and cautious. I knew during the trial that, whether or not I had acted with prudence and judgement in a matter of great difficulty, no reflection could be cast on my personal relations with this woman, and no attempt or breath of suggestion was ever made of that sort.

Since the trial at Liverpool, clergymen, solicitors and others have called at my house to congratulate me on my part of the trans-action. They all spoke to me in the same strain as did Father Brindle when he said to me, "I have read the whole of this case, and have sympathised with you in your difficult position, but you have come out of it with honour and credit." Strange to say, in the vanity of my heart I had come to almost the same conclusion till I read the paragraph which you allowed to appear in your issue of yesterday, and which caused me more annoyance than all the other incidents of this trial put together. It is as follows: "What do you think," said the convict, "on one of the nights on which the child was ill Dr Patterson asked me to go to the theatre with him."

I suppose if any of us, still unrepentant, had in our ears the ring of the hammer in the erection of our scaffold, and felt the rope tightening round our neck, we should be driven to strange excuses and strange devices. I will, therefore, not speak with harshness of the convict. To those who know my habits I do not need to give the statement a contradiction. They know that I am not a frequenter of the theatre, and none of them has ever seen me with a woman of improper or even doubtful character, either in the theatre or in any place else. To those who do not know me I will show the falsity of the statement by its impossibility. The girl was ill on the nights of Saturday, Sunday, and Monday. On Saturday night I visited her at 10.30, rather too late, I think, to go to the theatre. On Sunday night, I believe, the theatre is not open. On Monday and Monday night the girl was dying, and, as I believed, from the deed of her mother, and I was not likely to ask the honour of taking to the theatre a woman whom I believed to be a murderess. Besides, other people were in the sickroom, Miss Anderson in the morning and Mrs Sanderson at night.

I do not ask you for an apology for the publicity of this gross untruth. That, I suppose, would be too much to expect. But I do ask you to publish this statement, for I believe that even this convict, to whose lips truth is a stranger, would not have made this statement had she known it would have appeared in print.

Yours, &c.,

T. Patterson.

Beneath Dr Patterson's letter comes from the editor: 'We regret that our reporter, in his anxiety to supply graphic and accurate information, should have mentioned Dr Patterson's name.'

It was not only to Mr Emmett that Elizabeth Berry traduced Dr Patterson.

Earlier in this book (p. 54) I quoted from a letter from Mrs Berry to Dr Kershaw. A very long letter, it was written on 10 March from her cell, in an attempt, as she put it, to give 'a truer account' of the circumstances surrounding Edith's fatal illness. Dr Kershaw, in a last bid to save her, sent it at once to the Home Office, where a clerk made a copy, after which the original was returned to the doctor, at his request.

The copy of the letter has several textual errors of grammar, punctuation and omission, and there is no way of knowing whether such errors were made by Mrs Berry or by the clerk who was given the task of copying the letter out. Whatever the fact, I have added some punctuation here and there and the occasional missing word and upper-case letter where I judged it helpful for clarity.

The letter is a most interesting document. In it, as seen previously, she wrote of her first days at the workhouse, and of her early conflicts with Dr Patterson. And one thing that is clear from the letter's content is that she blamed Dr Patterson for everything, including her downfall. In her letter she is, of course, always in the right, always the victim, always presenting herself as the most caring and considerate of mothers, with her sick daughter's wellbeing always to the fore.

Of the events surrounding Edith's falling sick, she writes:

...All went well until Jan 1st. On Friday 31 Dec I had a confinement case. My patient was very ill when she came, she having been in pain all night Thursday at the Town Hall. I delivered her at 10 a.m. but she sank and died at 4.50. I sent for Dr Patterson at 3 p.m. but he did not come until 6.30. Of course the patient was dead.

On Jan 1st I came down about 8 a.m., had breakfast, went into the surgery, wrote out my reports for Governor's office, took the reports into the kitchen and left them on the table for Ben to take up to the office. [I] went through the wards. On coming to my bedroom I looked in to see if the children were up, saw them leave the room...I went on through the wards, came down, went into the sitting room. The children were sat at the table. Edith put her hand on her breast and said, I do feel sick, and vomited. I stayed with her for some time, called Alice Allcroft to bring some water and powders, I having the child on my lap. When I saw her vomit blood [I] sent Alice Allcroft to the lodge for ice which I gave her to suck. When Dr Patterson came [I] told him how she had begun to be ill and showed him vomit which I said I thought came from lungs. He said it might be from lungs but would not say. He went into surgery and mixed a bottle which he said contained iron and bark. While we were in the surgery he said, I should think your child has never been a very strong child. I said, No. He answered, No, she is altogether too fair and too fragile. I felt very sad when he said this. Then he said, Now do not be afraid, children are soon down and soon up again.

We left the surgery and went through the wards, then returned to the surgery [and] dispensed for House and Hospital. He left the building and I returned to my child and gave her a dose of the medicine and she lay very still for a little time but as soon as she moved she was sick and vomited the medicine, which was black. I removed her to my bedroom and when [I] found she was no better again sent for Dr that evening. He came and said, Do not give her any more of [the] iron mixture and I will mix something else for her as I go downstairs. I did not go down, thinking he would leave it in the surgery or send it up but he did not do so. On Sunday morning he asked me to go the surgery with him. While we were in the surgery he said, Now if we can give the stomach perfect rest for three or four days we shall have some hope.

She goes on to write of Dr Patterson making the medicine of the creosote and bicarbonate of soda, criticizing his actions and his way of making the mixture:

…I was not surprised at the manner in which Dr Patterson made the mixture because I have never seen him use a minim measure. I gave her a dose, a desert spoonful. After taking it I gave her an orange with sugar, this was about 2 p.m. on the Sunday. After I went upstairs after tea I gave her another dose and again gave her orange and sugar. After this the vomiting began worse and I let her vomit in towels. I sent for him at 6.30, [and then] sent again to see if he had come. I was almost distracted to see her and could not stop the vomiting. When Dr Patterson did come I said, Dr Patterson, save my child if possible for she is all I have. He appeared struck at the symptoms and said, Did you give her the medicine I mixed today? and I said, Yes, I gave it her twice. I said, Will you bring someone else? He said, Yes, now you keep calm while I come back with Dr Robertson.

Before he left the room I gave him three towels which were filled with vomit and I said, Will you take these and examine them for I cannot understand this vomit. When he returned with Dr Robertson I told them how much worse she had been that evening. As they were leaving the room I said to Dr Patterson, Shall I pay this gentleman his fee now? thinking he was a physician. He said, Oh no, not now. He went towards the window sill where the medicine bottles were and [said], Which is the bottle I mixed today? and taking up the one he had mixed that day, put it in his pocket. Dr Robertson had left the room when he done this…During Sunday night I remained up with her until 1 a.m. when I was called away to attend a confinement case, and was absent from the room until 3.30 a.m. At that time my patient was confined and when I [had] seen her safe I returned to my child. When Dr Patterson paid his visit on Monday morning I asked him what was Dr Robertson's opinion of my child and he said he and Dr Robertson could not agree upon the matter. When he paid a second visit in the evening I told him I had given her champagne. He said you ought not to have done so.

Her letter ending, she blames Patterson to the last:

…I acted entirely under his direction as to the treatment. Had he been as anxious about her life as I was he would have paid greater attention to her. Dr, I put full trust in him and poison never dawned upon [me] not even when I was told that during my absence on Jan 6 a second post-mortem had been held. Dr Patterson has acted as a traitor to me in every sense of the word. He made my life very unhappy during the greater part of my time at the Workhouse. Often and often have I felt terrified when I have heard his steps approach the place. The vile books he has brought me and his manner to me

– in a word had I consented to be his mistress I should not be where I am today. I have proof of this.

>   I am Sir,
>   Yours sincerely,
>   Elizabeth Berry

In a scenario rich with invention Mrs Berry sets out to destroy Dr Patterson's reputation, both professionally and socially, and in doing so attempts to boost her claim of total innocence in the matter of her daughter's death. In an 'incident' that she had never reported before, she has him mixing a medicine for her child and then later, after the child has taken the medicine and is found to be close to death, surreptitiously removing the bottle of medicine from the scene: '...[he] put it in his pocket. Dr Robertson had left the room when he done this...' In all, according to Mrs Berry, she was in her extreme situation solely as a result of his incompetence, his dishonesty and his lust for her as a woman.

By presenting to Dr Kershaw her 'truer account' of the circumstances surrounding Edith's terrible death, she hoped, of course, that he would use her letter in a bid to have her sentence commuted. And, whether he believed her or not, it appears that he did what he could, and forwarded her letter to the Home Office. What he wrote to the Home Secretary in support of Mrs Berry's 'truer account', we do not know, as his letter has not been preserved.

Whatever the Home Secretary's response to Dr Kershaw's approach, Mrs Berry's situation was not influenced in any way. As noted, her letter was copied, and immediately returned to the doctor. The Home Secretary was of course very familiar with the case, and he would have been likely to have concurred with Dr Patterson when writing that he was dealing with a woman, a convicted murderess 'to whose lips truth is a stranger'.

Mrs Berry's painstaking letter to Dr Kershaw, with all its lies and contradictions, was never made public, and so, likewise, Dr Patterson never became aware of her continuing scurrilous accusations.

And it was Dr Patterson who had the last word.

Today, as we are often reminded, the nation is divided on the matter of the death penalty, and so it has been for years. In those March days of 1887 there were those who, opposed to the extreme punishment, hoped that the Home Secretary would be moved to recommend a reprieve for the condemned woman.

One such was the editor of a journal called the *British and Colonial Druggist*, who, hoping to change a few minds in the prisoner's favour, wrote an article that was republished in the *Oldham Standard*. Under the title THE VERDICT QUESTIONED, the writer expressed deep concern at the trial and its outcome. He contended that there had been a miscarriage in the judicial system, saying that the coroner's inquest with a verdict of guilty should have been trumped by the magistrates, who had considered the evidence insufficient to warrant sending the prisoner for trial. Mrs Berry, therefore, he said, should have been set at liberty, instead of which, she had been found guilty of murder and condemned to death.

His main criticism, however, was with the evidence brought to convict her, saying that what stamped the case as 'eminently unsatisfactory' in its circumstances and in its result, was 'the vague, inexact, and conflicting character of the scientific evidence produced'. With no motive found, he said, it all came down to the jury's decision to accept the scientific evidence presented. And in this he strongly criticized the three doctors, Patterson, Robertson and Harris, focusing on Dr Patterson for particular calumny. No evidence had proved that the child had been poisoned with sulphuric acid, he maintained, and the testimony positing such was 'so transparently vague and conflicting that it [was] far from easy…to understand how a body of intelligent men could allow it to weigh with them in a matter of life or death'.

'Altogether we are at a loss to understand the grounds of the verdict,' the piece concluded. 'There may be a strong presumption of guilt against the woman, but presumption should not be sufficient in a matter of life and death.'

The article raised several questions, among them questions on Dr Patterson's part in the affair. The good doctor, however, as will have been noticed, was not one to take criticism lying down, and having read the article he took up his pen and wrote to the *Standard*'s editor. In his letter he set out the anatomy of the murder in such a clear and direct way that one would be hard pressed to challenge any part of it. His informative letter was printed in the edition of Saturday 12 March. In it – and not missing the chance to show his contempt for the magistrates who had cleared Mrs Berry at the police court – he wrote:

Sir: – In inserting a long quotation from the *British and Colonial Druggist*, a contemporary omitted to make one important statement, viz., that this paper is in no sense of the word a medical journal; that it concerns itself, not with diseases, but with the nature, supply and demand, market price, &c., of drugs; and that the opinion can be of no value from a professional point of view. Now, was the medical evidence in the above case conclusive?

1. It convinced the coroner's jury.

2. We have no evidence that the medical testimony did not convince the four amateurs who sat on the borough bench, led by their noses by Mr Hesketh Booth, their clerk.

3. It convinced the jury at Liverpool, where the case was properly thrashed out.

4. It convinced the medical men of Oldham, for of several of them solicited to give evidence, none of them would do so.

5. It convinced all the medical men of eminence in Manchester, for of all the men in Manchester who have special knowledge of this kind of work (Dr Collingworth and others) not one would take a fee for the defence.

6. It convinced the three doctors from Manchester for the defence. These gentlemen went to Liverpool; they were present during the four days of the trial; they were prepared to give evidence, but on the last day not one of them would go into the box for the defence.

7. It must have convinced Mr Cottingham, who (after the exhibition made by Mr Thompson, the chemist, who went as a witness for the defence, but admitted the case for the Crown), threw up the sponge on the medical side of the case.

I will briefly recapitulate the medical aspects of the case: – On Saturday morning, January 1st, the girl is in perfect health. She is found alone with the prisoner in the surgery by Dillon, who leaves the pair alone there. Five minutes later the deceased is in the next room vomiting urgently; the bloody vomiting continues for thirty hours, with great pain over the stomach, and thirst. In other words, the girl had inflammation of the stomach coming on violently in five minutes from perfect health, and in five minutes after being alone with the prisoner in the surgery. In the surgery, at the disposal of the prisoner, were substances that would produce the above symptoms. The jury found that these early symptoms were due to poisoning, and that the prisoner had administered the poison to the girl in the surgery on that Saturday morning. I may add, from a circumstance that has come to my knowledge latterly, that I know the bottle out of which the girl was poisoned that morning. All this matter vomited during that day went down the sink, except for a small portion which fell on the carpet, which the prisoner, with good judgement, ordered to be washed twice.

On Sunday the girl was poisoned a second time, under the following circumstances: – She had a good night on Saturday. On Sunday morning she was much better; the vomiting had almost ceased, and I told the prisoner her daughter would get well. Beatrice Hall read to her during the Sunday. She says the deceased was nearly well. Miss Anderson, a nurse at the imbecile wards, stayed for an hour and a half, going away at twenty past three in the afternoon. During that hour and a half the deceased had been sick but once; she looked well, and was comfortable; she was not purged. She complained of no pain in any part; her lips were not inflamed or blistered. At 3.30 Knight came into the room, sent for by the deceased. She put down the blind, lighted the gas, and had one sentence of conversation. The deceased said, "I would be better but for the vomiting." Then the prisoner came into the room, and ordered Knight out of it. She was then prepared to do the deed a second time. The prisoner is now alone with the deceased for fifty minutes, at the end of which, at 5.20, Miss Evett knocks at the bedroom door, goes in, and sits by the bed. During that fifty minutes, in which the prisoner and the deceased are *alone* in that room, there is a complete transformation. A strong corrosive poison is administered to the girl as she lies in her sick bed, which marks the time and method of its administration by burning the lips, and by other tokens given in evidence by Miss Evett. She finds the girl in great pain, she is every moment vomiting bloody matter, she cries for a poultice to relieve her belly, she begs to be placed on the chamber-pot, strains and cries, and evacuates blood. The prisoner, seeing the marks of her guilt on the mouth of her child, takes the initiative, and says, "See, Miss Evett, what the orange has done to Edith's mouth."

Later, Dr Robertson and myself note the above violent symptoms, the blistering of the lips, of a kind impossible in disease; the inside of the mouth painted white (from coagulation of albumen, as in boiling an egg), a state of things never due to disease, and always due to a corrosive; and on post-mortem we note the gullet corroded. The gullet had arrested for a moment the passage down of this blazing, red-hot draught, but the fiend pressed it down her child's throat. The jury at Liverpool found that in that fifty minutes the girl had been again poisoned, with this time a strong corrosive, and that the prisoner, who was alone with her, was the person who did it. And all the facts given in evidence against the prisoner, her attempts to insure the girl for £100, her wholesale lies for excuses, went in one direction, and that against the prisoner.

Talk of a petition to reprieve her, a woman who in twelve short months for greed of money, slew by poison her mother and her child. Who in Oldham will sign it, except it be her solicitor and Mr Hesketh Booth, the adviser of the magistrates who would not commit, and who are now in the hole which their lack of intelligence and comprehension digged [sic] for them?

With regard to the particular corrosive employed, we say probably sulphuric acid. We never said positively sulphuric acid, but not unlikely at all oxalic acid, or hydrochloric acid, or some other corrosive. We find a girl with her head cut clean off, and surely it is too much to ask the doctors to swear whether the weapon employed was a butcher's knife, or a carving knife, or a razor, or what other sharp instrument. The fact that the girl died of a corrosive is beyond a doubt to those that saw her. It has been established beyond a doubt in the eyes even of the defence. It is the exception to find a corrosive acid by analysis if the patient has lived for a short time, if there is violent vomiting and purging, and if, as in this case, the thirsty patient has swilled stomach and bowels cleaned out with frequent and copious draughts. I say, therefore, if a reprieve be sought for, let it be on fair and square grounds, not on any alleged weakness of the medical evidence, the strength of which the defence have admitted, nor on the pretext that the prisoner did not commit the crimes of Saturday morning and Sunday afternoon, for the jury at Liverpool, without a moment's hesitation, found that she did.

T. Patterson.

P.S. – Dr Stevenson, of Guy's Hospital, the highest authority in the kingdom on these matters, writes to me to say that from reading the evidence he came to the conclusion that the poison of Sunday was oxalic or sulphuric acid.

Dr Patterson's letter would have found great support among the public at large, and might well have altered the feelings of some of those who had supported the petition for clemency. Here, at last, for everyone to see, was a brilliantly judged, step-by-step account of how Mrs Berry had murdered her child. And not only did it show that the verdict had been a just one, but in doing so delivered a serious blow to any chance that she might have had of being granted a last-minute reprieve.

As noted above, Dr Patterson's letter was published on 12 March, and the day previously it was reported that further statements in connection with the case – statements that had not been put before the jury at the trial – were laid before the Home Secretary. It was not announced what was the nature of those statements, but it is possible that they included the letter to Dr Kershaw, the memorandum from Mrs Berry's female warden, and Mrs Berry's petition. What is very likely is that they also included official information on the inquest into Mary Ann Finley's death. Taken together, the Home Secretary would have been presented with precious little in any way favourable to the situation of the condemned woman.

24

Strange Reunion – After the Mazy Dance

While the Home Office considered the situation, preparations for Elizabeth Berry's execution continued. All had to be ready for the morning of Monday 14 March.

There had never before been an execution at Walton Gaol. Previously, the execution of condemned prisoners held at Walton had been carried out at Kirkdale Gaol, but following an Act of Parliament in 1886 this arrangement was discontinued. Executions from then on, it was decreed, would be carried out at Walton, which meant that if all went as scheduled, Elizabeth Berry would be the first felon to be executed there.

Following announcement of the proposed proceedings – not happily accepted by the local community – arrangements were put in place for the hanging. Public executions had ceased in 1868, and all those subsequent would be witnessed only by a limited number of invited persons. It was decided that executions at Walton would take place in an outbuilding known as the Coach House, a kind of large shed which had been used to accommodate the prison vans. The whole thing, it was claimed by the authorities, would be an improvement on the scaffold at Kirkdale. Not only would it be 'more in accordance with modern refinement', but the condemned woman would not have to undergo the testing operation of having to mount steps in order to get up onto the scaffold.

The initial task of the convicts who were given the job of building the structure was to dig the 'well' or 'pit', into which the body would fall, and over which the scaffold proper would be erected. Working all day, the men set about digging the ten-foot deep pit, after which bricklayers were brought in to brick and plaster its sides. Once the bricking and plastering was complete, the joiners came to set about their labours. Mrs Berry, hearing the sound of their hammering, inquired of her attendant what the noise was. With consideration for her feelings, she was told: 'Oh, they're only building outside.' Word of this being reported, it was decided to move the prisoner to a cell at the other end of the females' wing until the work was finished.

And there Mrs Berry waited, continuing to hope for a last-minute reprieve. And it was not considered impossible by some that such might yet be forthcoming – perhaps as a special act of clemency in that year of the Queen's Jubilee, for which Mrs Berry herself had pleaded. But it was not to be. On Saturday the 12th, the day that saw the publication of Dr Patterson's calendar of the child's murder, Mrs Berry's last hope vanished. She was informed that the Home Secretary did not see fit to interfere in the capital sentence.

At last everything was ready for the grim business. The gallows were now complete, their efficiency tested to the satisfaction of the visiting justices, and a room made ready for the visit of the executioner. He, James Berry (no relation to the condemned woman) would be travelling from his home in Horton, Bradford. He had been working as hangman since 1884, and would continue in his work till 1891. He had made a contribution to the ghastly practice by refining the 'long drop', originally developed by former hangman William Marwood, using a method by which the weight and height of the condemned prisoner more or less determined the length of rope required, all in an effort to ensure that the felon died quickly, and did not hang there dying slowly from strangulation.

Writing later in his autobiography, Berry said that he rather dreaded the event awaiting him at Walton. Of all the 131 persons that he hanged in his time, only five were women. 'I never liked to hang a woman,' he said. 'It always made me shiver like a leaf, but it was sometimes a consolation in those days to believe that I was carrying out the last dread sentence of the law on one who was not worthy to be allowed to live.'

It was soon after his arrival at the gaol on the Sunday that a rather remarkable occurrence took place. He was received by the governor, Mr Anderson, who said to him, 'I didn't know you were going to hang an old flame, Berry.'

James Berry, hangman.

'What do you mean?' Berry asked. He thought the governor's words were some sort of joke on account of his having the same name as the condemned woman.

The governor replied, 'She says she knows you very well. You'd better go and look at her tonight. I'll make the necessary arrangements.'

Following completion of the work on the scaffold, Mrs Berry had been returned to her former cell, and it was there that James Berry came later and peered through the narrow observation window in the door to look at her. He recognized her at once, recalling how, just the year before, he had met her in a crowded ballroom at a police ball in Manchester, when she had approached him and invited him to dance with her. So, he said, he had trodden with her 'the mazy dance'. He remembered her as 'a young woman of charm and vivacity', who had chatted gaily to him, telling him about herself and her work as a nurse at the Oldham Hospital. After another dance or two and some refreshment they had discovered that they would be travelling home in the same direction, and as a result she had ridden with him in his cab to the station, and then travelled with him for part of his train journey home.

Commenting later on the episode, James Berry said, 'The story goes to show something of the romance in my life.'

That Sunday night the prison chaplain, the Rev. David Morris, went to the condemned woman's cell and remained with her almost till dawn. She slept little, he later said, her slumber much broken, sleeping only fitfully and spending much of the night in prayer. With Monday's icy dawn a heavy hailstorm passed over the city, accompanied by lightning and thunder. This was followed by a snowfall, which would continue till shortly before the hour of the execution.

The executioner was early at Mrs Berry's cell. When the door was unlocked and opened she looked up and saw him. James Berry wished her good morning and she came forward, holding out her hand.

'Good morning, Mr Berry,' she said. 'You and I have met before.'

'Where was that now?' he asked, pretending to have forgotten.

'Oh,' she said, 'at the ball in Manchester, given by the police. Surely you haven't forgotten.'

'Oh, yes, I remember,' he said. 'It's a long time ago, and I didn't realize that I was to officiate at the execution of a friend of mine.'

'No, I suppose you didn't.'

'Well, I'm very sorry to have to do it.'

She gave a little toss of her head and said, 'You've no doubt heard a lot of dreadful things about me, but it isn't all true what people say about one.'

'Well, I've heard a great deal about you,' he said. 'But you must pull yourself together and die bravely.'

'Oh, I'll go bravely enough,' she said, with a shudder. 'You needn't be a bit afraid of me. You don't suppose I'd want to give you any trouble, do you?'

'I *hope* you won't give me any trouble.'

'You'll be easy with me, won't you?' she said. 'You won't give me any pain. You'll be gentle with an old friend, won't you?'

'I shan't prolong your life a single minute,' he said.

He asked her then whether she had made her peace with God, and urged her to make the most of what time remained to her. After that, he left her side.

Outside the prison the snow lay thickly on the ground and the wind was biting. Perhaps due to the weather, or to the relative inaccessibility of the gaol, a smaller number of spectators than anticipated had gathered. Most were men, stopping by on their way to work, though there were a few women there, generally sympathetically disposed, hoping that the culprit would yet be reprieved. The size of the crowd grew a little as the minutes passed, but at no time did the numbers exceed two or three hundred. At half past seven the prison gates were opened to admit eight representatives of the press to witness the execution. Once inside the Coach House they were marshalled in single file to within a few yards of the scaffold where they were joined by others concerned with the proceedings. Apart from the hangman, Mr Berry, there was Mr John Hughes, the under-sheriff; Mr W. Rutherford, acting under-sheriff; Mr J.L. Anderson, the governor of the prison; Dr Beamish, the senior surgeon, and Dr Hammond, assistant surgeon. There were also several male and female warders waiting in attendance.

When all were assembled they were informed by the chaplain that the condemned woman had partaken of the Sacrament the previous day at a special service held in the prison chapel, to which she alone had been admitted. Then, a few minutes later, at a quarter to eight, the passing bell commenced to toll, and James Berry left the Coach House to return to the condemned woman's cell, there to pinion her in preparation for the execution.

'Now, Mrs Berry,' he said, facing her once more, 'I've come back. Is there anything I can do for you before you leave the condemned cell?' At his words she shivered and shrank back. He asked her if she would like a drink of water, but she shook her head. 'All right, then,' he said. 'Time is getting on. Don't be afraid – I'm not going to hurt you.'

After he had pinioned her arms there appeared outside the cell door the governor, the chaplain, the under-sheriffs, the doctors and warders. Mrs Berry, her preparations complete, was led out to join them, and when all were assembled they formed a procession, and together they began to move towards the exit leading into the yard.

Standing near the gallows, the men of the press had become aware of the various officers going from the shed, and realized that the last moments of the prisoner must be close at hand. Then, just two or three minutes later, as the bell tolled out the hour of eight, they saw the head of the solemn procession come into view, emerging into the prison yard. Two male warders led the way, followed by the chaplain, who walked backwards while reading aloud the Prayers for the Dying to the desperate woman who walked facing him. The procession was brought up by the under-sheriffs, the doctors and the executioner.

From the condemned cell to the scaffold the distance was about sixty yards, the path taking the procession across the yard in the open air. Following the snowfall, sand had been hurriedly sprinkled over the ground to prevent any slips or falls.

Elizabeth Berry appeared to be in a very feeble condition. Wearing the black silk dress that she had worn at her trial, and with no covering on her head, she was supported by two female warders who, with womanly sympathy, were weeping. Keeping her eyes closed, she was led slowly and steadily on, as she walked repeating in a faint voice the responses to the chaplain's prayers. To the watchers she appeared to be holding herself together until the moment when, entering the Coach House, she opened her eyes and saw before her the great, looming structure of the gallows. In that moment she lost her self-control. With a wailing cry of, 'Oh, dear!' she staggered and almost fell. Quickly she was caught by the two female warders while at the same time the executioner rushed to her side and held her.

'Now, look here, Mrs Berry,' he said, 'you remember what you promised me in the cell. You promised me you'd give me no trouble. What d'you call this?' She gave a groan, and he, afraid that she would collapse, took hold of her again. Shrinking from his touch, she cried out, 'Let me go, Mr Berry. Let me go, and I'll go bravely.'

'All right.' With his words he released her, and she staggered on a few steps, supported by the warders. Then, looking at the gallows again before her, she halted and, terror-stricken, cried out, 'Oh, God forbid! God forbid!' With some difficulty, the warders managed to get her walking once more, while at the same time she tried again to repeat the responses to the chaplain's prayers. But it was too much, and at the foot of the gallows she gave a moan and fell to the ground. Quickly the warders lifted her, and hoisted her up onto the scaffold, and there they held her erect while Berry completed his arrangements, pinioning her feet and putting the white cap upon her head. Coming out of her swoon she cried out, 'May the Lord have mercy upon me,' and then, 'Into His hands I commend my spirit.' The chaplain, much affected by the scene, stepped away from her side. Just before Berry pulled the cap down over her eyes and adjusted the fatal rope, she muttered a few indistinct final words. A moment later Berry was pulling the lever, and in the next instant she fell.

Said the reporter from the *Liverpool Mercury*: 'The passage from life to death was swift. The woman passed out of sight into the well beneath the scaffold. Death must have been instantaneous; not a vibration of the rope was seen.'

A minute or two after the fall, the two doctors, Beamish and Hammond, followed by James Berry, descended by ladder into the well to ascertain that the condemned woman had died. That done, the black flag was hoisted above the prison, and the people assembled outside the prison walls dispersed.

The Rev. Dr Morris was later asked by one of the reporters what had been Elizabeth Berry's final words while on the scaffold. Had she made a last-moment confession? He replied that she had not. Her last words, he said, were, 'May God forgive Dr Patterson.' The chaplain then said that during an interview with her on Sunday night she had again protested her innocence, saying that she attributed the death of her daughter to the creosote mixture prescribed by the doctor.

An inquest on the body of Elizabeth Berry was held before Mr Clarke Aspinall in the prison shortly after two o'clock. Much of it was a formality. But it was the first ever execution to take place there, so for most of those assembled, with the exception of the executioner, the experience would have been a new one.

After all the testimonies had been given, the coroner addressed the jury, asking them to consider whether they were satisfied as to the identity of the body, whether the judgement of death had been duly executed on the offender, and that the execution had taken place within the walls of the prison. The jury, through their foreman, duly stated that they were satisfied on all points. With this the inquest was done.

With his part in the execution behind him, James Berry got the train back to Bradford. He was relieved to get away from the prison, he later wrote, as he was feeling far from well. His indisposition may have been partly psychological. In his account of the proceedings he said: 'I may say that on no occasion did I ever execute a woman without suffering as severe mental and bodily pains as my victim. It may seem a bold thing to say, but, nevertheless, it is true, and when I have been setting out from my house to carry out my duties I have broken down and turned back. My wife and mother on these occasions used to comfort me as best they could.'

Readers of James Berry's memoir might find such claims to be a bit rich. To say that he suffered mentally and physically just as much as the executed person is rather gilding the lily, and perhaps somewhat inappropriate as well was the manner in which he claimed to have spoken to Elizabeth Berry in her cell and on the way to the scaffold – rather as if she was putting him out. Also, his telling her not to worry, that he wasn't going to hurt her, might seem a little odd.

His autobiography reveals that he kept scrapbooks of cuttings about the various murder cases, his 'victims' and his work. Not only that, but he also kept mementoes of the different dark events. One such was of his execution of Elizabeth Berry. He tells in his memoir that after her execution he cut two locks from her 'beautiful chestnut tresses' to add to his memorabilia collection.

He also wrote that years later he sold everything, as the possession of it all was causing him stress. Afterwards, he said, he slept better.

The day after Elizabeth Berry's hanging the newspapers devoted many column inches to accounts of the gruesome happening, and of the terrible crime for which she had been convicted. There was no sympathy shown by the editors. Without exception they showed their approval of the execution of the sentence.

25

Last Words

The drama and horror of the execution was over, and Elizabeth Berry was dead and buried. Her name would continue to crop up in the newspapers occasionally over the days following her burial, but less and less frequently. Her bleak story was told, and soon her name would be largely forgotten and fade into oblivion.

Under George Robinson's authority, Joseph Whitaker's application for the dead woman's effects to be given him in lieu of payment due was eventually granted, and it was announced that they would be sold at auction, this to be held at a shop on Union Street, Oldham, at 6.30 p.m. on Thursday 24 March, ten days after Mrs Berry's execution.

In securing the venue, however, Mr Whitaker had clearly not foreseen the great interest that the event would foster. Well before 6.30 on the evening of the 24th it became apparent that the premises were much too small. The auctioneer arrived to find the shop packed to the doors while on the pavement outside an eager and curious crowd was gaining in number by the minute. Nevertheless, the auction went ahead, and continued until Mr Whitaker appeared and instructed the auctioneer to halt the sale. With prospective bidders being denied the chance to bid, he could see his much-wanted recompense dwindling before his eyes. His announcement was greeted with derisive cries, but he told the crowd that the sale would be resumed at a different venue, with word of its time and location posted in the next day's papers. Subsequently, Friday's early edition of the *Chronicle* gave out the news that the sale would be resumed that evening at the Temperance Hall on Horsedge Street, a far more spacious venue.

There the proceedings were got under way, and continued until the last of the effects were knocked down. An array of articles was sold, among them an ink stand with bottles of ink, gloves, curling tongs, a workbasket, a pair of cufflinks (gold or not, the auctioneer couldn't say), pieces of fabric and the bonnet that Edith had worn on her last visit to the workhouse. The pieces that claimed the most attention, however, were the dead woman's clothes, the prize of all being the dress that she had worn to the workhouse ball the day after Edith's arrival, the dress of ruby red silk, draped with black lace and ribbons, and with it the black fan, the pink silk gloves, pink silk stockings and dainty, elegant shoes. It went for the great sum of £7 – over £800 in today's money.

It later transpired that some of Mrs Berry's clothes went to a buyer from a waxworks museum, and others to a group of theatrical players. These latter would, just two weeks later, put on in Liverpool centre a dramatization of Mrs Berry's last hours. Complaints about it were made, naturally, and members of the Liverpool Watch Committee were called upon to ban the show and have the city's Chief Constable prepare a report on the subject for the attention of the Home Secretary. Said the *Huddersfield Chronicle*:

> Not a single detail is omitted which is likely to impart the requisite ghastliness to the performance, and even a number of the articles of clothing worn by Mrs Berry prior to her execution are brought into prominence on each occasion of the mock execution. The chaplain is in attendance reading the prayers, the prison warders are present to witness the carrying out of the death penalty. The result is that a large number of persons are regularly attracted to the hideous exhibition, and watch each performance with manifest delight and satisfaction.

It was reported elsewhere that in the interests of science and medicine Dr Thomas Harris, whose evidence had been so crucial at the trial, put on exhibition at a meeting of the Medical Society the charred gullet of Edith Annie.

As for the waxworks, while Mrs Berry was to receive no pedestal at the famous Madame Tussauds, an effigy of her was on display for many years at the popular Reynolds Waxworks in Lime Street, Liverpool, where she shared her grim surroundings with likenesses of other killers, among them Landru, the French Bluebeard, and Charlie Peace, executed in 1877 for the murder of his neighbour. Mrs Berry's effigy, which remained on show until the museum closed in 1923, presented her in a tableau with two other murderesses, Margaret Higgins and Catherine Flanagan. Sisters, they were executed in 1884 for poisoning Higgins's husband, though the unfortunate man was in fact just one of their many victims. Elizabeth Berry, with her superior attitude to those whom she believed to be her inferiors, would have been horrified to be seen with such low-class women, though it can't be denied that she was, in truth, in good company.

What became of the effigy of Mrs Berry, I doubt we shall ever know. Though perhaps somewhere in some forgotten file or shoe-box there lies a photograph of it, perhaps showing the petite murderess with her Piccadilly fringe, and wearing her ruby-red ball gown or the black silk mourning dress that she wore at her trial.

And what, too, of those photographs of Mrs Berry and Edith that were taken during one of their trips to Blackpool, one of which holidays ended with the death of little Harold – will they, along with others of Mrs Berry's treasures, surface one day in some forgotten archive?

Today there is almost nothing to remind us of the tragedy and the drama that featured in Elizabeth Berry's eventful life. The Oldham Workhouse, scene of Edith's death, has been gone almost thirty years. Demolished in the 1980s, it was replaced by the Oldham Hospital.

What became of the greater part of Elizabeth Berry's effects after Joseph Whitaker's auction, we shall never know. On 26 March the solicitor's clerk, George Robinson, wrote to the Home Office to say that the sale of them was complete, and that after all expenses had been paid – his own and those of the auctioneer – there was a net sum realized of only £18 (a little over £2,100 today). He wrote: 'I may say that the only creditor is Mr Whitaker, Solicitor for the defence of Mrs Berry, and he will be one for £50 or £60 after deducting the amount paid to him on account by the deceased.'

So Mr Whitaker, for all that he had worked so untiringly on Mrs Berry's behalf, was left considerably out of pocket. Further, and very sadly, he did not long survive his most infamous client. He died of a brain tumour only two years later, aged just thirty-nine, his young wife Sarah Ellen at his side.

Dr Thomas Patterson, bête noire of the murderess, and responsible for her downfall, did not see old age either, dying at his home in Chadderton in 1894 at the age of forty-four. Although in some ill-informed, lasting myth he is still sometimes blamed for Edith's death, there surely can be no doubt that, in spite of the calumny heaped upon him from some quarters, he acted most properly and courageously, and that without his tenacity and his brilliant mind, the murderess Mrs Berry might well have gone on to kill again.

The mystery surrounding Elizabeth Berry's father persists. There is no evidence whatsoever that he left the country and died abroad, and records reveal more than one man living in England at the time who might fit the bill as regards name and age, and who lived through the time of Elizabeth's execution. This being so, and assuming that one of them was her errant father, it is tempting to believe that he would surely have read about the case in the papers. And had he done so, and read a little of the felon's history then he must, at some point, have seen a connection, and realized that the callous, murderous woman was his own daughter. If so, he had an even greater reason for keeping his secret safe.

And, lastly, what of Edith Annie, a major player in the drama, whose cruel death brought about her mother's execution?

With Joseph Whitaker being granted all the proceeds from the sale of Mrs Berry's goods, his clerk George Robinson was denied any chance of carrying out her wish, that the sale of her effects be used to pay for the erection of a stone for her 'darling'.

Today, in the windswept Chadderton Cemetery, it takes careful, diligent search, and help from kind cemetery assistants, to find little Edith's last resting place. Her small plot lies in an area of the cemetery where the graves have lain undisturbed for a century and a quarter. Those who once came to mourn her, standing at her graveside that day in the bitter January wind, while her cheap little coffin was lowered into the hard earth, are themselves now long beneath the soil. In this part of the graveyard, nature, unhindered, has come back to take hold and reclaim her own. Here the graves are overgrown with shrubs and weeds, while ivy, long unchecked, climbs and spreads and hides from view the stone angels and the fallen crosses, and mosses and lichens obliterate the names and loving tributes once so painstakingly carved into the marble and the granite.

Edith Annie's grave has no engraved quotation from Longfellow's 'Resignation', it has no stone, it has not even an empty flower pot. Looking down at the girl's last resting place one sees nothing at all to indicate who rests in the bare, unkempt, shabby little plot. Untended and forgotten under the bleak winter sky, she lies long forsaken.

Select Bibliography and Sources

Books

Berry, James, *My Experiences as an Executioner* (David & Charles, 1972).

Doughty, Jack, *Come at Once – Annie is Dying* (Pentaman Press, 1987).

Evans, Stewart P., *Executioner: The Chronicles of a Victorian Hangman* (Sutton, 2004).

Flanders, Judith, *The Invention of Murder* (Harper Press, 2011).

Glaister, John, *The Power of Poison* (Christopher Johnson, 1954).

Hempel, Sandra, *The Inheritor's Powder* (Weidenfeld & Nicolson, 2013).

Knelman, Judith, *Twisting in the Wind* (University of Toronto Press, 1998).

Rose, Lionel, *Massacre of the Innocents* (Routledge and Kegan Paul, 1986).

Smith, John, *The Register of Death: A History of Executions at Walton Prison, Liverpool* (Countyvise, 2007).

Thompson, Charles J.S., *Poison Romance and Poison Mysteries* (Scientific Press, 1899).

Watson, Katherine, *Poisoned Lives: English Poisoners and their Victims* (Hambledon & London, 2004).

Documents

HO 144/289/B830. Home Office file held at the National Archives, Kew, London.

ASSI 52/9. Papers from the relevant Assizes, held at the National Archives.

Journals

Evening Mail (London)

Evening News (London)
Huddersfield Chronicle
Liverpool Mercury
Manchester Evening News
Manchester Guardian
Oldham Chronicle
Oldham Evening Chronicle
Oldham Express
Oldham Standard

Index

Alcroft, Alice 73, 77, 80–2, 96, 135
Anderson, Sarah 80, 95, 136
aortic regurgitation 186
arsenic 185

Banks, Alexander 129
Bartlett, Adelaide 52
Berry, Edith Annie 2, 24–5, 36
  birth 18
  funeral 73, 84–5
  grave 234–5
  illness and death 59–64, 188–90,
    214–15, 219–21
  inquest 71–6, 79–86
  insurance policies and 65, 67, 84–5, 90,
    137–9
  magistrates' hearing *see* magistrates'
    hearing
  Oldham holiday 56–8
  post-mortem 66–7, 72, 74, 75
Berry, Elizabeth (née Welch) xi–xiv
  appearance 8–9, 19, 71, 80, 89, 211
  apprehension of 2–3, 72–3
  arrest and remand of 76–7, 79, 87,
    105–6
  birth 5–6
  breach of promise case and 27–9
  children 18–20, 24–5, 131, 181, 183–4
    see also Berry, Edith Annie *and*
    Berry, Elizabeth Jane *and* Berry,
    Harold
  clemency petition 203–4, 209–10, 224
  current affairs and 51–2

death certificate and 65–8
death sentence 157, 193–4, 198–200,
  209
disposal of effects 165–6, 194–6, 200–1,
  205–6, 231–4
dramatization of 232
education 7–8
employment as housekeeper 24, 25–6
execution 223–30
illness 53–6, 163–4, 179–80
imprisonment 162–6, 193–4, 196–203,
  211
inquest, and the 86
insurance policies and *see* insurance
  policies
intelligence 9
magistrates' hearing, and the 89, 96
marriage 17–21, 24, 26
mill work and 8–9
mother (Mary Ann Welch) and 40–2
murder and 183–92
nursing career 26, 31, 34–40, 43–5,
  95–6, 173–4
Oldham Union Workhouse and 44–7,
  49–59, 95–6
Patterson, Dr Thomas and 44–5, 53–6,
  65–6, 210, 212–17, 229
personality 8–9, 19, 20, 49, 52–3,
  177–82
personality disorder and 53–6, 179–80
pregnancy 205
religion 27, 196
romantic liaisons and 27–9, 50–1

statement of 139–40
stepfather (Joseph Welch) and 15–16
trial, and the 111–12, 123, 126, 155–7, 165
wax effigy of 232–3
widowhood 23–4
Berry, Elizabeth Jane 20, 184, 185, 188, 191
Berry, Harold 24–5
    birth 18
    death 36, 131, 181, 187–8
Berry, James 224–30
Berry, Thomas 17–21, 23, 131, 186–7, 191
bigamy 14
Blackpool 36
Booth, Hesketh 127
Braden, John 185
breach of promise 28–9
Britland, Mary Ann 52, 159
Burton-upon-Trent Union Workhouse 37
Byrne, Henry 127

careers 26
    women and 26–7
Chadderton, Joseph 171–2
child murder 138
Chorlton, Alice 119
convulsions 184
Coombes, George 172
Cottingham, James 71
    inquest, and the 81–5
    magistrates' hearing, and the 89, 96–101, 103, 106
    trial, and the 127, 129–32, 141–3, 149–52
cotton industry, the 8

death penalty, the 217–18
Dillon, Ann 91–2, 133–4
Dorrick, Harriet 119–20

Eaves, Alice 118–19
education 7
    females and 7
Emmett, Joseph 210–12
Estcourt, Charles 76, 82, 85, 94, 147
Estcourt, Philip 82

Evett, Lydia 54–5, 61, 80, 95, 136
executions 223

Finley, Mary Ann (previously Welch, née Bevan) 5–7, 11–16, 38–42
    death 41–2, 88, 174–5, 191
    exhumation 113–16
    inquest 114–23, 127, 167–73
    insurance policies and 42, 122, 171–2, 175
    relationship with daughter (Elizabeth Berry) 40–2
Finley, William 11–12, 38, 181–2
    Berry, Elizabeth and 14–16, 182
Flanagan, Catherine 233
Fletcher, Mr 197–8, 201
funeral insurance 25 see also insurance policies

Hall, Beatrice 56–8, 62
    inquest, and the 74–5, 82
    magistrates' hearing, and the 94–5
    trial, and the 132–3
Harris, Dr Thomas 74, 93–4, 115, 169–70, 232
    trial, and the 52, 146–7
Hawkins, Mr Justice 126, 153–5, 157
Higgins, Margaret 233
Hodgkinson, Charles (Chief Constable) 67, 68
    inquest, and the 84–5
    magistrates' hearing, and the 97
    trial, and the 137, 143

infanticide 138
inquests
    Barry, Edith Annie 71–6, 79–86
    Finley, Mary Ann 114–23, 127, 167–73
insurance policies
    Berry, Edith Annie and 65, 67, 84–5, 90, 137–9
    Berry, Harold and 36
    Berry, Thomas and 23
    Finley, Mary Ann and 42, 122, 171–2, 175
    funeral 25

Jackson, Henry 122, 137–8, 148

Kershaw, Dr John 18, 25, 54, 214, 217
    Patterson, Dr Thomas and 106–11
    trial, and the 127
Kleppell, Brother 113–14
Knight, Mary Jane 82, 96–7, 136

Landru, Henri Désiré 233
Lawson, William Henry 45–6, 122, 129
life insurance *see* insurance
Longfellow, Henry Wadsworth
    'Resignation' 198–200, 202
Lyons, Mary Ann 114, 116

magistrate's hearing, the 88–90, 96,
    101–3
    Alcroft, Alice and 96
    Anderson, Sarah and 95
    Cottingham, James and 89, 96–101,
        103, 106
    Dillon, Ann and 91–2
    Estcourt, Charles and 94
    Evett, Lydia and 95–6
    Hall, Beatrice and 94–5
    Harris, Dr Thomas and 93–4
    Hodgkinson, Charles and 97
    Knight, Mary Jane and 96–7
    Patterson, Dr Thomas and 97–8, 106
    Robertson, Dr George and 98–9
    Sanderson, Ann and 90–1
    Thompson, Ellen and 92–3
marriage 26–7
M'Connell, William 126–7, 128–9, 152–3
medical careers 26
Mellor, J. W. 89–90
Minahan, Mr 197–8
Molesworth, F. N. (District Coroner) 71,
    114, 127
Morton, Henrietta 120–1
murder trials 52

newspapers
    Berry, Elizabeth and 177–82, 196–7,
        211
    Patterson, Dr Thomas and 212–14,
        218–22
    trial reports 159–60, 218

Oldham Union Workhouse 1–2, 32–4,
    48–9, 233
    Berry, Elizabeth and 44–7, 49–59, 95–6
    scarlet fever and 135

Partland, Ann 136
Patterson, Dr Thomas 44–5, 53–6, 60–2,
    234
    criticism of 53–6, 106–11, 210, 212–22,
        229
    death certificate and 65–6, 84
    inquest, and the 71–2, 73–4, 82–4
    Kershaw, Dr John and 106–11
    magistrates' hearing, and the 97–8, 106
    trial, and the 139–43, 148
Paul, Dr Frank 168, 169
Peace, Charlie 233
Pemberton, Sarah 170–1, 194
Pickford, James 67, 137
poisons xi, 185
professions 26
prostitution 27
Purser, Charles (Detective Inspector)
    136–7

'Resignation' (Longfellow, Henry
    Wadsworth) 198–200, 202
Robertson, Dr George 61–2, 75, 98–9
    trial, and the 144–5
Robinson, George Henry 126, 162–6,
    205–6, 233

Sanderson, Ann 17, 25, 62–4, 194
    Berry, Harold and 187–8
    inquest, and the 71, 84
    magistrates' hearing, and the 90–1
    trial, and the 129–32, 143
Sanderson, John 17, 63, 202–3
serial poisoners 191–2
Sharples, Dr William 168–9, 174
Shaw, Dr David 24

Shaw, George 167–8
Smith, Albert 110–11
strychnine 185

Taylor, John 121–2, 145–6
Taylor, William 172
teething 184
Thompson, Ellen 75–6, 92–3, 134–5
Thompson, William 148–9
Thorpe, William 136
trial, the 126–8
    Alcroft, Alice and 135
    Anderson, Sarah and 136
    Berry, Elizabeth and 111–12, 123, 126,
        155–7, 165
    Banks, Alexander and 129
    Booth, Hesketh and 127
    Byrne, Henry and 127
    Cottingham, James and 127, 129–32,
        141–3, 149–52
    defence case 149–52
    Dillon, Ann and 133–4
    Estcourt, Charles and 147
    Evett, Lydia and 136
    Hall, Beatrice and 132–3
    Harris, Dr Thomas and 146–7
    Hawkins, Mr Justice and 126, 153–5,
        157
    Hodgkinson, Charles (Chief Constable)
        and 137, 143
    Jackson, Henry and 137, 148
    jury 148
    Kershaw, Dr John and 127
    Knight, Mary Jane and 136
    Lawson, William Henry and 129
    M'Connell, William and 126–7, 128–9,
        152–3
    newspapers and 159–60
    Partland, Ann and 136

    Patterson, Dr Thomas and 139–43, 148
    Pickford, James and 137
    prosecution case 152–3
    Purser, Charles (Detective Inspector)
        and 136–7
    Robertson, Dr George and 144–5
    Sanderson, Ann and 129–32, 143
    summing up 153–4
    Taylor, John and 145–6
    Thompson, Ellen and 134–5
    Thompson, William and 148–9
    Thorpe, William and 136
    verdict 156–7, 161, 218

Waddingham, Dorothea 37n
Wallwork, Frederick 122
Welch, George 6
Welch, John 6
Welch, Joseph 5–7, 12–14, 234
Welch, Mary Ann (née Bevan) 5–7, 11–16,
    38–42
    death 41–2, 88, 174–5, 191
    exhumation 113–16
    inquest 114–23, 127, 167–73
    insurance policies and 42, 122, 171–2,
        175
    relationship with daughter (Elizabeth
        Berry) 40–2
welfare 23–4, 31–2
Whitaker, Joseph 71, 116, 162, 201–2, 233
    clemency petition and 209–10
    fees and 125–6, 194–6, 205–6, 231, 233
Wolfenden, Sarah 39–40, 114, 116–18
Wood, C. Granville 108
workhouses 1, 31–4
    Burton-upon-Trent Union
        Workhouse 37
    Oldham Union Workhouse see Oldham
        Union Workhouse